WORLDS of the FUTURE

Merrill Sociology Series

Under the Editorship of

Richard L. Simpson
University of North Carolina at Chapel Hill
and
Paul E. Mott
University of Pennsylvania

WORLDS
of the
FUTURE

Exercises in the Sociological Imagination

Bernard S. Phillips

Boston University

Charles E. Merrill Publishing Company
A Bell & Howell Company
Columbus, Ohio

Published by
Charles E. Merrill Publishing Company
A Bell & Howell Company
Columbus, Ohio 43216

ISBN: 0-675-09085-7

Library of Congress Catalog Card Number: 72-75763

1 2 3 4 5 6—78 77 76 75 74 73 72

Printed in the United States of America

Contents

To Aristotle

It was way before the crash in the beginning. In the beginning when time was time and there was always time. There was time and it was sequential and monotonous and always saying and shaving off minutes from the whole. And there was time to be, to be before, be forward and backward or lost; and then a something began. A something different of loss and gain. Something happened behind the mind. A difference sensed, felt, and slowly—ever so—quietly the mind acknowledged and the thing spread from behind and it spread through the mind. Throughout the mind. And the mind didn't understand. And time didn't understand and there was the spreading point, and pressure, and time expired slowly. Time was bent and broken and everything was changed.

And everything changed and language vanished and the mind thought in pure and perfect concept. A crystalline concept that streamed and merged into an immense totality, and no thing was everything and nothing was everything. And the mind acquiesced and relaxed and merged mingling in the drifting waters of a timeless totality. And every thing seemed right—The Rite of Spring—and all was movement and beginning and all was suggestion. Everything out-of-time was an infinite suggestion to the mind and the ripples played in linear dimensions upon the objects in the mind. And the mind saw all. In everything the infinite waited and the mind-in-motion touched the infinite with rippling urgency and release.

And the sound was every thing and in every thing and the objects moved in infinite motions of a perfect pattern. And the sound moved in light and was light: an exquisite web of gold with light-blue-water notes. And the mind merged with the sound and radiated blue and the harmony was pure.

And the harmony beckoned and the mind yielded and watched the sound. It watched the sound through the body's left ear and the purity beckoned beyond the body and the mind obeyed. The mind poured out the ear into spatial freedom and floated there as pure thought. And it saw the body shell below, and the sound beckoned. And the mind turned in tempo and glowed in colored counterpoint with the sound. And was the sound in a purely patterned dimension of timeless spatial harmony. And was the sound!

DAVID M. KUIECK

Preface

Sociology was, is, and will be. Sociology was born a child of the industrial revolution, has grown into adolescence in the midst of the world revolution of early post-industrial society, and perhaps will grow into manhood along with the development of late post-industrial society. The future of sociology is inextricably tied to the future of society. Yet why is it that just now so many of us are so deeply concerned with envisioning the future? What is so special about this moment in history? What does it tell us about past, present, and future?

I remember a time not so long ago when I considered myself to be an observer of the facts of human behavior. I was not able to observe the future, and so I ruled it out as being of no importance. I was not even conscious of having ruled it out. I was looking for observations which would lead me to laws of human behavior that were beyond time, that applied to all past, present, and future instances of behavior, that were universal. And so I ruled out the past along with the future, for observations could be made most easily in the present, and the universal laws to be derived from those observations would certainly apply to the past anyway.

The world changed rapidly, and I along with it. The observations I and other social scientists made were observations of a world running downhill at an increasing rate. And our observations didn't seem to help matters very much. We were unable to anticipate the rapid changes all around us, let alone do anything about them. The purity or unbiased nature of our observations was called into question. What we saw was partly constructed by ourselves. It was based on an interaction process between investigator and environment. And if such intangible factors were intrinsic to research, there was no longer a need to focus on the hard facts of the present. The present was built up from the past, and an understanding of historical context could yield insight into the nature of the present. And the future—something even more intangible than the past—could be examined.

There was a growing urgency to make substantial progress on society's major problems, an urgency which made itself felt in every classroom. No longer could we in the social sciences dispense the faith we had lived by for so long without having its pitiful inadequacy thrown back in our faces. And so we changed along with our students and our society. Change and problem solving became important topics among those who formerly had seen little of a creative nature in them. The nature and future of the scientific method itself became problematic. The narrowness of all the disciplines became more obvious when we began to face the business of solving problems, since piecemeal "solutions" proved almost invariably to be failures. In short, we began to see the inadequacies of what we had been doing previously, but we had as yet little sense of direction concerning what to do about it.

I find myself now, located in the present, conscious of several alternative futures. In one of these, man's problems continue to increase until man himself becomes his own victim. This is a future which I no longer believe will materialize. In another future, man learns to gain control over those forces which presently are shaping his existence. I believe that the development of this future depends on man's consciousness of his ability to construct the future.

We all construct the future by everything we think, feel, and do, but we tend to do it unconsciously and with a limited spatial and temporal vision. We are futurists without knowing it, and we tend to extrapolate the limited present into the future. I invite the reader to become another kind of futurist, one who is conscious of the ways in which he is creating the future, and one who creates a future more conducive to his own development than the present is.

Because I am convinced of the importance of metaphors for integrating knowledge, I have chosen to alternate chapters of nonfiction and science fiction. I also make substantial use of metaphors in the nonfiction chapters. My emphasis is on a system of metaphors which are linked with one another, just as a scientific theory comprises a system of propositions. This system is also linked to abstract ideas taken from the literature of sociology and the social sciences.

Parts one and two sketch the basic framework of ideas on which the book rests. The subsequent parts—Man and Society, Groups, Social Category Systems, and Institutions—focus on the fundamental topics within sociology. The approach I take goes beyond describing and illustrating sociological ideas. I attempt to apply these ideas to an analysis of the transition from industrial to post-industrial society. The fictional characters—Basil Kornish, Ben Zorn, Ian Zenski, and Bart Khayyam—represent stages along this path from present to future.

The book may be read in different ways, depending on the purposes of the reader. By reading in sequence from beginning to end the reader moves by stages to more concrete views of a transition to the future. He may choose to read all of the fictional chapters in sequence (2, 4, 6, 8, and 10) for a metaphorical perspective, or he may choose the more abstract perspective of the nonfiction (1, 3, 5, 7, 9, and 11). If he desires the most concise statement of the fundamental abstract ideas presented here, he might begin with chapter 7. Chapter 2 would give him a concise metaphorical statement.

The appendix illustrates ways in which ideas developed throughout the book might be applied. "From Beaker Metaphor to a Dynamic Mathematical Model of Human Development" focuses on the transition to a post-industrial world. I believe that the techniques illustrated here—such as computer simulation—can open doors to understanding how to construct or discover diverse kinds of theories.

The individual whose confidence in my work was absolutely essential at every step of the writing process, whose knowledge I relied on ahead of anyone else's, and who devoted the time necessary to put the book together is—myself. This acknowledgment is not meant to be facetious but, rather, to be consistent with the fundamental ideas between these two covers. Of course it is true that my ideas are largely the product of innumerable ideas put forth by others, but I as an individual have pulled together these ideas in my own way, just as everyone's life is a unique synthesis of his own experiences. It is this uniqueness that I wish to acknowledge—and, by so doing, the uniqueness of each of my readers—for the book would never have been written if it were an eclectic conglomerate of the ideas of others. But it had a center in my own life, and that enabled me to reach outward to the ideas and experiences of other individuals.

Bernard S. Phillips
Boston, Massachusetts, 1972

ONE

INTRODUCTION

Sociology and science fiction have gone their separate ways. We believe that the two together constitute more than the sum of the separate parts. They interact in multiplicative fashion and the result is a wider view of man's past, present, and future.

By uniting these two modes of communication we are only making explicit what is already implicit. Every sociological theory contains at least the seeds of a vision of the future, even if it is only the near future; and every piece of science fiction contains implicit assumptions about the nature of human behavior. Yet by moving toward explicit ideas there is something to be gained. What formerly remained unexamined comes under close scrutiny. Questions are raised which would not have been asked, and doors are opened to a wider perspective.

In part one we state our fundamental aims and assumptions with respect to sociology and science fiction, and then we try out our perspective by discussing the transition from the industrial to the post-industrial world. We ask the reader not to abandon his present perspectives on sociology and science fiction, but to forge links between the two.

1

Sociology and
Science Fiction

Worlds of the Future is mostly about worlds which already exist to a degree, just as elements of industrial life are present in pre-industrial societies and elements of the post-industrial era exist in the industrialized world. This book represents an attempt to develop our vision so that we can see what is already here. And what seems to be here already is man's *ability* to construct the future, just as man's biological development has given him the *capacity* to construct his future. To the degree that he becomes conscious of this ability he will be able to gain control of those forces which already are shaping the future.

Any successful search for understanding yields tools for controlling one's fate. By learning what causes a given phenomenon, whether through studying the sciences or through personal experience, we gain knowledge which can be used either to control that phenomenon or to affect the way we act toward it. There is, then, nothing at all mysterious about our ability to construct the future. It is something we have been doing all the time.

Pre-literate man is greatly limited in his experiences in comparison to literate man. An advantage we have is our ability to move outward conceptually to encompass an ever-expanding number of forces which affect a given phenomenon and to reach far back into the past to gain perspective for reaching ahead into the future. This comprehensive and dynamic view constitutes the basic approach we take in *Worlds of the Future.* There is a choice involved here: to see man's future as one of expanding possibilities, or to see it more pessimistically. Our vision interacts with the world, and whichever option we choose helps to create that kind of world.

In this chapter we take up three topics: aims, assumptions, and an illustration. We attempt to join an open-ended and dynamic view of society through the lens of sociology with a view through the lens of science fiction, and the chapters of the book alternate between these two modes of communication. As for assumptions, at least some can be made explicit. Indeed, this is essential if the reader is to be given the option of relating his own ideas to the ones presented. Our illustration is a rather complex and dynamic process, that of the societal shift to the post-industrial era.

AIMS

Sociology and science fiction are modes of communication, but it remains to specify the particular approach we intend to take within each mode. The general approach is to achieve a broad and open view of man. Rather than take sides with this or that theory or method, we try to present a framework in which there is a place for a wide and widening number of theories and methods. Rather than see the future as an extrapolation of man's physical technologies, we attempt to capture the dynamic of change in such technologies *in addition to* the dynamic of change in man himself and in his institutions. We believe that these two views together—the sociological and the science fictional—constitute more than the sum of the separate parts. They bring together science and art, and we have yet to explore and assess the consequences of this kind of union. In our discussion of aims in this section we shall outline the particular kind of orientation we adopt toward sociology and science fiction.

Sociology

We would like to define sociology in such a way that we avoid a common tendency to draw boundaries between it and other disciplines and to defend that definition against changing ideas about sociology. We see sociology as a study of the dynamics of human behavior, with special attention to social systems such as groups or institutions. Facets of this definition which bear further comment are: (1) the definition's relation to the context in which it is being used, (2) the focus on human behavior as distinct from an exclusive concern with the social system, (3) the focus on dynamics, (4) the intangible nature of social systems, and (5) the types of social systems.

1. Context: A definition may be useful to some and not to others, and may be useful in one time period but not in another. Thus, we believe that readers should approach definitions quite critically. From our own perspective, the definition communicates a number of our fundamental ideas about the nature of sociology.

2. Human behavior: In our view human behavior is a phenomenon which should be understood holistically. Although we have succeeded in creating a variety of distinct disciplines within the social sciences, it does not follow that deep understanding will emerge if each looks to its own. Indeed, we see this division of labor as tending to stand in the way of such understanding. We believe that a kind of specialization is required which will recognize not only different kinds of emphases, such as an emphasis on the social system in sociology, but also responsibility for taking into account the best available information from the different disciplines in order to arrive at a holistic view.

3. "Social system" is a modified noun and, as such, we tend to think of it as something material and relatively static. However, a social system is best seen as something dynamic, like a river which has a structure and yet is in continual flux. For example, we may locate a group by noticing who interacts with whom, but these patterns of interaction encompass all kinds of changes, and the patterns themselves change. If we do not focus attention on these changes, then we miss what is most human about groups, and what remains is the kind of repetitive behavior which is more characteristic of lower forms of life or, better yet, of nonliving systems.

4. Intangible nature of social systems: If a group is defined by patterns of social interaction, and if social interaction is determined by the effect individuals have on one another, then the group comes out to be an intangible entity. The sociological "group" is different from the solid, material thing implied in the context of everyday speech. For example, a prime feature of the group is the patterns of influence among individuals. The same kind of intangibility is to be found in the other kinds of social systems to be discussed below. The bases for such patterns of influence are still other intangible elements. For example, there are the shared goals or values of the individuals involved as well as their shared expectations or norms. When we shift from the commonsense materialistic view of the group to this intangible view, we also shift from a conception of a phenomenon which is largely solid and immovable to one which is

fluid and open to alteration. If values and norms can be changed, then groups can be changed.

5. Types of social systems: We distinguish three types of social systems: groups, social category systems, and institutions. As indicated above, a group is organized around patterns of interactions, which are types of *action*. A social category system, such as a system of ethnic groups, economic classes, age categories, or sex categories, is a social system defined by norms creating boundaries for the various categories and governing behavior within them, and norms are shared expectations or *ideas*. An institution, such as the scientific, educational, political, military, economic, or religious institution, is a social system defined by values or shared *goals* (for example, power in the case of the political institution, knowledge in the case of the scientific institution). The three types of social systems, then, emphasize different elements of human behavior, although each includes elements of the other: action, ideas and goals.

Instead of thinking of the three kinds of social systems as distinct from one another, it is useful to think of three different perspectives from which to view any given social system, with the result being a richer understanding of that system. For example, we might view the family as a group, a social category system, and an institution. The group perspective alerts us to the boundaries of the family, to the various subgroups within it, to its relationship to groups outside of it, and to the ways in which individuals interact within and between groups. Seeing the family as a social category system, we pay attention to the various kinds of hierarchies within the family (for example, with respect to status, power), to the norms which regulate the relationships among the categories (such as parents and children), and to the relationship between the norms within the social category system and those in its environment. The institutional perspective alerts us to the goals which form the bases on which people interact with and influence one another and on which they develop norms for behavior. Thus, we might view the family from an economic point of view, focusing not only on its relationships to material wealth but also on whatever nonmaterial phenomena the family considers desirable.

To summarize, orientation to sociology points toward comprehensiveness and change. The breadth is illustrated by a desire to incorporate information from other disciplines, by an interest in including knowledge from the humanities, by a holistic approach to human behavior, and by our concern with viewing any given social system from the three foci of the group, the social category system, and the institution. As for change, we see the social system as analogous to a river. It has a structure and yet is in constant flux. Our conception of social systems as intangibles enables us to become oriented to their fluid nature, since ideas—which are basic to these intangibles—can be changed.

Science Fiction

In the physical sciences, a number of science fiction writers now seem to be devoting the bulk of their time to writing nonfiction, just as scientific technology has overrun a great many of the science fiction predictions of the past. This mixing of science fiction and nonfiction is illustrated by Professor Nikolai Amosov, Soviet heart surgeon and cybernetician. In the midst of his distinguished career as a medical scientist, Professor Amosov produced his fictional *Notes from the Future*[1] describing a physician's successful attempt to freeze himself and awaken in the future, and his subsequent establishment of an institute to develop technologies for producing immortality. Following the book's publication, Professor Amosov announced to his Soviet colleagues his intention to develop a gerontological institute focusing on longevity.

It seems that Professor Amosov was able to construct a world in his imagination, and this enabled him to partially construct that world in his own life. Why should this seem to be unusual? A great deal has been said and written about the powers of the imagination. Sociologists have written that situations which are defined as real become real in their consequences, and that prophesies can be self-fulfilling. Indeed, almost all of us are intuitively aware that we have some control over the shape of events to come, that our own actions help to bring about what we desire.

Perhaps what is so unusual about Professor Amosov's experience is the result of his great temporal and spatial extension of familiar processes in everyday life. Temporally, we can understand our ability to influence what occurs from one moment to the next, but we have difficulty envisioning a long chain of such moments stretching out into the future. Spatially, we are able to see the cause-and-effect process in operation when it involves physical movements which are visible, but when we have to deal with intangibles like the imagination—the tool that binds phenomena normally separated in time and space to a given situation—we tend to be at sea.

We are describing a process of constructing the future with the aid of the imagination, a process which enables the individual to help create himself and his environment, just as he in turn is partially created by environmental forces. Social science has taught us very well the latter lesson, but it has tended to neglect the former. We might distinguish three aspects of the process by which an individual or group proceeds to construct the future: (1) viewing the past from the vantage point of the present, and linking one to the other with imaginative tools such as comprehensive social science theories of change; (2) viewing the present from the vantage point of a vision of the future and linking the two as above; and (3) acting in the present so as to take what appears to be the most effective next step in moving toward the future.

This process has far-reaching consequences. For example, beginning with (1) we might focus on the shift from the pre-industrial to the modern industrial era, viewing it as a movement away from material scarcity and toward a situation where man has made great strides in his ability to obtain food, clothing and shelter. As for (2), we might envision the post-industrial era as one in which we look beyond material scarcity to the intangibles of life, to the scarcities within man's imagination which prevent him from achieving what he might achieve. In moving toward such a future, as called for in (3), man will try to develop technologies which can monitor, locate, and progressively eliminate such scarcities. This book itself illustrates, in a small way, step (3). The basic tools used are ideas. The scarcities involved are incorporated in our language and thought and spread, thereby, to personality and social structures.

In our view, it is possible for any individual to learn to consciously construct the future. For example, the writing of each chapter was followed by definite changes in the way the author conducted his classes, and those changes in turn influenced the writing of subsequent chapters. The author also noted certain personality changes in himself as he moved from Basil Kornish to Ben Zorn to Ian Zensky to Bart Khayyam, the protagonists of the fictional chapters.

To break away from the past without rejecting it wholly we must learn to detect which aspects of the present are in the past and which are in the future, and this requires a comprehensive and distant vision of the future. Anything less will lead us to foist the past on the future or neglect the future in the present. The commonplace nostalgia for the close-knit group, such as the pre-industrial family, illustrates the former, and the emphasis by many "radical" thinkers on the power and worth of the group as opposed to the individual illustrates the latter.

Although sociology emerged in an era when man was seeking to understand and control the vast forces being released by the industrial revolution, that understanding and that control has been limited, in our estimation, by a limited conception of the sociologist which has been dominant during the past forty or fifty years. He has been seen as an observer and not as a doer, an analyst and not a problem solver. However, we see these roles not only as mutually supportive but as essential to one another. Ideas are tested by action, and action leads to the development of ideas. To ignore or deemphasize any basic element of human behavior is to dehumanize whatever is accomplished. In employing science fiction we hope to help generate a sense of problem and urgency, which is often sorely lacking in sociological analyses, and to point toward the construction of technologies based on such analyses.

ASSUMPTIONS

A number of our assumptions about human behavior have been stated or implied in the foregoing section. These include beliefs that all phenomena are interrelated, that all phenomena are in continual flux, that man's capacities are limitless, that man can continue to improve his ability to construct the future, that a holistic orientation is essential if we are to understand man, that intangible forces have shaped history, that a sense of history is vital both for understanding the present and for constructing the future, and that as far as possible we should take into account the uniqueness of any human situational context.

Taking a self-critical view, these assumptions appear to be overly abstract. This analysis suggests a remedy: to balance these assumptions with views that are more concrete and that emphasize existing situations. We can achieve this by centering on those aspects of the future which have already emerged, along with those forces which favor and block this emergence. Let us take up four topics which span the spectrum of sociology: (1) the relationship between man and society, (2) groups, (3) social category systems, and (4) institutions.

Man and Society

Our basic orientation can be stated simply enough. Sociology has helped us to come a long way in understanding the power of social forces in shaping the individual, but the time has come to devote attention to another phenomenon as well: the individual's power to shape his environment. We might think of both kinds of understandings as stages in the development of man's freedom. On the one hand, there is man's freedom from biological forces which were once believed to constrain him so greatly as to determine a very large portion of his behavior. On the other hand there is man's freedom from social forces which he believes are so powerful that they inevitably determine his fate, a belief which helps to create the reality, a prophesy which helps to fulfill itself.

Let us illustrate this orientation by examining David Riesman's *The Lonely Crowd,*[2] where four personality types or, correspondingly, types of societies, are discussed. The tradition-directed social order or personality is characteristic of pre-industrial agricultural societies, relatively unchanging, and marked by conformity to norms that have endured for generations and centuries. A new orientation, inner-direction, helps to equip man to master his physical environment as he moves into the industrial era. An ability to cope with novel situations is required, and it is achieved by channeling behavior through a rigid though highly individualized personality structure. The "rugged individual" who emerges is subject to a different kind of conformity than was characteristic of tradition-directed man: conformity to the rigid dictates of the iron cage of his personality. Other-directed man emerges during a later stage of industrialization when economic problems shift from extracting raw materials and manufacturing processes to distributing goods and developing an ever-widening variety of services. The principal requirement is to get along with others, to sell others, to sell oneself. Other-directed man sends out radar signals to discover what others would like him to do and then conforms to these desires.

These three types of men and societies are oriented to conformity, whether to the way things have always been done, to rigid principles which the individual dares not to question, or to the wishes of others. The power of social forces to shape the individual is illustrated in each of these cases. But there is another kind of man and society which we would do well to pay more attention to, the society of autonomous men. Man is still socialized in such a society, that is, he still learns to incorporate within his own personality the fundamental tenets of the society. But those tenets require that he does not respond to situations through automatic conformity to tradition, to his own rigid principles, or to the dictates of others.

Riesman says something about autonomous man, but little in comparison to his treatment of the other types, and there is little in the literature of sociology that deals with this type of individual or society. Autonomous man is the individual who does not conform in those sociological experiments designed to test for conformity, and who, by his behavior, helps to transform existing norms and values. By attempting to learn about autonomous man we also devote attention to the individual's power to shape society. And if man's history is the history of increasing freedom available to more and more individuals, then autonomous man is the man of the future. He has learned, first of all, to escape from the constraints which limited traditional man to devote his life to extracting a bare subsistence from nature in an agricultural society. He has learned to escape from the iron cage of personality which trapped inner-directed man into rigid responses which were insensitive to the context of a given situation. And he has learned to free himself from a dependency on others which would tie him to a life of subjugation to their desires. In response to his efforts, the society in which autonomous man resides will change more rapidly than any previously existing society.

Groups

Man's pattern of relationship to groups has changed dramatically as we have moved historically from traditional agricultural to industrial societies, and we can see what has happened by noting the changes in the family in Western society. From a situation in which most of life's functions took place within the context of the family grouping, man has learned to live his life in a great many kinds of groups, each focusing on one or a few functions. The same kind of thing has occurred in community and neighborhood settings. In place of the continuing face-to-face relationships with a group of individuals in a given locale, man has learned to venture out to engage in face-to-face relationships in a variety of locales. And it is the organization, with its limited focus, which has come to be man's new home when he departs from his family and neighborhood.

Historically, sociologists generally have decried this shift from the *primary group* to the *secondary group,* or from *familistic* to *contractual* relationships.[3] However, they have tended to accept the supposed inevitability of this transition, speculating about the continuation of the trend, with ever larger organizations, steeper hierarchies in society, and a finer division of labor.

There is an alternative way of viewing what has occurred. We can see man as having widened his spectrum of relationships with others, at the same time placing limits both on the diffuseness of emotional impact involved in any one group and on a continuation of the widening process. From this perspective, the process involves both increased freedom for man to venture outside the narrow confines of one or a few groups and increased constraints on the depth or fullness of the interaction process occurring within the groups he finds himself in. Then one possibility open to man is to continue to increase his freedom or autonomy by opening up the narrowness of these confines and by continuing the widening process. In other words, it may be possible for man to have the best of both worlds and avoid the worst of both to an increasing degree. He can move toward increasing diffuseness or depth of relationships and also toward an ever-widening range of interaction with others.

To illustrate this, let us turn to a recent trend within organizations, one which seems to be reversing the "inevitable" trend toward ever steeper hierarchies and ever finer degrees of specialization. A number of organizations have discovered that somehow efficiency can be increased by giving managers more scope for decision making, and managers have learned that the same kind of thing can work when they give more scope to their employees. This appears on the organization chart as a flatter pyramid, with each official having to supervise a larger number of individuals under him. In this way he has less time to breathe down any individual's neck. If this process continues, pyramids of organizations will increasingly flatten, and we can look toward ever greater degrees of autonomy for the individual in the organization.

This autonomy goes hand in hand with the individual's ability to bring into his work situation more and more of whatever is important to him, as distinct from the confining situation where he must gear himself to conforming to the dictates of his superior. In this way, he converts his work situation into one which is more meaningful to him, one in which he feels more involved, and one in which he is more effective. Increasing effectiveness legitimates what he is doing to his superior. And if the individual can learn to continue this process, the rolling snowball will move toward an autonomy-centered society.

We might see the same kind of trend occurring in the family. Rising divorce rates can be viewed as symptoms of a sick society in which individuals no longer are able to relate to one another within a sustained and close relationship, the end-result of an inevitable march into industrialization. From another perspective, however, we can see this trend as an indication of greater freedom for the adult male and female. In the same way, increasing numbers of runaway children can be seen as symptomatic of increasing freedom for children. And if we attempt to look beyond the present, we might envision the individual learning to develop the kind of autonomy which would enable him to use his freedom for his own development instead of attempting to escape from it into other kinds of conformity.

Social Category Systems

Social categories function in a manner directly analogous to groups in that they create in-groups and out-groups, that is, sets of individuals who belong to a given category and sets who are outside of it.

Whatever the categories—male and female, under thirty and over thirty, black and white, rich and poor, educated and uneducated, white collar and blue collar—we find that they serve both to unite and to separate people.

Pursuing our analogy between groups and social categories, a society which is highly differentiated in terms of the latter can serve to give the individual a wider range of experience than one which is not, just as an industrial society with multiple groups can. But just as groups in industrial society have become quite specialized, so it is with roles, and the result tends to be a narrowing of the range of behavior open to the individual within any given role. As he moves from one role to the next, he can easily find that what he was required to do in one role is anathema in the next. For example, the dependencies that he learns as a youth contrast with the independent stance expected of him as an adult, and that in turn contrasts with the dependency associated with the role of the aged in industrial society.

If we look for the social category systems within a group, such as an organization, we shall find grid patterns extending horizontally and vertically which tend to narrow the individual's experience. If group membership as a whole tends to limit him to a concern with a few functions and a separation from other groups, then he is much further limited within the group by these grid patterns. He is subject to special constraints associated with his sex, age, race, religion, economic status, level of education, and a host of other characteristics which have been socially defined as important. He learns to stereotype himself and others according to these characteristics instead of treating each person as a unique individual.

How can we escape such stereotyping? There is a great deal of talk within education about treating each student as an individual, and the same kind of talk about individual uniqueness is heard with respect to race relations and sex roles. By and large, however, we are only beginning to take seriously this question of how to learn to interact with individuals as individuals and not as stereotyped roles.

Perhaps our ability to interact with others in this manner is dependent on our ability to see ourselves in this way. If our self-image is a string of roles—student, female, young adult, radical, well-to-do, intelligent—then we cannot help but see others in the same way. Perhaps in an autonomy-centered society the individual will learn to avoid placing himself and others into static categories, and will see himself in continual flux. Perhaps he will learn also to see himself not as one thing, depending on the role which is expected in the particular situation, but as many things simultaneously. Perhaps this kind of self-image and view of others will prevail because, by enabling the individual to use more of his resources in a given situation, he will act more meaningfully, more expressively, and more effectively.

Institutions

Let us add to the foregoing analysis the lens of an institutional analysis. Institutions are social systems which emphasize a particular value or value cluster. We might relate the major institutions to the three fundamental elements of human behavior: ideas, goals, and action. Science and education emphasize the first, the economic institution focuses on the second (this is broadened to include not only wealth but also whatever is valued, tangible or intangible), the political institution centers on the third, and the religious institution straddles all three in its efforts to provide man with an integrated and comprehensive world-view and way of life.

Once again we can draw a parallel, this time between social category systems and institutions. If we think of social category systems as imposing grid patterns in two dimensions on any given group, then institutions impose a grid pattern of their own in a third dimension. The result is that the individual always finds himself in a small cubicle. Not only is he limited to the context of some in-group contrast to out-groups, and not only is he confined to some specialized role which is at some level in a hierarchy within that group, but he also learns to emphasize whichever aspect of human behavior is emphasized by the institution involved.

In our discussions of groups and social category systems we described a number of factors producing poor communication among individuals. Now we are in a position to examine results of this kind of communication. We can start with an illustration of communication within an organization. The overriding feature of the organization, for present purposes, is a high degree of scarcity. There is a hierarchy of status, and only some can have high status. We do not imply that this situation represents a historical throw-back, for in pre-industrial times a much smaller minority was privileged to share in whatever was valued by the society.

Given this situation, communication on the hierarchical ladder in an upward direction would tend to be distorted by the communicator's desire to place himself in a favorable light to gain favor and achieve scarce entities. Communication downward would tend to be distorted by the desire of the higher-status individuals to retain their position over those of lower status. Lateral communication, from one functional category or occupation to another, would tend to be minimal because of the general belief that such a division of labor is highly effective for purposes of production.

From an economic standpoint, such an organization tends to be quite inefficient, with its actions based on sparse or distorted information, and with little utilization of its human resources. From a political perspective, these weaknesses reveal themselves by the organization's helplessness relative to its total environment. The organization tends to be shaped by anonymous forces, such as the marketplace, instead of shaping these forces itself.

As for science and education, we have already noted the distortions and barriers associated with the flow of information up, down, and across the organization. Finally, if we define religion as concerned with an integrated and comprehensive world-view and way of life, then the organization will tend to provide very little that is satisfactory to the individual. During earlier phases of the industrial revolution in Western society a work ethic was indeed tied to a comprehensive religious ethic, with business success being seen as a sign of salvation. During the present phase, however, these two have come to be separated, with man tending to look elsewhere for something to make his life meaningful.

In our emphasis on the negative effects of groups, social category systems, and institutions on the development of the individual, we do not mean to imply that there was some rosy period in the past when the individual truly flourished. The individual has indeed achieved a great many gains throughout history. Yet at the same time he has also created forces which threaten to erase these gains along with man himself. He has started a snowball rolling downhill, but somehow he has attached himself to that snowball, and as it moves downward it threatens to crush him under its increasing weight. If he becomes conscious of the situation before he is crushed there is a great deal that he can do. Perhaps his primary mistake was to make himself dependent on the snowball and to avoid facing up to the problem of his own continuing development.

TOWARD THE POST-INDUSTRIAL WORLD:
AN ILLUSTRATION

Much of this book represents an effort to explore the future, and a basic perspective is a dimensional, as distinct from a dichotomous, approach to language and thought. For example, instead of thinking of an individual as either oriented to conformity or to autonomy, we might think of him as somewhere on a continuum between the two. We see these dimensions stretching from the past into the future. We shall focus on three dimensions which emphasize, respectively, the heart, the head, and the hand (goals, ideas, and actions), treating them in the context of the transition to a post-industrial world.

Heart

Our evolutionary perspective implies that things continue to improve in the long run. Yet the short run may be different. Suppose our own situation is no less desperate than that of the dinosaurs. Suppose that we have so firmly boxed ourselves in with a combination of tradition-direction, inner-direction, and other-direction that we have become too inflexible to adapt to changing conditions. Suppose that we are so deeply conformist that we do not have time to turn the tide.

The gravity of our emphasis on conformity may be dramatized with the aid of a series of experiments performed by Stanley Milgram.[4] Milgram worked with pairs of individuals, one a naive subject who ostensibly aided him in training the other individual, who was actually a confederate of Milgram's. Milgram ordered the naive subject to administer an escalating series of electric shocks (actually, the electric chair apparatus did not transmit these shocks) to the confederate when he failed to perform properly, and the results were groans, agonizing shrieks, shouts that the pain was unbearable, and pleas about a weak heart. A panel of psychiatrists previously had predicted that only four percent of the naive subjects would administer a shock greater than 300 volts, but actually seventy-eight percent did so, and sixty-five percent administered the maximum shock of 450 volts.

If these results might equally well apply to all of us, then it becomes very hard to keep one's mind on how far we have come within the past thousand years. What seems most relevant is that it would be difficult to go much further unless somehow our orientation to conformity is altered. Yet what could possibly produce this? Despite occasional questioning which most of us do from time to time, we tend to legitimate our groups, social category systems and institutions. We tend to believe that they have much to offer us in their present state, and we rarely toy with the idea of alternative types of social systems.

Yet suppose all of these social systems began to be seen as having results quite analogous to that described in the Milgram experiments. Suppose that each of us comes to see himself as the person in the electric chair, and suppose we come to see our torturer as the various social systems surrounding us. Far-fetched? Perhaps. Yet let us at least explore this possibility. Let us go back over the various groups, social category systems and institutions which we discussed earlier. Let us see to what extent we are able to classify basic relationships between these social systems and the individual as comparable to torture. If it is possible to do this, then it is also possible to deprive these social systems of their legitimation.

We return to our view of the individual residing in a cubicle determined by his position at any given time in certain groups, social category systems, and institutions. The particular role we play, although it offers us new possibilities from an evolutionary perspective, at the same time confines us very narrowly relative to our potential. We may have succeeded in creating a beehive world for ourselves with the kind of specialization we have erected, yet we are far more than insects. Suppose, now, we begin to become conscious of what we have done, that each of us might be so much more than what we are, yet we have not yet learned how to escape from our prisons. We submit that this is a kind of torture analogous in intensity to what we just described in the Milgram experiments.

To break free we must conceive of a continuum encompassing a series of goals taking us beyond a rejection of our existing situation to increasing levels of freedom. One such continuum—appropriate within the context of the present discussion of goals—takes us from "GOODNIK" at one pole to "MAN FOR HIMSELF"[5] at the other. GOODNIK implies a conformist orientation, such as the compliant subjects in the Milgram experiments demonstrated. MAN FOR HIMSELF implies an autonomous orientation, illustrated by the dissenters in the Milgram experiments. The dimension we refer to may be designated by GOODNIK–MAN FOR HIMSELF. Capitals and dashes are used to emphasize that this dimensional approach to language and thought, although certainly not new to our experience, sufficiently contrasts with most of the ways in which we think and speak to justify a special mode of designation.

Our path now is based on a rejection of a dichotomous orientation of in-group versus out-group or male versus female or power versus religion. The walls separating the cubicles begin to break down, and we learn to move around more freely. We no longer consider ourselves as residing in any one cubicle, and we learn increasingly to see ourselves in a larger number of places simultaneously. There is a parallel between this process and the function of language generally in helping the individual to bind space and time, bringing other situations as well as the past and the future into the present, thus expanding his consciousness. A dimensional orientation represents an extension of the symbolic process we have already learned.

The reader may wonder why we present ideas in a metaphorical mode, using terms like "goodnik," paralleling our chapters of science fiction. Is not poetry or fiction less exact and less scientific than nonfiction? Why must we resort to what appears to be a "gimmick"? What can fiction possibly add to nonfiction? Maybe it's good for people who have not learned to think abstractly, but for the more intelligent among us it certainly is not required.

There are several ways we can respond. Science and art are separate cubicles, and by using both modes of discourse we hope to free the individual to widen his range of experience. The abstractions of ordinary discourse may appear to be exact, but they, like metaphors, mean different things to different individuals. By using a variety of metaphors along with abstract speech we hope to focus more exactly on what we wish to communicate. Finally, we might return to the Milgram experiments. Most of the compliant subjects pleaded with the experimenter to allow them to stop applying electric shocks to the screaming confederate *while they continued to escalate the shocks they were administering.* We submit that this seemingly irrational behavior is typical of a disparity between head and heart which is an almost universal disease in industrial society. We may *think* we understand fully a point of view presented in abstract language, yet our *feelings* may refuse to let that point of view penetrate deeply enough to take it seriously. The heart as well as the head must somehow be reached, and the language of poetry is a useful tool to this end.

Head

Let us begin with the cognitive situation the individual faces as the walls separating the cubicles begin to crumble. In the movement for community control of the public schools, for example, the professional competence of the educational establishment to make all necessary decisions is questioned, and the professional competence of a teacher to know all the answers about what and how to teach in a given discipline comes under fire. All this is happening in a societal context in which the traditional division of labor is increasingly seen as inadequate to the task of meeting existing problems in society. Worse yet, students in a variety of disciplines who have trained for many years to become specialists are finding that they are "overqualified" for available positions. We are reminded here of Thorstein Veblen's acid comment about the "trained incapacity" which higher education tends to foist on the young.[6]

These teachers and students may think of themselves as betrayed by a society which has taught them to value specialization. We have learned to accept the life we lead in our cubicles. It is the only life we know, and we think we are happy with it, just as a caged bird who has been well cared for learns to accept and even enjoy its cage. If the cage is removed suddenly, the bird may see its new freedom as a desperate situation full of danger, and he may fear to make use of it. He will have to learn, by degrees, to forage for himself.

What appears to be required is movement along a dimension, from GOLDFISH BOWL to CONSCIOUSNESS, a dimension which stretches from an inability to step outside of oneself and see oneself confined to a goldfish bowl or cubicle to an ability to continually step outside of one's former self and bring into the present more of human experience, including the past and the future. This process of stepping outside of oneself and seeing oneself as an object is at the heart of the socialization process, that is, the process by which we learn to become human by incorporating the ideas, goals, and patterns of behavior within our social milieu. We see this process as one which can continue indefinitely. Instead of becoming socialized to play certain fixed roles, much as machines are constructed and utilized in a repetitive manner before they become obsolete and are scrapped (like the aged in industrial society), we can learn to turn around and continue to alter ourselves.

But how are our teachers and specialized students to learn to forage for themselves? One important ingredient has to do with the heart: a deep realization of the inadequacies of the beehive or bureaucratized society (in the sense of steep hierarchies and a fine division of labor). A sense of problem is required, a delegitimation or negation of a good portion of what exists, and a legitimation of efforts to search for alternatives. A second ingredient has to do with the head, a third with the hand, and they develop together. It is difficult to negate, to abandon a branch supporting oneself, unless one can cognitively see another branch to leap to, and unless one believes and feels he has the strength to make the leap. Yet we also see heart, head, and hand developing by degrees. If one waits to negate totally, one never will do so. A little negation, cerebration, and construction lead, cyclically, to a little more, and so on, much as a snowball rolling downhill enlarges by degrees, with each enlargement leading to further acceleration.

One direction for the teachers and specialized students—indeed, for all of us—involves taking into account an ever-widening array of systems, including personality, social, biological, and physical systems. In this way no major aspect of the human environment is neglected. A temporal, as well as spatial, dimension is encompassed by a concern for enlarging the present with more and more of the past and future.

This systems approach may be illustrated by the way in which we defined and discussed the various social systems in society. We recognized the importance of a holistic approach, and we proceeded by discussing social systems in relation to personality systems, attempting to lay bare a basic biological assumption about the nature of human capacities. Also, the various social systems were related to fundamental elements of human behavior: ideas, goals, and action. In this way, any instance of human behavior can be seen in relation to the various social systems. This contrasts with, say, a definition of the religious institution in such a way that it applies only to a narrow class of behavior. In the former case, the barriers separating the cubicles crumble, while in the latter case they remain erect and make it difficult for us to see the larger significance of any instance of human behavior.

Our dynamic orientation is based on an attempt to think gradationally along dimensions such as GOODNIK–MAN FOR HIMSELF and GOLDFISH BOWL–CONSCIOUSNESS. We assume that there is continuing movement along the various dimensions, and that man can learn to direct his own movement instead of moving almost completely in reaction to external forces. Further, we believe that such directed movement can be developmental for man, that is, he can learn to locate his goals along these continua and thus learn to achieve them as he moves along them. Even to those who are uninterested in human development but are interested in understanding the process of social change, such an orientation might prove to be fruitful.

Hand

If the stuff of social and personality systems is intangible—norms, values, expectations, goals, patterns of action—then to learn to alter these systems we must develop technologies which deal with intangibles. It is all too easy to assume that visible elites in the various social systems make them go or stop, or that laws move society, or that money is what makes the world go round, or that what happened in the past will also happen in the future. When a nursery school class was asked about how a war would be ended in a scenario they were developing, they decided that it would be accomplished by the prince with "a magic sword, a scary mask, and a law." Tangibles are certainly important, and we must take them into account, but we believe that it is the relatively neglected intangibles which play a far greater role in social change. However, if people have learned to live mainly on the basis of tangibles, ways must be found to make the intangibles more tangible.

The dimensions GOODNIK–MAN FOR HIMSELF and GOLD-FISH BOWL–CONSCIOUSNESS illustrate a mode of thought, something which is rather intangible. This dimensional mode of thought is concretized or made more tangible by the metaphorical content of the language used. A goldfish bowl, for example, gives us an immediate visual image of the narrowness of a specialized approach to thought. We might also add a third dimension to illustrate the hand in addition to the heart and the head: CONFORMITY–AUTONOMY. Another illustration has to do with discussions of the future. By writing science fiction, we are once again attempting to make the intangible more tangible. This mode of communication, in common with literature in general, is dependent on a healthy dose of metaphors.

There are other forms of communication which can go even further in concretizing intangibles, such as audio-visual techniques. For example, the passive watching of television might function to move the individual toward the CONFORMITY pole of the CONFORMITY–AUTONOMY dimension. Alternatively, the individual might use the video tape medium to turn the camera on himself and learn to monitor his various modes of conformity, thus moving toward autonomy. Or he might construct animated cartoons of the future he envisions and reveal many of his implicit assumptions about himself and the nature of human behavior.

We are not limited to these modes of communication. On the one hand we are able to deal with intangibles at a more abstract level using, for example, the language of computer simulation. On the other hand, we can become still more concrete or tangible, shifting from video tape or film to physical models or architecture. To illustrate how the latter might take intangibles into account, we offer the following passage from a short piece the author constructed in a science fiction workshop.

The first thing I noticed as the fuzziness of my vision of the future
began to disappear was a peacefulness. I had experienced that
same feeling once before, on the island of Chappaquidick. A
strange new way of life spread out before me, covered in soft mist.
Every part of the landscape asked to be explored, and yet there
seemed to be endless time to do everything.

As I moved to examine something that looked like a dwelling, as I
touched it, the thing altered its shape. It seemed to be alive, aware
of my presence. The new shape was much more familiar to me. I
no longer had any question that it was a house, and yet I could see
that it was built in such a way that it could be re-shaped in a
variety of ways. It was constructed out of transparent panels which
could join to one another. As I examined them I saw changes in
their degree of transparency. Now they let in no light, now they
were translucent, now they were transparent. . . .

The first paragraph attempts to set the mood of a natural environment in which man can be at peace with himself and at the same time have endless opportunities to explore his environment. Although the environment is being described directly, it is man who emerges at its center. The second paragraph carries this emphasis on man one step further, this time in the context of a man-made environment. What we wish to convey is a vision of an environment that is responsive to man, one that alters itself on the basis of his needs, one that is sensitive to the intangibles which make up man, as distinct from the kind of architecture designed to harmonize only with some external material environment.

Is this the way the post-industrial world will look? Perhaps. Or perhaps it will have many different faces. We believe that how it will look depends on our imagination in the present. We may be able to construct the future in this way. If we fail to do so, we will surely find that the future is being constructed for us. And the forces which will do the job are blind and impersonal, forces which care no more about the fate of man than the fate of the dinosaur. And we ourselves will be the helpless tools of those forces.

NOTES

1. Nikolai Amosov, *Notes from the Future* (New York: Simon & Schuster, 1970).
2. David Riesman, *The Lonely Crowd* (New Haven: Yale University Press, 1961).
3. For a brief discussion of these dichotomies, see John C. McKinney and Charles P. Loomis, "The Application of *Gemeinschaft* and *Gesellschaft* As Related to Other Typologies," in Ferdinand Tönnies, *Community and Society* (New York: Harper & Row, 1963), pp. 12-29.
4. Stanley Milgram, "Behavioral Study of Obedience," *Journal of Abnormal and Social Psychology* 67 (1963).
5. The phrase is taken from the title of Erich Fromm's book by the same name (Greenwich, Conn.: Fawcett, 1969).
6. Thorstein Veblen, *The Theory of the Leisure Class* (New York: Mentor, 1953).

SUGGESTED READINGS

HAMPDEN-TURNER, CHARLES. *Radical Man.* Cambridge, Mass.: Schenkman, 1970. Hampden-Turner presents a powerful and well-documented argument against bureaucratic social science. He calls for "a new philosophy for the social sciences—a complete reassessment of what a science of humanity should be."

PHILLIPS, BERNARD S. *Sociology: Social Structure and Change.* New York: Macmillan, 1969. The body of sociological ideas is vast and sharply compartmentalized, with a specialized vocabulary for describing each of the many kinds of social systems. This book attempts to achieve an integration around a small number of core concepts. The focus is on a historical and dynamic perspective, with the central question being how to understand social change.

REICH, CHARLES A. *The Greening of America.* New York: Bantam, 1971. Reich argues compellingly that youth's counter-culture is part of a process of cultural revolution which will transform all social systems in industrial society and produce a more humanistic world. He has been sharply criticized by those who see social change as necessarily stemming from political change or change in the educational institution; see for example Philip Nobile (ed.), *The Con III Controversy* (N.Y.: Pocket Books, 1971).

VAN VOGT, A. E. *The World of Null-A.* New York: Berkley Medallion, 1970. This classic piece of science fiction introduced general semantics to a wide audience in the mid-forties. Van Vogt states: "In *World,* we have the Null-A (non-Aristotelian) man, who thinks gradational scale, not black and white—without, however, becoming a rebel or a cynic, or a conspirator, in any current meaning of the term."

TWO

CONSTRUCTING THE FUTURE: A FRAME OF REFERENCE

We are already constructing the future. Rather than wonder whether this is possible or desirable, we move to the fundamental question of what kind of future we are constructing. Is it one where we move in a dream-like state along the Indian paths laid out for us by our predecessors, where we look downward for fear of tripping or of meeting someone else's eyes, and where the earth heaves until it finally opens up to swallow us? Or is it the kind of future in which we can consciously construct the future of that future, where we look forward, backward, sideways, upward, and inward as well as downward, and where we have made the environment our ally in our path toward continuing growth?

In the first of our science fiction stories, Basil Kornish opts for the latter kind of future. He attempts to take us from where we are now to where we might be. Should we take him seriously? If we do, then we will have to question most of our fundamental assumptions about man and society.

In the nonfiction chapter paired with the Kornish story we focus on a frame of reference which will enable man and society consciously to construct the future. We go out on a very long limb, but we believe that the limb is supported solidly by the trunk of social science, bolstered by the trunks of the humanities and the physical sciences.

25

2

The Public Life of
Basil Kornish

THE DISCOVERY

The jumble of excited voices of the news media representatives suddenly compressed itself into whispering followed by a tense silence as Kornish stepped to the podium.

"Gentlemen," he began, "I have called this news conference to announce a discovery which is of greater importance to our species and to the entire universe than any other previous discovery since the origin of life."

Kornish's statement produced near-panic in his audience. Individuals who would pay little attention to a declaration of war were shouting wildly to one another, leaping about, or rushing to the nearest phones. Kornish's reputation belied any cynicism about even his wildest ideas. It was not simply that he was world-renowned in a given discipline, such as mathematics. Kornish was brilliant in a dozen disciplines ranging over the sciences, humanities, and technologies, and the list was growing at an increasing rate.

Kornish waited until the seats in the immense auditorium were once again occupied and the suspense was becoming unbearable. He then waited a full two minutes longer until Upsnow of the *Guardian* started to tear her hair out in huge clumps, *Pravda's* Varnishky began to babble in a low, even voice, and Klutz of *Die Zeitung* stood on his chair with arms outstretched baying like an Irish wolfhound.

"Gentlemen," Kornish continued in his characteristic calm voice, "I invite each of you to suggest what would be the most earth-shaking discovery you would like to see made at this time."

No one dared speak. The hardened newsmen behaved, in the presence of Kornish, like a bunch of schoolboys with a new teacher who had just asked his first question. Finally, Jessick of *Beautiful Is Black* stood up and said, "An end to war."

Kornish bent down, took off his shoe and his red sock—the other sock was blue, to keep him continually conscious of violating the norms of an insane world—and began to scratch the planter's wart on his big toe, waiting for others to speak. Gretchen Klump of *Abolish Chastity Now* was next with "Saving the environment." The floodgates had opened, and statement followed statement very rapidly, dealing with the whole range of human problems.

Kornish stepped forward, holding up his hands for silence, and paused for a few moments to allow the hush that followed to penetrate the entire auditorium. "Within evolutionary history we have failed to solve even one of these problems, yet even if we could solve them all, the world is producing new problems at an accelerating rate. What we require, and what I have succeeded in uncovering, is analogous to the granting of a wish that all future wishes be granted. It is the discovery of the process of discovery itself."

Pandemonium broke loose in the auditorium. Everyone was shouting at once and no one was listening. A few recovered sufficiently to dash to the nearest phones. Basil Kornish scratched his wart again absent-mindedly as he tried to decipher what was being said. But he could hear nothing intelligible, and he raised his hands for silence.

"I choose not to reveal at this time the exact nature of my discovery," Kornish continued. "Action speaks louder than words, and I intend to speak loudly for a period of one year. I will then call another press conference. That conference will take place in a world very different from the world of today, a difference which will have been produced by man's conscious intervention."

Klutz, who had long since abandoned his baying, jumped to his feet. "Mr. Kornish, cannot you give us *any* further clue at this time about your discovery?"

Kornish tugged at his left earlobe as he cogitated. Then he spoke.

"Yes, I can describe the chain of events which led to it. This morning when I was sitting in my john I glanced at my watch and realized that I would have to be out the door in exactly three minutes in order to catch the train. From long experience I have learned that it takes a full five minutes for me to exercise these bodily functions properly. At that point I concentrated fully on the specific sequence and rate of contractions which would be required to complete my task in time. Three minutes later I was surprised to find myself closing the front door.

"Two additional events combined with the first to produce the discovery that prompted this emergency press conference. The first took place while I was in the men's room of the Columbia University administration building, where I was seized by a fit of diarrhea. On the partition next to my seat was scrawled in bright red paint, 'As a john wall, I am becoming conscious of myself.' Something clicked in my mind. There was an association between this experience and my earlier one that morning, and it was not simply the fact that both took place in johns. But what was the relationship?

"A third experience enabled me to solve the problem. As I was thumbing through a series of books in the stacks of the Butler library at Columbia I lost my footing and fell forward, crashing into the shelves. A book fell from the top shelf and hit me on the cranium. It was *Parkinson's Law* and it was opened to the first page. I glanced at the page, noting the familiar statement of the law: Work expands so as to fill the time available for its completion. As I was replacing the books which had fallen, I chanced upon an illustration of a man on a toilet seat in a little known sociological study on the origins of grafitti. The picture was upside down. Then I had a blinding flash of insight as I linked my three experiences together.

"The upside down picture, along with my first experience of the day when I was able to complete in three minutes what would normally take five, suggested to me a corollary of Parkinson's Law: Work contracts so as to fill the time available for its completion. As for the statement, 'As a john wall, I am becoming conscious of myself,' that suggested the vast context in time and space where this corollary can be applied. The wall's movement toward consciousness—and of course I do not imply that the wall itself wrote this statement—suggested a unity among all nonliving and living phenomena in the vast reaches of the universe. Most important, it suggested a direction for man's future development: the attainment of ever-widening consciousness of self and of the universe. Then and there it dawned on me that this corollary could be the tool enabling man to move toward infinite consciousness."

Edgar Halsey of the *Scientific American* was on his feet. His voice was highly charged, and its pitch changed frequently. "We who are men of science are all aware of serendipity as the key factor in scientific discovery. I need not go into a very long list which includes Madame Curie, Alexander Fleming, Louis Pasteur, Henri Bessemer, Louis Daguerre, Elihu Thomson, Joseph Priestley, Luigi Galvani, Wilhelm Roentgen, and William Perkin. Are we to understand that you are contradicting this scientific principle that discovery occurs by chance?"

As Halsey was talking a twinkle appeared in Kornish's eyes and a broad grin soon covered his face. "I am not smiling at you," said Kornish, "but at the pretentiousness of what we take to be science. The concept of serendipity, in common with most other scientific concepts, is a device we use to erect our ignorance into a scientific principle and then to preserve the *status quo.* When we use chance as a basis for explanation, we are simply saying that we refuse to look beyond what we already know. If Newton had not prepared himself properly, he would have eaten the apple that fell on his head and we would have heard little of him. If I had not spent much of my life attempting to expand my own consciousness, I would not have seen the significance of a john wall's moving toward consciousness."

With that, Kornish whipped out a huge handkerchief that had been bulging in his hip pocket, blew his nose loudly four times to the theme from Beethoven's Fifth Symphony, and departed as quickly as he had arrived.

KORNISH'S TV SPECIAL

After two months of intensive preparation, actor-director-composer-author Kornish is ready to present his first TV special to an estimated worldwide audience of ninety million.

The show opens with an ear-shattering and blinding explosion, with the Eroica theme in the background. It seems as if an infinite number of suns are shattering simultaneously under the impact of some unknown and overwhelming force with their fragments hurtling outward in every direction at unbelievable speeds. Initially the viewer is in the very center of the explosion, but then the camera moves outward so rapidly that the fireballs emanating from the explosion soon become no more than one pinpoint of light, and then there is darkness. After a full minute, the pinpoint of light reappears and rapidly grows larger, overtaking the camera. It is a single vast fireball, and we can dimly make out several other fireballs moving in different directions at the outer edges of the screen. We are soon within its center, and we can see tiny specks of matter permeating it. It appears to have cooled down considerably during its long journey through the universe.

The particles vary in size. They are swirling about rapidly in a huge revolving cloud. A close-up inside the cloud shows how far apart the particles actually are: the screen is mostly empty space with a very few minute specks scattered throughout. Now the paths of several of the larger particles nearly cross, and they seem to exert a pull on one another, bringing them together into the largest mass on the screen. The camera zooms out and we see this mass, which is actually very tiny, gradually accelerating its growth. The bigger it gets, the more rapidly it pulls in particles. The more rapidly it pulls in particles, the bigger it gets. During the last moments of the process the rate of growth of the mass is phenomenal as it succeeds in pulling every last particle into itself.

Once again the camera moves rapidly outward, and the mass, which is still white hot, becomes a distant speck. But now we are not immersed in darkness. There are many other specks of light around us, and they appear in the familiar patterns of the constellations of the Milky Way galaxy. We move back toward the mass we just came from, barely in time to witness another explosion, with strains from the Eroica in the background. This one produces huge chunks of matter which are ripped outward from the mass. These chunks vary in size and also in the distance they are able to travel from the central mass before they are pulled into orbit around it. The chunks now become distinctly recognizable as the planets of the solar system, and the central mass as the sun.

Pointing directly toward the third planet from the sun we move rapidly down to a point in the Indian Ocean and then just below its surface. Moving closer and closer, we see air bubbles magnified to the entire surface of the screen. The magnification process continues for some time until we are able to detect the geometrical patterning of large molecules. Huge numbers of them swarm around one another. They are not self-propelled, but are pushed and pulled by the swirling currents around them. Now we focus on one particular set of molecules, somewhat isolated from the rest, located in a place where the underwater currents go around it leaving it undisturbed. A peculiar feature of these molecules is that they appear to fit into one another like pieces of a jig-saw puzzle, although they are slightly separated. Abruptly, currents from three different directions push into these molecules simultaneously and fit the pieces of the puzzle together tightly.

The picture suddenly changes from black-and-white to color and we become conscious of the theme from the Eroica symphony as the super-molecule begins to move under its own power. On the screen we witness another kind of explosion. The super-molecule, as it seemingly dances around, grows rapidly. Then a split appears down its center, and it divides. The multiplication process continues with the camera moving further away as we witness the generation of hundreds and thousands of living molecules.

As the viewer is transported out of the ocean and into the atmosphere, the voice of Basil Kornish is heard above the now muted music. "What you have just witnessed are scenes taken from a computer simulation of the origin of the universe, the origin of the solar system, and the origin of life in our solar system. Just as it is possible to simulate events of the distant past, we are able to simulate events distant from us spatially, basing such simulations on available knowledge. We are now embarking, via computer simulation, on a journey throughout the universe in search of intelligent life, and we shall return several years in the future.

"The first portion of our journey," continues Kornish, "takes us around the Milky Way. We shall explore the twelve existing solar systems in our own galaxy." Stars whiz past the viewer in rapid succession. "We are travelling at an apparent speed which is 367 trillion times that of the speed of light. We shall now slow down for our first stop."

The first solar system to make its appearance contains four planets. As the viewer speeds over the surface of each, the central fact that emerges, more impressive than the unusual topography, is that of barrenness, silence, emptiness. There is no life here, and none will ever emerge. The planets are huge chunks of matter, and that is all. The remaining eleven solar systems present a similar picture. They vary greatly in their physical characteristics, but the story is always the same: cold, lifeless rock, devoid of atmosphere, motion without meaning.

"From among the trillions of galaxies in the universe,"
Kornish continues, "we are heading toward the one which—with
the exception of the Milky Way galaxy—contains the most
advanced form of life. Scattered widely throughout the universe
there are several billion solar systems and several million planets
with an atmosphere that is capable of supporting life. Several
thousands of these planets do in fact contain forms of life.
However, although the level of life attained on these planets
varies substantially, nowhere does it go beyond the microscopic
level. In order to reach this galaxy in a short period of time, we
must increase our apparent speed to ten to the twenty-third
power times the speed of light."

As the speed picks up, the stars rushing past merge into
galaxies, the galaxies themselves merge into super galaxies, and
even these combine in a blinding blur of light and darkness. The
process is suddenly reversed, with super galaxies and then
galaxies becoming distinct as the camera decelerates. Finally the
viewer heads toward a very large but dim star in a gigantic
galaxy, and soon an enormous planet appears. The nature of the
life on the planet shortly reveals itself in the form of spidery
beings of perhaps one foot in length along with vast hive-like
structures a dozen stories high and several miles in diameter,
each one housing several million creatures. The body structure of
these overgrown insects consists of a round head attached to a
thick cylindrical body and eight oval-shaped appendages, four
near the top of the cylinder and four near the bottom. Beyond
these few uniformities, there is a great deal of variation in
physiological structure. One kind of creature has an unusually
large head. In a second variation the top appendages or arms are
unusually long, and in a third variation the size of the bottom
appendages or legs is increased. Each biological type is engaged
in a different kind of work suited to its biological capacities, with
special tools taking into account these differences.

"The creatures on this planet have created societies similar to
those of the social insects on earth," Kornish explains. "The basis
for such societies is the kind of overspecialization which led to
the extinction of the dinosaurs on our planet and now threatens
us with extinction. Specialization which is functional in one era
can be harmful in another if the environment changes
sufficiently. These creatures have developed the kind of
physiology which does not allow them to adapt very much to
change. Although they have produced civilizations far superior to
those of our own social insects, they are much inferior to our

own. The problem here is closely related to the immense gravitational force on a planet of this size. It becomes very difficult for living forms to go beyond a certain rather small size, and as a result the brain size remains quite limited. There is almost no chance for further evolution on this planet. Its sun is dying, and temperatures on the planet have already fallen considerably. The weaker ones among these spider creatures have already died. Those still alive do not appear to possess the kind of mental capacity that can deal with these changing conditions, let alone escape to a more hospitable planet elsewhere in the universe."

The image of the creatures becomes smaller and smaller. Kornish's voice can be heard as the galaxies pass across the screen. "We are now heading back to earth. We shall return several years ahead of our own time, making use of this computer simulation to scan the future. The question to be examined is easy to state and difficult to answer: why is it that our own species, with its fantastic brain capacity, is having such great difficulty in surviving? What can man do to take advantage of his unique situation as the most advanced form of life in the universe? In our exploration of the universe we have learned how rare life is, and especially how rare is intelligent life. We are the leading edge of an incomprehensibly vast universe. If we cannot answer this question—and there is very little time left for us to do so—then perhaps the universe itself is devoid of meaning."

Earth finally comes into view, and the scenes can easily be a composite from all the end-of-the-world films that had been produced during the preceding decade. There are nuclear missile attacks and counterattacks, great black clouds of radioactive matter spreading across the surface of the earth, cities everywhere in flames, human and animal bodies lying around in every conceivable position, children screaming for their parents. Just like the one-horse shay, every aspect of civilization seems to be falling apart simultaneously. The story of what is happening is written on the faces of the small pockets of survivors: fear, hate, greed, envy, guilt, despair, hopelessness. In one scene in a fallout shelter these emotions are portrayed as the survivors battle over the remaining supplies of food and water.

"This is only one possible future for mankind," breaks in Kornish. "Whether or not it actually occurs depends on our ability to understand the forces which are bringing us closer and closer to it. We face extinction no less than the spidery creatures in another part of the universe, but our tragedy is much greater than theirs. We presently possess the capacity to alter our situation, whereas those creatures are severely limited biologically. They have created a beehive world with an intricate division of labor in which their capacities are well utilized. Our own beehive world does violence to the fantastic capacities of the individuals of our species." Kornish's voice is punctuated by views of mammoth housing projects, crowded highways, committee meetings, organization charts, prisons, mental institutions, hospitals, military salutes, uniformed flunkies, the singing of national anthems, political rallies, a huge crowd in a football stadium, workers on assembly lines, families watching television, and the hierarchy of desks in an office.

Kornish appeared on the screen, balding, grinning at himself, dressed in a purple T-shirt, green shorts, and red sneakers with matching socks. "We're back again in the present, and if we don't like that future we have a chance to construct an alternative one." Kornish paused to scratch his groin, no longer conscious of his effort to free himself from conformity to the meaningless norms of a society heading for chaos. "We now begin the second part of our special. This time the viewing audience gets an opportunity to participate. The telephone operators are now taking calls. If humans do indeed have the fantastic untapped capacity portrayed in the first part, then why should I be monopolizing all the time on the show? As highly developed as I am," Kornish grinned, "there are still things I can learn from you, and things you can learn from one another. As a matter of fact, if I keep going on in this way and refuse to shut up, I'll get in my own way." Kornish did shut up, waiting for the first call to come through.

"Mr. Kornish, I have been an active member of the women's liberation movement for five years. I've spent a lot of time in consciousness-raising sessions, and I've come to learn what a desperate situation most women are in in modern society and how much encouragement they need to view themselves as people and not only as women. Frankly, I'm getting very discouraged because I see how long it takes for most women to do something about themselves and how few women dare to take any steps at all. Looking at the special you just presented I get the impression that you are so optimistic about the human potential that you expect very rapid changes. But I can't see how this potential could apply to the specific problems I'm having with consciousness raising. Do you have any concrete suggestions?"

KORNISH: I can't think of anything more concrete than our communicating with one another right now, which is analogous to what you try to do in consciousness-raising sessions. You've just alerted me to a way of applying my ideas that I was only slightly aware of before. Specifically, it's how the question-answer or problem-solution approach applies to women's lib. If every answer is only a partial answer and only partially effective, and if we expect much more from an answer, then we're in for a big disappointment. I think that's been your experience. But if we learn to expect less of any given answer, then we can keep going and continue to develop. You've just communicated something that helps my understanding, and I hope I've done the same for you. If we expect no more than some help from one another, then we're able to keep going indefinitely without discouragement.

QUESTIONER: But I'm beginning to feel so helpless about the whole thing. Women expect me to help them, and I can't do much for them.

KORNISH: (Kicks off his sneakers and dances a few bars of a polka.) An orientation to conformity frequently is hidden behind what the individual believes is an effort to help others, to be altruistic, and that may apply to you. You've referred to your efforts to help others, and I suggest that maybe you need to focus more energy on developing yourself as an autonomous human being if you expect to help others. The operator tells me that I have a young man on the line now.

YOUNG MAN: Mr. Kornish, I'm going absolutely crazy with my parents. My mother is all the time trying to make me feel like I'm some kind of worm. I got dirt on the refrigerator, I forgot my lunch, I don't have enough friends, I'm too slow, I'm selfish, I sass her—a million things every day. My father just stays out of it and lets my mother make all the decisions. When I try to talk to her or complain that maybe she isn't right about something she makes me feel like I'm betraying her, like I'm stabbing her in the back, being ungrateful, questioning her honesty. I don't know what to do, but maybe some of your ideas can be applied to me. I feel terrible, like crawling into a hole.

KORNISH: I haven't heard your mother's side of it, so what I say may be off base. But I suspect that she's suffering from the Jewish mother syndrome, which is found in all ethnic groups and among males and females of all ages. It's based on scarcity, namely, her feelings of inadequacy in reaching her goals unless she can get you to perform according to her wishes. But each time she gets you to jump through one hoop she finds that she's not any closer to her own goals, and the same thing holds true for all the hoops she puts out for you to jump through. And when you start balking, that's another indication to her of her own helplessness. She blames you for her own inadequacies, and no matter what you do, it's not enough to give her whatever she wants out of life.

YOUNG MAN: But what can I do about her?

KORNISH: Her power over you is based on what's in your own mind. Why don't you start thinking about what *you* want out of life, and not so much about satisfying her desires, which are insatiable. She makes you conform to her wishes because she uses all the tricks about how to make you feel guilty, although I think she applies them unconsciously. If you were conscious of how her demands conflicted with your own paths toward personal development, then you would feel less guilty about disobeying her, and her power over you would begin to disappear.

Kornish continued hour after hour, on through the night. The TV special was also a twenty-four hour marathon. At about two A.M. Kornish retired behind a screen—the network had refused to let him change on camera—to change into pajamas and a bathrobe, saying that he felt more comfortable that way at that hour of the night. When the show was almost over the next evening, Kornish made his famous announcement. "All this has been great fun for me, but I'm also trying to face up to the question of where does it go from here. I don't see this as just a Victor Borge kind of entertainment, something that's quite pleasant and is repeated every once in a while. So here is what I plan to do, here is my announcement. I'm starting a human liberation movement, related to all the other liberation movements: women's liberation, the black revolution, gay liberation, the prison rights movement, welfare rights organizations, the student movement, efforts to achieve community control of schools, the antiwar movement, children's liberation, and many others. What all those have in common was illustrated by the first two people who called in: a sense of oppression or injustice felt by the individual in his relationship to some segment of society. For the women's liberationist it was the inadequacy of the feminine role in giving a woman enough latitude to be a person as well. For the young man, he felt torn apart by parents who neglected his own needs for development.

Human lib won't compete with these other movements but will
help them to draw together and gain strength from one another.
My next step is to arrange, via cable TV, a communications
network throughout the world where people in each of these
movements can communicate with one another and with those in
the related movements. Adios!"

KORNISH'S SCHOOL

"Instead of talking in detail about any one aspect of the school,
I'm going to give you an overview of it. Then you can wander
around and explore what interests you." Ann had not known
quite what she would say until the moment came. This was the
first group of visitors from among the large number wanting to
find out about Kornish's school, and neither Ann—who had
volunteered to explain the school to visitors—Kornish, nor any of
the other students had discussed possible strategies of
presentation.

"To get this overview, let's use the general approach of the
school itself. In addition to talking about the philosophy of the
school, let's live it. Why don't we start by rearranging our chairs
to form a circle, and let's partition the room so that we get rid of
most of the empty space. In this way we construct a physical
environment which is focused on the human beings in the
environment, we begin to overcome the traditional split between
student and teacher or between student and student, and we
structure a sense of urgency into the situation."

Ann allowed the visitors to rearrange their chairs and then
operated the partitioning mechanism from her console. "We have
attempted to construct a flexible physical space in our school,"
Ann explained, "and we are experimenting with many
approaches to automation. We tend to view these devices the way
most people think of pencils. They are no threat to us. Rather,
we see them as ways of extending ourselves and creating more of
a null-A environment.

"What I've just mentioned—the concept of null-A—is the key
concept which we use to construct our total environment. We try
to create more and more of a null-A situation in the physical,
biological, social, and personality systems here. To explain what I
mean by this, I'll begin with an illustration: the sentence I just
uttered."

Ann typed it out on her console and it appeared on the display
boards of the other ten consoles attached to the visitors' chairs.

The group had been limited to ten for the same reason that Kornish had invited only ten students to participate in the school: to achieve rapid and widespread diffusion of the ideas behind the school. When this was initially explained to the entering students it had sounded like a contradiction. Yet they soon learned that what is most important for the diffusion of ideas is not the number of individuals involved but the depth of communication achieved, even if it is only between two individuals. This depth yields increased power to solve problems which in turn lays the basis for wider communication.

" 'Null-A' is a concept popularized by A. E. Van Vogt in his classic science fiction novels, *The World of Null-A* and *The Players of Null-A,*" continued Ann. "A null-A world is one that is opposed to or—more accurately—goes beyond Aristotelian modes of thought. Van Vogt based his novels on the ideas developed by Alfred Korzybski, the founder of General Semantics, in *Science and Sanity.* In a null-A world the individual does not stereotype phenomena by lumping them into some category. Rather, he is aware that such categorizing abstracts only one piece of information from the infinity of potential information about the phenomena. Thus, he sees phenomena on dimensions or continua as distinct from, say, dichotomies, and he is also aware of the interrelatedness of all phenomena and all information. To illustrate, notice that I said that we try to create *more and more* of a null-A situation. I did not say we try to create a null-A situation, which would have implied a dichotomous mode of thinking. Once people understand the null-A mode of communication, it is no longer necessary for them to qualify everything that they say in this way so long as they do not get trapped by the Aristotelian or A connotations of ordinary language."

Ken Yoshada, director of the Cultural Institute of Japan, interrupted with a question. "Will we have an opportunity to learn about how you use computer simulation for creative work in the visual arts?" Yoshada, along with artists generally, had been greatly impressed by the computer techniques Kornish had demonstrated in his TV special. He was already familiar with the pioneering work of the world-renowned architect, Kenzo Tange, which utilized computer techniques to create graphic outputs on the basis of a set of functional and artistic constraints, and he viewed Kornish's work as a major step forward.

"Yes," Ann responded, "although you will find this work going on in a number of our workshops. In keeping with our null-A orientation, we refuse to specialize narrowly. Thus, the workshops do not center on any one particular technique, such as computer simulation, but rather are organized around basic problems. Four of the workshops deal with the problems of reconstructing the four basic systems of the universe: physical, biological, social, and personality. One of the social systems we deal with is that of the community of artists, and our approach to that system emphasizes computer simulation as a device for linking science with art. The simulation is based on an integration of available scientific information as well as on principles of artistic presentation. We believe that the two together result in something superior to either alone from the standpoint of scientific communication as well as that of artistic expression."

Walter Jordan, Special Associate to the President of the United States, who was known to be a participant in the President's daily volleyball game, had been deeply concerned about Kornish's activities ever since his press conference, and the TV special raised further suspicions. He wondered whether Kornish's activities would encourage dissident groups and tend to subvert the authority of the President. He felt that Kornish was becoming much too powerful, and that this was a rather undemocratic development, since Kornish had neither been elected nor appointed to any important governmental office. "Exactly what are you people trying to do?" he asked. "Let me make myself perfectly clear. I am deeply concerned about violence in this country, and I am also deeply concerned about revolts in the schools of this nation. I am also deeply concerned about law and order. Does this school teach individuals to have faith in a democratic way of life?"

"With all due respect, Mr. Jordan," responded Ann, "you're taking a very A approach. One characteristic of an A orientation is a static view of the self and the world. If we tend to see everything in black-and-white terms instead of as shades of gray, then there is no reason to budge from our present position. We are white. Others—the enemy—are black, and we have nothing to learn from them. We have already discovered the perfect approach to existence: the democratic way. Therefore, we must seek to preserve it. The way to preserve it is to prevent enemy ideas—black ideas—from destroying our white perfection.

"A null-A view of the world does not see cowboys and Indians, good guys and bad guys, enemies and friends, democracy and communism, or being perfectly clear as distinct from being perfectly unclear. The value of this approach centers on its openness to communication, learning, or development. The good guys are not so good, nor are the bad guys so bad. But we won't be able to see ourselves as partly bad if we stay with the notion that we are relatively static creatures and are unable to change or improve. For this would imply that we are stuck with these features indefinitely. Thus, a key aspect of the null-A orientation is the individual's conviction that he can change.

"To illustrate how this approach works with reference to the concept of democracy, we begin with the idea that democracy is not a static state but is rather a process, and we then inquire about how conducive a null-A world is to this process which gives people a voice in the political decisions that affect their lives. Such a world carries forward the democratic idea to every aspect of life and, ideally, every moment of time. We are all aware of the undemocratic aspects of our political life, let alone our family, business, educational, military, scientific, community, and religious life. We are also aware of how infrequently the individual has the opportunity to exert his influence in political systems as well as in most other social systems. In addition, we are all aware of how pitifully uninfluential the individual can be in his attempt to make his weight felt in social systems. In a null-A world, every single social system comes to be structured in such a way that the individual shapes his social environment, as well as his physical, biological, and personality environments, at every moment."

"But how do you deal with conflicts of interest?" queried Jordan. He had been listening and watching intently and had begun to realize that Ann was not trying to talk down to him as so many intellectuals had been doing in the recent past. She was actually trying to communicate with him, and he had responded in kind.

"Now you have hit upon a key purpose of our school. I could talk for hours about how a null-A world is built on values that are potentially infinite, such as information as contrasted with status. But unless we can demonstrate in practice—in this school —that one person's gain can be the gain of others, then we expect to convince no one of the value of a null-A world. Since I am now conducting a null-A session, I will use our conversation to illustrate the point. I could have seen your point of view as bad or harmful, falling into the kind of stereotypical thinking which is universal in the A world. The result would have been an escalation of ill will between us. Instead, I chose an approach which is quite Gandhian by nature. I tried to show you how your

own fundamental beliefs and goals with reference to democracy
might be furthered in a null-A world. Rather than rejecting your
beliefs and touting my own, I tried to present a synthesis of both.
In so doing, I came to realize more than I had previously the
great advance which this country's political system has
demonstrated to the world. At the same time, I tried to convey
the importance of continuing to advance this democratic spirit.
The result was an expanding pie of rewards for both of us,
instead of a limited or scarce pie in which my gain is your loss. If
the pie is expanding, then everyone gets more and more.
Conflicting interests which prevent the pie from expanding work
to the detriment of all concerned."

Elyan Tanuski, who had just become a member of the USSR
Politburo after many successful years as an industrial leader,
made use of the momentary pause in the discussion. "Is the
null-A world a capitalist or a socialist world? So far, I have not
noticed from anything you have said that Kornish will attempt to
lead a revolution that will seize power from the capitalists in the
nonsocialist world and give it to the people. They certainly will
not give up their power peacefully. If this is true, then Kornish's
cultural revolution or information revolution—whatever he calls
it—is a mere sham. It is a front which hides the same kinds of
exploitation of man which capitalist countries are noted for."

"Everything I just said to Mr. Jordan applies equally to you,"
Ann responded without hesitation. "The way you phrased your
question reveals your dichotomous or A orientation: capitalist
and socialist, revolution and lack of revolution, exploitation and
lack of exploitation, power and lack of power. This dichotomous
way of thinking is, in my view, the product of a world which
values scarce entities, whether that world is labeled as capitalist
or socialist. Both of these political systems have resulted in rapid
industrialization and the expansion of a bureaucratic way of life.
The noble ideas of Marx and Jefferson have failed to become
translated into societies which hold as their central purpose the
development of each individual. Neither capitalist nor socialist
political systems have been successful in directing the
fantastically powerful forces within the continuing industrial
revolution to produce a humanistic way of life. Your Black Sea is
polluted no less than our lakes and rivers, and your society
values the scarce commodity of status no less than does ours.

"To answer your question more directly, the null-A world
includes important elements from both capitalism and socialism.
For example, in this school we are learning how to eliminate to

an ever greater degree the sense of alienation about which Marx had so much to say. But it is not only the worker who is alienated or separated from the fruits of his labor and becomes thereby only partly human. It is also you and Mr. Jordan, as well as your respective societies, who are alienated from one another, and both of you are the lesser for it. As for elements from capitalism, I cite the political rights and, indeed, the sanctity of the individual. Is not this another way of looking at what Marx was so concerned with? Yet in the A world we tend to learn nothing from those who are located in the other part of a dichotomy."

Tanuski was surprised at Ann's knowledge of Marx, but he thought she was quite naive about the workings of an industrial society. "But how do you propose to achieve your null-A world if not by revolution?" he resumed. "General Motors is not going to give up its plants without a struggle. All your idealism about the individual is fine, but society is a collective unit. Marx himself shifted from his early concern with alienation to the task of arming the proletariat ideologically for the inevitable class struggle."

"It might interest you to know that your statement, with certain substitutions, could equally well have been made by one of our capitalist entrepreneurs. Instead of saying that society is a collective unit, he would have referred to a much smaller collective unit, the business firm or corporation. Instead of saying that General Motors is not going to give up without a struggle, he would have insisted that the Soviet Union would not compromise. He too would have found my ideas to be idealistic. He, just as you, has years of practical business experience behind him. And he might be concerned about arming the free enterprise system in its struggles against communism. You both give priority to the collective unit over the individual.

"Both you and Mr. Jordan have emphasized conflicts of interest, but I maintain that both of you base this emphasis on an image of a fixed pie of rewards. Both you and Mr. Jordan do not have sufficient faith in the capacities of the ordinary individual to envision him as learning how to develop an expanding pie. And it is the primary purpose of this school to demonstrate—not simply teach—that it can be done. As a matter of fact, my own ability to communicate with you constitutes a partial demonstration. I was interested in learning when I first came to this school, but I had little knowledge or confidence, and my level of aspiration was rather low. Now I believe that I am shaping the universe, and I increase rather than diminish my own self-confidence when I encourage each of you to think of yourself in the same way."

"But how much does Kornish's work speak to the needs of the oppressed people of the world?" Tanuski continued. "If they don't have enough to eat, are they going to need Kornish to raise their level of aspiration? They don't need fine words, they need action. Kornish may be able to help educated people, but he can't do anything for the masses. They don't need pie, they need bread."

Ann was slow to begin speaking. "I wish I had a good reply, but I don't," she said. "So far, it is much easier to communicate these ideas to people who have already gone through the industrial revolution and feel how limited a materialistic way of life is. But it seems to me that there ought to be a way for people who have not experienced this to learn from the mistakes of those who have. In the United States many of us thought for a long time that the answer to problems of poverty and unemployment was to give more and more power to the federal government. The Roosevelt administration did many humanitarian things for people, but at the same time it helped to develop a vast governmental bureaucracy which was antihumanitarian in a variety of ways. Maybe the individual can't depend on some large, well-organized group to protect his interests. Maybe he has to learn to depend much more on himself."

Tanuski's response was immediate. "Then what I had suspected is true. Kornish is simply restating the old Social Darwinism, the idea that only the fittest will survive, with the fittest being defined as the wealthiest. And his supposed humanitarianism is simply a cover for his elitism."

"Not at all," Ann responded. "By stressing the importance of the individual in his own development Kornish does not neglect social factors. We don't have to choose between these two. A given effect can have many causes. The Social Darwinists have emphasized the individual while neglecting the power of his social or economic situation in shaping his behavior. You, on the other hand, take the reverse position. Both views are partial truths, and Kornish's attempt at synthesis is also a partial truth, since he assumes that there will always be more factors to take into account than are known at any given time.

"Before we go into the different workshops I'd like to look back at our discussion. The way in which we've related to one another is rather unusual. The atmosphere here has encouraged each individual to develop his own ideas without feeling constrained to agree with others. It's not a play on words to say that we are learning to conform to norms of autonomy, and the same is true for the school. Another facet of this group and the school is that the dimensional approach to language and thought leads to continuing development by the participants along these dimensions. The workshops do the same kind of thing, only the emphasis is less on working with traditional modes of communication and more on developing new tools for communication, such as games, dramaturgical techniques, and computer simulations.

"And now, please step this way to the workshops. . . ."

KORNISH'S SECOND NEWS CONFERENCE

Interest in the news conference Kornish had scheduled for one year from the date of his first conference was so great that it was being carried live by every network in all parts of the globe. Everyone was talking about it, just as they had talked about his TV special and about the "new drama," the "new science," and the human liberation movement which followed in its wake. Cynicism and despair about the human condition were everywhere changing to the kind of hope and optimism which man had not seen since the height of the Renaissance. Indeed, the New Renaissance—as some had designated the recent events —was based on earlier discoveries no less than the Renaissance had been based on the discoveries of Classical Greece. And just as Greek discoveries had been almost completely buried for over a thousand years, so had the discoveries of the modern period been buried by an age of specialization. Kornish stepped forward to the microphone. The world had indeed beaten a path to his door.

Edward Constable of CBS was first to speak. "We are all aware of a fantastic number of changes, large and small, going on in every part of the globe—the new art-science-technology to be found in every occupation, the educational games that are sweeping the world and are proving to be far more effective than traditional modes of education, the new man-centered architecture which is functional for man's inner space just as older forms focused on outer space, the sudden spurt of major discoveries in every field of knowledge, art and technology, the new computer communications technology which is enabling man to use more and more of his life experiences as experiments and pass along the resulting information to his fellow man, the new humanism which has swept every aspect of organizational life and which seems to be transforming all social relationships, the creation of computer-controlled physical environments which can be responsive—via reprogramming—to the continual development of the individuals using them. It is as if someone had written a science fiction story about what he would like to see happen in the world, and suddenly the world changed to meet his specifications. We all have some ideas about what is now happening, but I think we have very little notion about why or how it is happening. Perhaps you can enlighten us."

Kornish was happy to hear this question first. If he had indeed built a better mousetrap, it was logical that people would want to know how he had managed to build it.

"The situation that confronts us in this latter part of the twentieth century," Kornish began, "is similar in certain respects to the situation in the latter part of the nineteenth century. At that time the industrial revolution was sweeping through the world and producing a rate of change unparalleled in history. At that time, also, people were confused about the new forces that had been created. The origin of sociology during that period was a reaction to man's inability to understand his situation.

"Unfortunately, no one discipline by itself was equal to the task of uncovering the nature of the forces that had been set loose in the world, forces which eventually succeeded in pushing that world to the brink of destruction. Today we are taking part in a revolution which is so vast and rapid that it dwarfs the industrial revolution into insignificance, and it is natural that the same kind of question about the origin of the transformation should be asked.

"To answer your question completely in null-A style, I would have to describe the entire universe over infinite time, but let me select a few of the crucial factors which are now operating to produce these changes. The evolution of the universe has produced after billions of years a creature—man—with the capacity to shape his own destiny. What we are observing in the world today is man's awakening to the nature of his capacities and the release of the unbelievable energies given to him by the evolutionary process. My own role has been that of a catalyst. A great many others have, in recent years, come very close to the null-A view, but they did not go quite far enough. My own work in a large number of disciplines enabled me to put more and more of my experiences within an ever-widening context of time and space. As a result, one year ago I was able to reach what might be called a take-off point in human development.

"This take-off point is analogous to the take-off point in economic development, which refers to the point at which a nation has created sufficient momentum as a result of its industrial revolution to provide itself with most of the capital it needs to continue its development. It is no longer dependent on other nations to supply it with needed capital. Of course, my own take-off point was based on human capital, or consciousness in a broad sense. But in an analogous way I was able to reach a point where I could continue to learn and develop even under the most adverse circumstances. Throughout human history no individual before me has been able to reach this point. The closest thing to it has been the scientific and industrial revolution.

"The result of my reaching this take-off point is what we are witnessing today. Change is so rapid because it can be consciously directed. Instead of man being pushed and pulled by the invisible forces of the industrial revolution, he becomes able to control the rate and direction of his own evolution. The forces involved are similar. In both cases it is the focus on values which are potentially nonscarce—infinite progress in science and technology, and infinite development of man—which provides the energy for the transformations. However, the progress of the industrial revolution has been slowed because of its dependence on the creativity of individuals who have come to view themselves as quite limited. My own development, by contrast, is not blocked by any such scarcity. More and more of my own behavior is producing growth in my understanding which then becomes the basis for more effective action. I have solved the problem of the divided self where man is torn by being so much less than he might be. My aspirations are, in the spirit of the null-A world, developmental: I take one step at a time rather than attempt to reach perfection instantaneously, and I retain all the while a vision of infinite development."

In a series of questions that followed, Kornish was asked to give more details on the mental process which enabled him to tap more and more of his potential energy. These were followed by a question from *Life* magazine's Arthur Prouty. "Can you explain this process of development in a more concrete way? How do you actually apply your theory to the ordinary events of the day?"

"Let me illustrate my approach by referring to my tennis game, which has always had a split personality. Either I would

swing like crazy and continually make heroic-type shots which
looked beautiful as they crashed into the top of the net or missed
the lines by inches, or I became what is known in the trade as a
poop artist, someone who softly pats back every ball hit to him
until he finally drives his opponent crazy. Whenever I resorted to
pooping I hated myself for it. This kind of tennis is viewed by
most players as despicable. Frequently, I would start off a match
with my desperate parody of the big game of the champions and
then, as my errors started to pile up and my courage failed me, I
resorted to the pooping tactics.

"For the past fifteen years I have played no more than once or
twice a year, never succeeding in getting my game back to where
it was in the early days, but this morning I played the best
tennis I have ever played in my life. To start with, I was
interested in developing my game far more than winning. Sure, I
wanted to win, but when the chips were down I would not run
around my backhand to take a return on my more powerful
forehand. Also, I never once resorted to pooping, which
previously had never helped me to develop any aspect of my
game and had been solely a competitive effort to win points.

"Just before the match started I thought for a few minutes
about my backhand stroke. Why had this stroke always been so
unsatisfactory? I began thinking about my tennis lessons, how I
had been taught to grip and swing the racket. I suddenly realized
that I was taught the right way to play tennis, as distinct from
the wrong way. One should grip the racket thus and so, swing in
a certain prescribed way, adopt a certain strategy of play, watch
the ball, place one's feet in certain positions, and so on. But
every player is different and every ball is at a different height
and a different angle with a different degree of spin, and every
opponent is different and every racket is different and every ball
is different and every court is different.

"As distinct from an A approach in terms of the right and the
wrong way to play, I began to think in null-A terms. I realized
that how well I was able to play would constitute a test of my
theory and therefore was related to my basic goals. I got away
from the scarcity idea associated with competitive play and
moved into the non-scarce approach of continually developing my
abilities. I started to think more situationally: every stroke
involved a unique constellation of factors which must be
understood as a total system in order to develop the most
appropriate behavior. I began to think more developmentally:
every stroke was an experiment in which there was something

important to learn about how to improve my game. As a result, I got stronger and stronger as I went along, winning 6-2, 6-0. And as I improved, I was able to keep shifting my tennis self-image to that of a better and better player."

"Do you mean to imply that any of us here in this auditorium can do the same thing in every aspect of our lives?" Jan Janssen, publisher of a chain of Swedish newspapers, was reacting to Kornish's statement. "But my tennis game is very poor, and I have no mathematical ability."

"You're being held back in each of these areas," Kornish responded, "by a sense of your own inadequacies. What holds you back—what holds us all back—was brilliantly expressed in Bergman's *The Passions of Anna.* We are all prey to a thousand-and-one humiliations which life heaps on us every day resulting from, in my own view, belief and value systems which structure scarcity, such as belief in fixed abilities or fixed intelligence or an emphasis on status. We tend to react to these humiliations in different ways.

"Some of us become cynical about life, convinced that it has no meaning. For these, no aspect of life can be approached very seriously, nothing can be entered into with intensity. Some learn to puff up the importance of others in inverse ratio to their own feelings of worthlessness. This magnifies their daily frustrations, for their lives become subject to the whims of others. They lack any central direction or thrust. Still others withdraw. These are the silent sufferers. They are all of us to a degree, insofar as we stop our growth and follow our own Indian paths of fixed routines and assured accomplishments. They—we—are afraid to venture out. We have already suffered too much. Finally, there are the Annas of the world. Intellectually they retain their ideals in the face of humiliations. But the result is a split personality. They cannot live up to these ideals and cannot face the reality of their failure. The result is a departure from reality which, if it continues, can lead to the total destruction of self and others. They have not learned a null-A approach where we move toward truth or any other virtue by degrees.

"Perhaps each of us reacts in all of these ways at one time or another, only we tend to mix them in different proportions. Your tennis game may be poor because you have been humiliated too many times, have not learned how to learn from your failures, and have withdrawn. Or you may have become cynical about the meaning or importance of tennis. Perhaps your failure to develop mathematical ability is based on a dichotomy which your teachers taught you dividing the genuises from the idiots, a dichotomy which held back their own development, and you cannot live with the reality of being so much less than your ideal. Possibly you have developed an exaggerated view of the mathematical ability of others."

The newsmen had become strangely silent. Each was thinking of personal hangups. Was it really possible that something could be done about them? If Kornish had changed the world, was there *anything* that was impossible?

EXERCISES

1. Follow Kornish's lead by negating basic ideas that almost everyone believes in, see where this process leads and explore the nature of conformity and autonomy. For example, take the phrase "We are alive" and transform it to "We are dead." In what sense is it reasonable to think of ourselves as dead? If we now think of the caveman as "dead" to the kinds of worlds which human beings are able to create, then we too may be "dead" to the kinds of possibilities which will be open to humans in the future and might even be open to us now. Or view the concept of death from another perspective. In null-A style, let us try to think of degree of life, as distinct from the dichotomy of life and death. Then an organism which can alter itself rather quickly in response to changes in its environment may be viewed as more alive than one which responds very slowly. If we accept this interpretation, then the traditionalist or conformist is more dead or less alive than the autonomous personality.

2. Write a piece of science fiction about Basil Kornish's Human Liberation Movement, tracing the successes and/or failures of the movement. Draw on your own personal experience with social movements as far as possible to provide yourself with images to draw on in constructing what you write. Be concrete, but at the same time retain your overall perspective of the situation, making use of whatever knowledge of human behavior you can command.

3. Assume that Kornish is somewhere on a continuum between the A and null-A worlds, and that much of what he says and does is not located in an extremely null-A world. Analyze some of Kornish's language, as well as the descriptions of Kornish's behavior, to locate examples of A, as distinct from null-A, behavior. Would Kornish be

more believable to you if he were more A or more consistently null-A?

4. Play the following game in a group which need not be limited in size; the game might be called "Constructing the Future." Adopt the rule that you are looking at some aspect of present-day society from a vantage point in the future. You might choose to talk about your classroom situation or situations quite far removed from the class-room, and you might choose a vantage point in the near or far future. Anyone starts with a sentence, then is followed by someone else with another sentence, and so on. Each participant is obligated to take into account what has been said before, yet he is free to turn the story in another direction. For example, the story may successively swing from an optimistic to a pessimistic interpretation of the present. After the game has been played for a period of time, it is often useful to discuss the similarities and differences among the various players.

5. Analyze your own behavior in one or more of the exercises out-lined above. In what ways do you reveal a null-A orientation, and in what ways an A orientation? Repeat the exercise, deliberately at-tempting to alter your behavior either in the null-A or the A direc-tion. Now, analyze your behavior once more. To what degree have you succeeded in achieving your goal? How do you explain this degree of success or failure? What, if anything, have you learned about yourself that you were less aware of previously?

3

A Dynamic Systems Perspective

INTRODUCTION

In contemporary society we seem to be going through a period similar to that which gave birth to sociology in the mid-nineteenth century. Forces have been set loose in the world which are overturning existing social forms, and men are losing confidence in their ability to understand what is happening. In the nineteenth century it was the industrial revolution which shattered the power of the aristocracy and the Church, a process which had been under way for several centuries. The individual could no longer depend on the pronouncements of nobles or priests for insight into what would happen in his life. Power had somehow slipped away from them and into the anonymous marketplace. In our present era we have a continuation of this industrial revolution, much accelerated by processes of automation, which joins the industrial awakening of numerous economically underdeveloped areas. Once again power is shifting, this time from the forces of the marketplace, which we have learned to understand at least partially, to processes which have not been identified. We are caught up in a post-industrial revolution in which the most fundamental norms and values of industrial society are under attack, and we neither understand what is producing this state of affairs nor where it is taking us.

In this chapter we shall set forth a frame of reference which specifies an evolutionary path from the distant past to the far future, and then we shall discuss three segments of this path or continuum: biological evolution, the scientific-industrial revolution, and the post-industrial revolution. The continuum may be extrapolated far beyond our present experience with the post-industrial revolution, and it will give us an outline of a possible future world, with details to be filled in in subsequent chapters. Even if this possible future never materializes, the construction does serve some function: by comparing existing cultures with one which is radically different we learn to bring to the surface some of our unquestioned assumptions about the forces at work in society. And these might prove to be the very assumptions which stand in the way of our achieving a deeper understanding.

In our final section, "Toward A Dynamic Systems Approach to Language," we take up where we left off at the end of chapter one where we discussed three linguistic dimensions (GOLDFISH BOWL–CONSCIOUSNESS, GOODNIK–MAN FOR HIMSELF, and CONFORMITY–AUTONOMY). In this section we locate this linguistic orientation within our general theoretical framework, focusing attention on the metaphor of the game.

Before proceeding with these topics, it is useful to place this frame of reference within the context of certain parallel developments in sociology and related fields. For example, there is a whole series of intellectual movements—going by such names as existentialism, phenomenology, the human potential movement, sensitivity training, reflexive sociology, and ethnomethodology—which attempts to probe more deeply than ever into the world within the individual.[1] From the physical sciences and biology come new attempts to integrate knowledge in the forms of general systems theory, cybernetics, and game theory.[2] From philosophy, the sciences, and the sociology of science come an increasing realization of the limitations of a traditional approach to the scientific method and a search for ways of widening this method's horizons.[3] From all disciplines—the physical and social sciences, the humanities, and the technologies or professional fields—comes a rapidly growing cry for relevance in an age when man's continued survival is at stake.[4] The recent interest in the future within different disciplines represents in part an attempt to find means for giving man the power to shape his own future. Wherever we look within academia and the professions we find thrusts toward dramatically new ways of thinking about the nature of man and society and of man's relation to society. It is squarely within this intellectual milieu that we may locate a dynamic systems perspective.

FRAME OF REFERENCE

In chapter one we presented our general approach or frame of reference with respect to sociology. We viewed human behavior as encompassing three fundamental elements: the head, the heart, and the hand (or ideas, goals, and action). In addition, our orientation pointed toward change more than stasis. Finally, we were interested in certain types of change, namely, change along various dimensions such as the linguistic dimensions cited above. Our task here is to carry each of these three ideas further.

Human Behavior

The child who learns the word "plane" and uses it whenever the occasion arises is pulling together what otherwise might have been quite disparate experiences. He does the same kind of thing for every other concept, and so do we all. Language is a powerful tool for integrating experience, and because society emphasizes language that is held in common by large numbers of individuals, we are able to pool the knowledge gained by others, past and present, along with our own.

Yet somehow, for all this, people seem to have serious difficulty communicating with one another. Language separates as well as unifies, erects barriers along with building bridges. Each concept divides phenomena into two classes: those which may be subsumed under the concept and those which may not. By lumping planes into a single category we tend to pay less attention to the unique characteristics of any given plane or to the phenomena for which no name has yet been invented. Furthermore, language tends to emphasize what is visible and tangible at the expense of the nonmaterial and intangible, and it may be that these latter are most useful for human beings to pay attention to.

If somehow all instances of human behavior were seen as having certain things in common along with whatever differences were recognized, then an important basis for unification would exist, just like the hub connecting the spokes of a wheel. Instead of getting completely lost in the differences we would see the similarities along with the differences. Every object differs from every other object in color, shape, position, weight, and any number of other characteristics, yet they are similar in that their behavior can be described by the laws of gravity and other physical laws. Such laws have been developed by the construction of concepts, such as time and distance, which can be applied to all physical objects.

The hub we use to understand human behavior is made up of ideas, goals, and actions; or the head, the heart, and the hand. With this extremely simple foundation, we can begin to see that all instances of human behavior bear some relation to one another, since all illustrate these fundamental elements. What may, on the surface, appear to be completely different kinds of behavior, may be described on the basis of variations in goals or ideas or actions.

A crucial test for this mode of viewing human behavior is the degree to which it helps us to see relationships we ordinarily would miss. That, after all, has been the power of language through the ages, and the development of language should carry this forward. For illustrative purposes, let us examine three types of concepts: scientific, economic, and political. We shall contrast the connotations of these concepts in ordinary usage, where our hub concepts are not generally brought into play, with their connotations when we pay explicit attention to the hub concepts.

"Scientific" generally implies a rather special mode of learning about phenomena, one which is developed after long educational experience. The scientist is a professional, a guardian of certain esoteric ways of dealing with phenomena, a powerful figure who has changed our world for good and for ill. But he is not the common man, and his work is different from that of everyone else. As for "economic," we tend to think of money, goods and services, supply and demand, large corporations, prices, inflation, cost of living, tangible things to buy, poor people, private property, competition, government ownership, banks, interest rates, mortgages, credit, and a host of other phenomena. But we fail to think of what each of us considers desirable and undesirable in a broader sense than goods and services. "Political" carries connotations of governments, laws, elections, representatives, speeches, courts, interest groups, and so on. But we don't tend to think of such things as power struggles within families.

Suppose we now view the scientific, economic, and political institutions as emphasizing ideas, goals, and actions, respectively, with no implication that an emphasis on one of these excludes the others. We will then begin to see relationships between what scientists and ordinary folk do, and the walls dividing human experience will begin to come tumbling down. The scientist attempts to put ideas together in a systematic way (theories or hypotheses), to test these ideas (research), and to communicate the results of these efforts (publication). But isn't this what all of us do, to a degree, all of the time? When we put our ideas together we call it thinking instead of theorizing; when we test these ideas we call it living instead of research; and in place of publication we simply attempt to talk, to touch, make gestures at, or write to one another. We submit that both scientist and layman have much to gain by seeing their behavior as similar. Perhaps the layman can learn to become more scientific in his behavior, and perhaps the scientist can learn to do the kind of research that speaks more directly to the problems which laymen are experiencing.

In the same vein, instead of viewing economic behavior as something rather special, we can view it—in the guise of human evaluation—as a component of all human behavior. The result might be that economists will learn to pay more attention to those human desires that are not directly translatable into monetary or material terms. Perhaps laymen will learn to see that all of their behavior takes place in an exchange situation, and their bargaining position depends both on how much they value what others have to offer as well as how much others value what they have to offer. As for political behavior, we can think of it as extending beyond governments to include all human action, for all action by any individual to a degree influences other individuals. As students of power learn to understand this, they will extend their knowledge beyond the narrow confines of the limited situations they tend to study. And when ordinary people see the breadth of political behavior, they will learn to see the relevance of academic knowledge.

Other examples of the utility of this mode of viewing human behavior can be given. Let us consider the sciences, the humanities, and the technologies. Once again we may note their emphasis on the head, the heart, and the hand, respectively. A narrow conception of the scientist sees him as a castrated man, bereft of those emotions which would otherwise indicate his humanity, and as a man who has bound and gagged himself. These images are implicit and not explicitly formulated. The scientist uses his heart and his hand, but he does it in such a way as to deprive them of their capabilities for helping him to be a scientist. Similarly, a narrow conception of the artist or technologist truncates head and hand, or head and heart. We see head, heart and hand as spokes in a wheel, and if any one is foreshortened the wheel does not function well. Their integration, represented by a rim around the spokes, provides the basis for extending the spokes beyond the rim, and additional rims and spokes can continue to be added *ad infinitum.*

Change along Continua

Concepts like time, distance, and weight set up dimensions or continua in physical science theory, and they in turn give us a basis for understanding change. We learn to view change along such dimensions, and powerful conceptual tools such as calculus are based on these foundations. We might contrast this dimensional approach to a nondimensional one that is typical social science. For example, sociologists see a large variety of phenomena as affecting human behavior: social class, ethnic group, education, political orientation, occupation, income, nationality, age, sex, religion, family status, group memberships, size of community, status, and so on. One way to deal with all this complexity is to ignore the changes and focus simply on classifying the individual into these different categories. Social science becomes, with this orientation, a search for stable uniformities.

But what if change is omnipresent, and what if our emphasis on stasis blinds us to the phenomena around us? In our view this is the situation that prevails today. An alternative way of handling such complexity is to locate ideas, goals, and actions along continua or dimensions. In this way we are able to take into account large numbers of goals in a simplified way, since there are an infinite number of points along any given continuum. And once we have defined such continua we can talk about rates of change easily.

To understand the significance of our distinction between a static and a dynamic orientation to social science, it is instructive to examine a transition from the static to the dynamic in mathematics and physical science. The former may be illustrated by Euclidean geometry and an Aristotelian logic, whereas the latter is illustrated by calculus. Geometry deals with fixed relationships and calculus deals with changing ones. What is most significant is that it was the latter which served far more than the former as a basis for the scientific revolution. We believe that part of the reason for this is that the universe is constructed along dynamic lines, and another part is that when human beings conceive of the universe dynamically it becomes even more so. We are far more than passive observers; what we see is based on an interaction between what is in us and what is outside us.

However, our own interpretation of the basis for the successes of mathematics and the physical sciences was not the prevailing one during the development of sociology. What came to be important was an Aristotelian logic of proof as distinct from a mathematics of change or a search for the process of discovery. The crucial question, at least within quantitative sociology, came to be *whether or not* one phenomenon was related to another phenomenon, and not to discover *degrees of relationship* or *the ways* in which phenomena changed and affected one another. The dominant metaphor has been a Euclidean geometry of static relationships far more than a calculus of change.

Sociology and the social sciences appear to be at the beginning of the kind of transition to a dynamic view of phenomena which characterized physical science many years ago. This is in part being forced on us by the increasingly evident disparity between the attempts to apply a relatively static orientation and the progress made on the large problems facing man. In part it is also the product of an increasing understanding of the transition undergone by mathematics and the physical sciences. In part it is due to the development of a new tool for working with complex and changing relationships, the electronic computer.

An Illustration of a Dynamic Systems Approach

From the preceding discussion of our frame of reference, the two key ideas that emerge are (1) an interest in taking into account the multiple aspects of any given situation, such as head, heart, and hand, and (2) a focus on process, or the dynamic aspects of the situation. One term we can use for the former is a "systems" orientation, viewing head, heart, and hand as systems of ideas, goals, and actions. Indeed, we have already used the concept of social system and differentiated among groups, institutions, and social category systems on this basis. By adding the concept "dynamic," we emphasize an orientation to change and development, with development based on movement along various dimensions or continua.

The concept we have selected to illustrate a dynamic systems approach is the continuum SHELL GAME–CONTINUING REVOLUTION, and our focus will be on the SHELL GAME end of the continuum. SHELL GAME refers to a mixed situation in which there is at least one end or goal and at least one means for moving toward that goal. The means and the end might each be conceived of as a continuum. To the extent that movement along one continuum interferes with movement along the other, we have SHELL GAME. To the extent that they are mutually supportive, we have CONTINUING REVOLUTION. In other words, the situations we will examine are sufficiently complex so that we may observe conflict or a kind of cooperation among two or more forces. Thus, SHELL GAME is our prototype of conflict, and CONTINUING REVOLUTION is our prototype of cooperation, that is, the joining of forces so that they mutually support one another.

The concept "shell game" is derived from a game of chance common at carnivals where the player attempts to guess which one of three shells a pea lies under. The house or dealer dexterously manipulates the shells and the pea and almost invariably succeeds in deceiving the player, whose weakness is that he becomes absolutely certain that the pea is under one shell when actually it is under another. From our more abstract perspective, in SHELL GAME a process which initially is a means to the furthering of some other end becomes by an invisible process (analogous to the dexterous manipulation of the pea and the shells) an end in itself which militates against the furthering of the original end.

In CONTINUING REVOLUTION, by contrast, there is a continuing examination of the impact of the means on the end. When the pea of the means shifts to a shell which is in opposition to the shell representing the original end, this shift is immediately detected. Whatever steps are taken as a result, efforts are made to do away with conflict between means and end.

The relation between means and end is an intricate one, involving many factors and extending over a considerable stretch of time. We warn the reader that any of our diagnoses could be changed on the basis of additional information.

Illustrations of SHELL GAME from Western history are readily available.[5] Going back to classical Greece, Athenian democracy and independence were ultimately subverted by the attempt to force obedience from small towns and to extend the Athenian empire—a strategy which was initially seen simply as a means for strengthening Athenian democracy and independence. In Roman times the Roman patricians acquired wealth by confiscating common lands from villagers, not forseeing that their generals subsequently would take over the patricians' properties in order to pay the soldiers' pensions which previously had come from these same common lands. The early Christians were only too happy to ally themselves and the Church with the Roman Empire, with the result that they absorbed an autocratic orientation which conflicted with their emphasis on the redeeming power of love in society. Closer to modern times, Philip II used the Inquisition to obtain religious and political obedience, which helped to provoke the men of the Spanish Lowlands to rise up against Spanish rule. The revolutionary and liberating impact which the French Revolution might have had on its dynastic neighbors was blunted by some of the means used to achieve this impact, namely, taxation, indemnities, and conscription. Moderate Southerners might have succeeded in retaining slavery in those states where it had already been established if they had not decided to join the extremists in secession and war. After World War I the conduct of the allies in forcing Germany to accept the sole guilt for the war, establishing a hunger blockade, and collecting large indemnities helped Hitler to build up a resentful nationalism and destroy democratic institutions. British attempts to prevent Indian independence through the violent suppression of the Gandhian movement stirred the British and Indian conscience to give great impetus to the independence movement. Some Southern sheriffs, in their attempt to deprive blacks of their civil rights, used cattle prods and police dogs in front of television cameras, and the resulting moral backlash helped to insure the passage of the civil rights law.

Our final set of illustrations of SHELL GAME is taken from the literature of sociology. These fall into two types: those focusing on cultural or goal displacement (head and heart), and those centering on social organization or interactional displacement (hand). Concerning goal displacement, a classic illustration is a series of three displacements which carry from the early Reformation to today, where each successive means that is transformed into an end is in turn displaced by a subsequent means. Whereas in early Calvinism —which was oriented to a dictatorship of ministers—good works were viewed merely as a means to atone for sin, they later became the basis for a religious calling upon the individual to orient his life around the effective discharge of secular duties.[6] This religious calling as an end was itself displaced by a secular ethic of hard work and achievement, an ethic which previously had served simply as a means to ascertain religious salvation.[7] Most recently, this ethic of achievement or production appears to be undergoing displacement by an ethic of success or consumption.[8] To cite an illustration of goal displacement outside of religion, we look to the field of community development. It has been observed that frequently an attempt to strengthen the integration and development of a community as a whole gets sidetracked or displaced by an immediate goal, such as an urban renewal program or the attraction of a new industry.[9]

As for interactional displacement, examples having to do with bureaucracy are numerous. Conformity to organizational rules down to the last detail, originally conceived as a means for achieving organizational ends, tends to become transformed into an end in itself, resulting in the familiar phenomenon of red tape.[10] According to one theorist, there is an "iron law" of oligarchy: no matter how egalitarian the principles of an organization, principles of reform are inevitably displaced by the task of strengthening the organization, a task which previously was simply a means for achieving organizational ends.[11] This process may be illustrated by any kind of organization, such as organized religion. A cult or sect, which initially develops out of dissatisfaction with existing institutions and is organized along spontaneous and informal lines, becomes transformed into a formal denomination or church dominated by empty formalities, the suppression of the personalities of church members, and an attempt to achieve respectability through conformity to societal institutions.[12] But interactional displacement need not proceed solely in the direction of strengthening an organization's interest in maintaining itself at the expense of its ideology. For example, a study of the Women's Christian Temperance Union shows that it has not acted to preserve organizational values at the expense of past doctrine.[13] Instead of changing its program of crusading against alcoholism to achieve greater harmony with dominant values after the repeal of Prohibition, it chose to sacrifice its potential strength, and organizational strength was itself displaced in favor of the original doctrine.

By presenting the above frame of reference, we have begun a process of explaining one type of social change which appears to be rather common. The purpose of the remaining sections of this chapter is to continue this process in greater depth. We hope to unearth more of the forces involved in the SHELL GAME—whether they involve goal displacement or interactional displacement—as we proceed to analyze biological evolution, the scientific-industrial revolution, and the post-industrial revolution.

BIOLOGICAL EVOLUTION[14]

A most significant contrast in evolutionary history is that between the vertebrates and the social insects. Vertebrate evolution led to increasing brain capacity. Mutants with increased brain capacity tended to be more effective in surviving and proliferating than non-mutants, and these mutants in turn were able to produce further mutations with still larger brain capacity. With *homo sapiens* a species was produced with a biological capacity for developing complex languages, a capacity closely related to a complex nervous system which had evolved. For the vertebrates this evolutionary process resulted in an unprecedented ability to change or control the environment, an ability based on an increasing capacity to extract and make use of information obtained from the environment. For example, language—along with the thought processes which it helps give rise to—offers man the opportunity to apply to any momentary situation vast amounts of information obtained from others or from his own personal experiences.

As for the social insects, their fate is wrapped up in an initial failure to develop vertebrae. On a planet of this size, such a failure implies a severe limitation on the possible size of an organism due to the forces of gravity. And a limitation of total size implies a limitation in the size of the nervous system. The result has been a severe limitation in ability to control the environment.

We can also use the evolution of the social insects to illustrate the SHELL GAME. Operating within the size limitation stemming from a lack of vertebrae, they nevertheless managed a degree of positive development which has enabled them to adapt admirably to a very wide range of conditions and to multiply. Although the individual insect's size was limited, a biological division of labor might develop —for example, into workers, drones and queens—which might in part make up for this deficiency. Such a biological development seems to constitute both a success and a failure. On the one hand it improved adaptability if we accept the size limitation as given, but on the other hand it handicapped the social insects in their ability to alter themselves and thus achieve greater control over their environment. If we view the social insects as a step toward the development of highly intelligent forms of life, then their successive mutations which improved their adaptive ability and preserved their lack of vertebrae may be seen as means which became ends in themselves. Their success in one sense became a failure in another.

THE SCIENTIFIC-INDUSTRIAL REVOLUTION

Our focus in viewing the scientific-industrial revolution will be on specialization, and we will obtain our picture through the lens of SHELL GAME. We begin with an analogy from our discussion of biological evolution: between the development of physical science and technology and vertebrate evolution, on the one hand, and between social science and technology and the evolution of the social insects, on the other hand. We are talking about CONTINUING REVOLUTION and SHELL GAME as they relate to biological revolution. Just as in the case of vertebrate evolution, physical science and technology have been developing systems of men and ideas which represent continuing advances both in the ability to utilize a widening range of information and in the ability to change or control the environment.

By contrast, as in the case of the social insects, the rate of development in social science leaves much to be desired. To carry the insect analogy a step further, our specialized approach to the scientific method results in a social division of labor which operates in the same general way that the biological division into the castes of queen, worker, and drone operates. Both serve to create boundaries around the activities of the individual member of the species, boundaries which work against the individual's opening himself up to a wider range of information and increasing his ability to solve problems and control the environment.[15]

These boundaries condition the individual to accept without question a vast number of common understandings or assumptions which, as a result of their implicit nature, are not open to being tested and improved. For example, the survey researcher in sociology tends to accept the many limitations associated with this mode of research. He works within these limitations, yet rarely challenges the basic premises of the approach in an effort to transcend their limitations in an important way. Suppose that he opens up channels of communication to philosophy, law, and history. From the philosopher he might learn techniques for bringing to the surface his own implicit assumptions. From the lawyer he might learn to subject his data to rules of evidence more stringent in certain respects than those he had been accustomed to employing. And from the historian he might learn something about the process of establishing the credibility of a given source of information, a process which would make him think twice about his respondents' ability and willingness to tell the truth. As a result, the survey researcher might come to spend more time doing something to overcome the limitations of his method.

There are different ways of specializing, and they vary in the way they close off options. For example, there is the division between theory and methods. Advances in methods, as illustrated by the development of survey research techniques, tend to become ends in themselves and frequently displace in importance the theoretical development which constituted their original purpose. Then there are the formidable barriers dividing the sciences, humanities, and technologies from one another, formalizing Western civilization's trichotomy of the head, the heart, and the hand. Science tends to be defined as a value-neutral or value-free enterprise. One result is that it encourages the scientist to ignore his own implicit values rather than bring them to the surface so that he can take into account the ways in which they affect the conduct of his investigations. Also, he will tend to avoid any probing into the sources of his own creativity, since his own personal motivations are to be kept apart from his research. In the attempt to separate science from technology, the results of each will not be geared to the development of the other, and both will lose as a result.

In our analysis of the SHELL GAME within the scientific-industrial revolution we have focused attention on the severe limits imposed by a narrow view of the scientific method on the development of social science and social technology. We believe that this assumption is also impeding the development of the physical sciences and physical technology, but not to the same degree. For one thing, physical science developed very far before this narrow interpretation was erected, and it could continue to be carried by its own momentum. For another, the social sciences deal with phenomena which appear to depart much further from the limiting and static assumptions of this view.

THE POST-INDUSTRIAL REVOLUTION

At the risk of oversimplification, we might characterize the emerging post-industrial society as a society where the individual is both the central means of solving problems and the most important end, a consistency characteristic of CONTINUING REVOLUTION. For purposes of illustration we shall take up two social movements under way in industrial society: the black revolution and the women's liberation movement.

The black revolution in the United States is partly a continuation of the industrial revolution, a movement which lifted individuals out of lives totally involved in survival. Much of the effort is in the direction of better opportunities for employment, better housing, improved facilities for obtaining credit, the kind of education which improves employment opportunities, cooperatives which offer goods at lower prices, opportunities for starting businesses, and so on.

But there is much more than this to the black revolution, for it is taking place in a world where the industrial revolution already has reached an advanced stage. It is analogous to the "revolution of rising expectations" of the so-called underdeveloped areas of the world. The problem is not merely to achieve an industrial revolution but to do it in a world where one starts far behind in the competitive race and where the emptiness of material success as an ultimate rationale for existence is being felt in "advanced" economic sectors of the world. The new media of communication have vividly brought home to the black (and to the nonindustrialized world) the contrast between poverty and affluence. At the same time, the "culture of poverty" has communicated to them despair and hopelessness. When other groups (or nations) were ascending the economic, political, educational, and status ladders, they were mired in an endless cycle: a narrow range of personal experience and poor linguistic development in the home, a lack of knowledge and ability to obtain further education, a poor self-image and lack of motivation to achieve a better life, poor jobs and housing, and means of withdrawal from life. Each aspect of the overall process feeds back to and reinforces the others, and the repetitive cycling continues.[16]

As a consequence of these and other problems, the black revolution focuses not only on material well being but also on the development of self-esteem, and therein lies its significance as part of the post-industrial revolution. The rejection of integration and the attempt to develop separate black institutions is related to this goal, for in an integrated world it is too easy for both whites and blacks to slip into the old Uncle Tom patterns of behavior. Slogans like "Black is Beautiful" have significance in this overall effort to create the kind of society where the black is no longer an invisible man. The black struggle for human dignity is part of the long struggle for freedom from the domination of feudal forms of society which the industrial revolution represents. But the deficiencies inherent in the modern bureaucratic society which militate against man's achievement of such dignity make the black struggle a part of the larger post-industrial revolution.

The women's liberation movement is more completely a part of the post-industrial revolution than is the black revolution. Throughout the history of Western society the role of women has shifted to accommodate the twists and turns of the industrial revolution. Victorian romanticism had its roots in part in an interpretation of Christian, Aristotelian, and Platonic thought which saw the renunciation of physical pleasures as movement toward the supreme good. In St. Paul this renunciation was a means to the end of spiritual development, but this means became an end in itself in Victorian England (SHELL GAME). With the decline of domestic industry a large surplus of women was created in the labor market. The Victorian conception of marriage helped to take women out of the labor market and at the same time provided a context where a sexual relationship could be viewed as part of a virtuous life. Samuel Richardson's *Pamela* provides a clear illustration: she is too delicate to soil her hands with work, and she faints at any sexual advance. She is the embodiment of purity, modesty, decency, and propriety. In the *Pamela* role a means was provided by which the Victorian middle-class woman could distinguish herself from the working class and also from the supposedly licentious aristocratic woman.[17]

The decline of the Victorian role for women—and this role had spread to the status-striving segment of working-class women—is associated with a change from an emphasis on mining and manufacturing in the very early industrial period to the service occupations at a later time. The demand for typists, clerks, and saleswomen provided the middle-class woman with a genteel alternative to a life of "leisure" in the home. Ibsen's Nora in *A Doll's House* illustrates the new role of the emancipated woman. Nora decides to leave Helmer after eight years of marriage. To Helmer's statement, "Before all else, you are a wife and mother," Nora replies, "I don't believe that any longer. I believe that before all else I am a reasonable human being, just as you are—or, at all events, that I must try and become one."[18]

The self-esteem that Nora is searching for corresponds to the most recent quest of women in the industrial society, just as it is also part of the modern black revolution. Yet this search seems to have experienced a much slower rate of progress than that associated with the black revolution, and once more we might note the workings of the displacement process. As we have moved into a consumption-oriented society in the later stages of the industrial revolution, the role of women has been altered to provide widespread markets for the quantities of goods we are able to produce. The home is the center of consumption activities, and with the carrying-over of the office-home division of labor, women have come to be the chief consumers in the "advanced" industrial societies. Also, in a civilization that is shifting from task-orientation to leisure and play, women have come to be a primary object for emotional release. They constitute a major device for selling the products of industrial society both via advertising techniques and via the *Playboy* philosophy of their role as playmates. Thus, as consumption has become an important end in society, women have developed the kind of role where they are either "consumed" as sexual objects, where they help to induce others to consume, or where they themselves are the consumers.

The success or failure of the women's liberation movement may be linked with all other efforts to move toward an individual-centered post-industrial society. As yet, we know very little about how to design the kinds of social structures within which the individual —whether his role is that of a black or a woman—can be treated as a developing individual who is an end in himself rather than as a stereotype who is primarily a means to other ends. In the foregoing discussion of the black revolution and the women's liberation movement, there is a common emphasis on achieving self-esteem. There is also emphasis on treating women as unique individuals rather than as stereotypes, and this is similar to the efforts by blacks to eliminate prejudice. In a world where paths to achievement and success generally take precedence over the treatment of individuals as unique ends, however, such movements face severe difficulties. Perhaps a key problem these movements face lies in the process of displacement or SHELL GAME. Under what conditions can they avoid the kinds of displacements which have derailed so many humanistic movements in the history of Western society?

Let us conceive of a society in which *both* the dominant means and the key ends focus on the development of the individual, and let us not be deterred by the fact that we are able to see such a society only very dimly. In such an integrated culture[19] there would be little or no displacement of the type which subverts the end for a means which is moving in another direction. This would constitute a continuing revolution in which man would continually assess the relationships between ends and means, and act accordingly.[20]

How might this come about? By degrees. Suppose that women, blacks, students, and others who are concerned about breaking out of narrowing roles which society has traditionally prescribed learn —as they are—about how these various societal problems are all of a piece. Suppose they and others learn to see their opportunities in life as being opened up or closed down on the basis of how frequently and intensely they play CONTINUING REVOLUTION. For this to occur, the playing of this game would have to produce opportunities that are highly valued by the players. Concerning the head, for example, suppose that the individual's understanding of himself and his relation to the universe continued to grow deeper. As for the heart, we might think of increasing ability to feel deeply and to express oneself emotionally. With respect to the hand, an example would be the growth of abilities which are ever more effective in solving problems.

To probe more deeply into the nature of games such as SHELL GAME and CONTINUING REVOLUTION requires that we take the time to examine more thoroughly the linguistic orientation which produces such dimensions as SHELL GAME–CONTINUING REVOLUTION.[21] In addition, we must examine the meanings implied by the metaphor of the game.[22] This we intend to do in our final section.

TOWARDS A DYNAMIC SYSTEMS APPROACH TO LANGUAGE

By a dynamic systems approach to language we mean one which carries forward what appears to be the central function of language: to extend any situation to incorporate knowledge of phenomena in other situations separated spatially and temporally from the given one.[23] A dynamic systems orientation to language is one which selects from ordinary usages those which emphasize both seeing a given situation in relation to many other phenomena and seeing it as a process with antecedents stretching far backward in time and with immediate and long-range consequences in the future. To state the matter another way, such an approach emphasizes the interrelationships among all phenomena as well as the ever-changing nature of all phenomena. It also represents an application of C. Wright Mills's concept of the sociological imagination—with its historical orientation and breadth of vision—to language.

There are a great many ways in which one can use a given language to emphasize these qualities. In English, we can use nouns and pronouns in a context which indicates that they are not fixed. For example, "I am changing," "Sociology today is much different from what it was five years ago and what it will be five years from now." We can describe the context of a given situation and relate it to factors seemingly distant from it in time and space, such as our illustrations of the displacement process from different cultures and periods of Western history. We can avoid verbs like "is" and passive constructions in favor of more dynamic ways of constructing sentences. We can relate value judgments to particular situations instead of keeping them at an abstract and timeless level. We can avoid simple dichotomies and deal, insofar as possible, with dimensions or continua. We can use the metaphor of the game to help us attain the required breadth and dynamism. It is to this latter possibility that we shall address ourselves in greater detail.

Let us begin by comparing two seemingly equivalent phrases: "the hypothesis of displacement" and "the SHELL GAME." The game metaphor differs from the specialized scientific language of hypotheses in at least three important respects:

1. The game metaphor conveys the idea of a process which will be continuing to produce new outcomes, integrating thought, motivation, and action. By contrast, the language of hypotheses connotes a causal relationship between two or more factors at a given point in time, with the factors not necessarily constituting a continuing behavioral sequence.

2. A game has explicit rules which provide the context for any given play of the game. However, the language of hypotheses does not refer us to the myriads of implicit rules which provide context for them.

3. The rules of a game are in a certain sense arbitrary, and they can be changed if the players agree to do so. But the language of hypotheses conveys no similar implication that the rules governing the behavior of phenomena can be changed.

It is on the basis of these three differences that the game metaphor seems to illustrate a dynamic systems approach. As a process, the game connotes continual change which takes into account basic units of behavior, that is, ideas, motivation, and action. The explicit rules of the game provide a context which interrelates phenomena in certain ways, and because the rules are explicit we can obtain evidence of the utility of the rules. Perhaps most important, the rules of the game can be changed: man can alter his situation if he takes into account the rules of the game as well as the changes in phenomena. This is crucial because the consciousness of this possibility gives the player leverage to bring to bear his own personal experiences on the game situation, and to see both as changeable.

With this brief view of a dynamic systems approach to language, let us apply these ideas to the question raised previously, namely, by what process does movement toward CONTINUING REVOLUTION take place on the SHELL GAME–CONTINUING REVOLUTION continuum? What is required for CONTINUING REVOLUTION is a continuing reassessment of the relationships between means and ends and continuing action to alter one or the other to achieve consistency. This demands the ability to step outside of one's situation mentally, and from this new perspective reevaluate means and end. It also requires the ability to act on the basis of such new evaluations. But this is exactly what the game metaphor helps the player to achieve. The rules are fairly explicit, and he can view them from outside, from the perspective of everyday life. And the game encompasses action and motivation in addition to thought.

Suppose that we learn to apply the game metaphor to everyday behavior, that is, to view life as comprising various kinds of games. Then the individual would begin to develop corresponding abilities to step outside of any given situation and reevaluate it, and to act on the basis of such reevaluations. But this is exactly what is called for in CONTINUING REVOLUTION. Our overall point is that the use of the game metaphor in ordinary language can facilitate movement toward CONTINUING REVOLUTION. What is also required, however, is that certain connotations which frequently accompany this metaphor—the repetitive nature of games, their competitive aspects, their separation from everyday life—be disassociated from it.

NOTES

1. See for example Charles Hampden-Turner, *Radical Man* (Cambridge: Schenkman Publishing Co., 1970); Stanford M. Lyman and Marvin B. Scott, *A Sociology of the Absurd* (New York: Appleton-Century-Crofts, 1970); Joseph R. Royce, *The Encap-*

sulated Man (Princeton, N.J.: D. Van Nostrand, 1964); Nathan A. Scott, Jr., *The Unquiet Vision: Mirrors of Man in Existentialism* (New York: World Publishing, 1969); and Alvin W. Gouldner, *The Coming Crisis of Western Sociology* (New York: Basic Books, 1970).

2. See for example Walter Buckley, ed., *Modern Systems Research for the Behavioral Scientist* (Chicago: Aldine, 1968); Ludwig von Bertalanffy, *General System Theory* (New York: Braziller, 1968); Norbert Wiener, *The Human Use of Human Beings* (Garden City, N.Y.: Doubleday, 1954); and John McDonald, *Strategy in Poker, Business and War* (New York: Norton, 1950).

3. See for example J. Bronowski, *Science and Human Values* (New York: Harper, 1965); and Thomas S. Kuhn, *The Structure of Scientific Revolutions* (Chicago: University of Chicago Press, 1962).

4. See for example Leonard Goodwin, "The Historical-Philosophical Basis for Uniting Social Science with Social Problem-Solving," *Philosophy of Science* 29 (1962): 377-92; and Bertram M. Gross, ed., *Social Intelligence for America's Future* (Boston: Allyn & Bacon, 1969).

5. Most of the following historical illustrations are taken from Hilmar S. Raushenbush, *Man's Past: Man's Future* (New York: Delacorte, 1969).

6. This thesis has been advanced by Richard H. Tawney, *Religion and the Rise of Capitalism* (New York: Mentor, 1963).

7. The classic work on this subject is Max Weber's *The Protestant Ethic and the Spirit of Capitalism* (New York: Charles Scribner's Sons, 1958).

8. For some evidence of this process see Leo Lowenthal, "Biographies in Popular Magazines," in William Petersen, ed., *American Social Patterns* (Garden City, N.Y.: Doubleday, 1956), pp. 63-118.

9. Roland L. Warren, *The Community in America* (Chicago: Rand McNally, 1963), pp. 330-31.

10. This process is analyzed by Robert K. Merton in "Bureaucratic Structure and Personality," in Merton, *Social Theory and Social Structure* (New York: Free Press, 1957).

11. Robert Michels, *Political Parties* (New York: Free Press, 1949).

12. See for example David O. Moberg, *The Church as a Social Institution* (Englewood Cliffs, N.J.: Prentice-Hall, 1962), pp. 118-25.

13. Joseph R. Gusfield, "Social Structure and Moral Reform: A Study of the Women's Christian Temperance Union," *American Journal of Sociology* 61 (November 1955): 221-32.

14. This discussion is based on the analysis of the evolution of vertebrates and social insects in C. Judson Herrick, *The Evolution of Human Nature* (Austin: University of Texas Press, 1956).

15. For recent discussions of some of the problems involved in specialization see Ernest Becker, *The Structure of Evil: An Essay on the Unification of the Science of Man* (New York: George Braziller, 1968); and Marjorie Grene, ed., *The Anatomy of Knowledge* (Amherst: University of Massachusetts Press, 1969).

16. This sequence is described in Bernard S. Phillips, *Sociology: Social Structure and Change* (New York: Macmillan, 1969), p. 263, based on a study by Phillips, *The South End Survey: A Report to the South End Neighborhood Action Program, Inc.,* 1967, Department of Sociology, Boston University, mimeo.

17. This analysis of the *Pamela* role is based on Ian Watt, *The Rise of the Novel* (Berkeley: University of California Press, 1957), pp. 138-49, 154-64.

18. Henrik Ibsen, *Four Great Plays* (New York: Bantam Books, 1965).

19. Edward Sapir develops the concept of an integrated culture in his "Culture, Genuine and Spurious," in Sapir, *Culture, Language and Personality* (Berkeley:

University of California Press, 1962), pp. 78-119. For a more recent view see Herbert Marcuse, *Eros and Civilization* (New York: Vintage, 1962).

20. This idea that man and society have the ability to direct the course of human evolution falls within the framework of a newly developing literature on the social construction of reality. See for example Peter L. Berger and Thomas Luckmann, *The Social Construction of Reality* (New York: Doubleday Anchor, 1967); and Burkart Holzner, *Reality Construction in Society* (Cambridge: Schenkman Publishing, 1968).

21. Such a linguistic approach is within the tradition of symbolic interactionism, as illustrated by George Herbert Mead, *Mind, Self and Society* (Chicago: University of Chicago Press, 1934); and Herbert Blumer, *Symbolic Interactionism* (Englewood Cliffs, N.J.: Prentice-Hall, 1969).

22. There is an interdisciplinary literature on game theory, as illustrated by: McDonald, *Strategy in Poker, Business and War;* Anatol Rapoport, *The Essential Ideas of Two-Person Game Theory* (Ann Arbor: University of Michigan Press, 1966); and Rapoport and C. J. Orwant, *Prisoner's Dilemma: A Study in Conflict and Cooperation* (Ann Arbor: University of Michigan Press, 1965). There is a close relationship between the game metaphor and the dramaturgical approach to sociology, as illustrated by the work of Erving Goffman. See his *Encounters* (Indianapolis: Bobbs-Merrill, 1966), *Stigma* (Englewood Cliffs, N.J.: Prentice-Hall, 1963), *Asylums* (Chicago: Aldine, 1962), and *The Presentation of Self in Everyday Life* (Garden City, N.Y.: Doubleday Anchor, 1959).

23. The dynamic systems approach to language is very close to the non-Aristotelian or null-A approach as described in Alfred Korzybski's *Science and Sanity* (Lakeville, Conn.: Institute of General Semantics, 1958) and *Manhood of Humanity,* and also in A. E. Van Vogt's *The World of Null-A* and *The Players of Null-A.*

SUGGESTED READINGS

CLARKE, ARTHUR C. *The City and the Stars.* New York: Harcourt, Brace & World, 1956. Diaspar and Lys are two cities a billion years in the future. They represent two cultures, a computer culture, and a mind-reading culture. How can these two systems learn to communicate with each other, and how can this communication establish the basis for an evolution which had been stifled for a billion years?

GOULDNER, ALVIN W. *The Coming Crisis of Western Sociology.* New York: Basic Books, 1970. Of special interest is chapter 13, "Living as a Sociologist: Toward a Reflexive Sociology," where Gouldner describes a direction which academia seems to be moving toward. For those who want to obtain an intimate picture of what has been happening in the private world of the sociologist, the remainder of the book represents a good beginning.

MILLS, C. WRIGHT. *The Sociological Imagination.* New York: Grove Press, 1961. Mills castigates equally the specialization of sociology into camps of theorists and methodologists and the bureaucratic ethos of the large research project and the research institute. The sociological imagination helps the individual to reach outward in time and space: to see his personal problems as tied to issues in society, and to see his situation in historical perspective.

ROYCE, JOSEPH R. *The Encapsulated Man.* Princeton, N.J.: D. Van Nostrand, 1964. According to Royce's preface, "This book represents one encapsulated man's views as to why 'specialization' is a profoundly serious problem in today's world, why we must remove some cobwebs in our thinking on this matter and at least seriously entertain the idea of developing 'generalists' as well as 'specialists.'"

THREE

MAN AND SOCIETY

Poets and playwrights have been saying for many years what social scientists are finally learning to say: man's being is at least partially destroyed by his experience in society. In the past the sociologist has emphasized the importance of society in the process of shaping man's humanity, the socialization process. He is now beginning to add to this picture. However, a fundamental question remains unresolved: can the creative forces win out over the destructive ones? Poets and playwrights tend to be pessimistic. Yet perhaps there is room for optimism if we are able to probe deeply into the nature of these forces.

Ben Zorn, the hero of chapter 4, attempts to find a way out of this dilemma, just as his predecessor Basil Kornish did. Zorn comes up with a new approach to language, one which builds on Kornish's dimensional orientation, specifying these dimensions with a set of game concepts or metaphors. This points directions for extending the socialization process so that the individual develops far beyond the point where the sociologist might say that he has become "socialized."

Chapter 5 elaborates this idea of extending the socialization process. Illustrations are presented within the contexts of the classroom and the family. And to the one-sided notion of socialization as a process in which society shapes man is added the reverse: a view of man shaping society. We conclude with a discussion of the development of charisma in everyone and speculation about the kind of society which might result.

4

Ben Zorn

IMMERSION

Ben Zorn began his immersion in the world of the 1970s in front
of the New York Public Library. He stood there during the
morning rush hour attempting to catch the eyes of any of the
passers-by as they hurried past. People were looking straight
ahead or down, carefully avoiding one another's eyes. A portly
man with a briefcase glanced at Zorn for an instant, pretending
that he was really interested in something else and had just
happened to see him.

Zorn was wondering just how much this failure to
communicate was occurring all over the world. If so, it was an
important clue relating to the problem he had selected to work
on in the seminar. From the vantage point of his studies in the
twenty-sixth century he was well aware that in exactly one year
almost all of the earth's human population would be destroyed,
and that the repercussions of this catastrophe would produce a
dark ages lasting for five centuries. Zorn was working on the
problem of how to alter a chain of events that ends in war. His
interest was far from academic, for World War IV appeared to be
imminent.

Zorn turned around and walked up the steps toward the library entrance. His six-foot height was not unusual among the other ten-year-olds he knew. This acceleration of physiological development had been achieved at the beginning of the twenty-sixth century. It constituted only one of the ways in which man was learning to shape his own biological development. He felt the wind against his face, the steps against his feet, and the traffic noise on his ears. Just as with his other computer simulations, it was very difficult for him to believe that he really was not in the world of the 1970s.

The best analogy to these computer simulations, Zorn thought, is the dream-adventures of the people of Diaspar in Arthur Clarke's *The City and the Stars.* These individuals could have any imaginable experience, and it would be quite real to them because of the direct involvement of all of the senses. Yet at the same time there was no risk, since these "adventurers" would only be dreaming. For Zorn the computer simulation had a distinct advantage. By pitting himself against a problem of the magnitude he had selected he was pushing himself to grow mentally and emotionally. By contrast, dream-adventures were a safety valve for the inhabitants of the domed, computer-run city of Diaspar, helping them to avoid changing either themselves or their environment for a billion years.

As Zorn continued to climb his mind travelled from Arthur Clarke to Stanley Kubrick's film *2001,* based on a Clarke story, and then to Kubrick's earlier film, *Doctor Strangelove.* Something about the Strangelove film was related to his observations in front of the library. Was it the Doomsday Machine, triggered by the radiation from a nuclear attack, and connected to enough super bombs to destroy all life on earth? Once programmed, there is no way to reprogram it. And those individuals walking past him, weren't they also programmed to react in specific ways to specific stimuli? Taken together, weren't they also a Doomsday Machine? Wouldn't their reactions produce the kind of escalation which would erupt in a universal holocaust one year from that date? Yet if it were not possible to reprogram the Doomsday Machine, perhaps it was possible to reeducate *homo sapiens.* But how does one set about removing the blinders which narrow everyone's vision, or at least widening the angle at which the blinders are set?

Zorn decided to follow through with his present line of thought rather than do what he had originally planned. He headed to the current newspapers section where he located a listing of a revival of Fellini's *8½*. A leisurely walk to the theatre gave him time to collect his thoughts. The fascination which *8½* held for him was based on its play within a play structure. Fellini was constructing a movie about his own life, and through this kind of construction it was possible for him to pierce the blinders which normally constrained himself and others. He was reprogramming himself, as the Doomsday Machine never could.

As Zorn took his seat he noted that the film was almost over. Guido was giving the order to have his huge launching tower— the one designed for his movie depicting the escape of the survivors of a nuclear war to another planet—taken down. He could no longer stand the idea of making a film which, in the words of his writer-collaborator, "will leave a mark on the sands of time like the deformed footprint of a cripple." Guido decided to make a movie about himself, his personal life, and the making of movies. Taking up his director's bullhorn, he started to arrange the characters in his life—wife, mistress, actors, producer, technicians, aquaintances, even himself as a boy. They walked up from the sea and down from the launching tower, linking hands and dancing to the blare of a circus band, all led by the ten-year-old Guido. The film ended while Guido was still in his dream sequence. Guido's solution to the problem of doing a creative film while being harassed by almost everyone has been provided in his dream.

As the audience filed out Zorn remained seated, thinking of Fellini's own life, a third level behind the movie and the dream sequence in the movie. According to *The New Statesman,* Fellini had begun a film which was to be a sequel to *La Dolce Vita,* with costly sets and stars under contract, when he realized that things weren't working out. At the last minute—he still hadn't made up his mind how to end it two weeks before it opened in Rome—he switched to *8½*. The solution provided by the dream sequence not only was a solution for Guido but also for Fellini. And perhaps now there is a fourth level if it suggests a solution for me, thought Zorn. And why not a fifth, a sixth, a never-ending number of levels, if I continue to move outside of any given level of reality or consciousness?

Zorn headed out of the theatre, walking downtown along Third Avenue. His pace was leisurely, but his mind raced madly ahead. He was thinking of a number of others whose approach was related to that of Fellini: Arthur Clarke, who designed a therapeutic dream-adventure to enable the people of Diaspar to conquer their fear of leaving the city, and who wrote non-fiction and fiction about man's future; Soviet heart surgeon and cyberneticist Nikolai Amosov, whose fictional *Notes from the Future* describing a physiologist's search for the secret of immortality was followed by Amosov's "real-life" volunteering for brain experimentation to investigate this secret; Ayn Rand, who created in John Galt of *Atlas Shrugged* a hero of epic proportions and who attempted to apply her ideas through the founding of the Objectivist Society; Ingmar Bergman, whose transition from films of the '50s with exalted hopes to films of disenchantment in the '60s was influenced by, and in turn influenced, awareness of the accelerating problems of the era; and Basil Kornish, who was equally at home in the imaginative worlds of art, science, and technology.

Zorn attempted to pull together the various threads of his thoughts. What these individuals had in common with Fellini was a belief in the power of the human imagination to create worlds which have an impact on the everyday world. How could he use the imaginative construction of reality as a basis for enabling individuals to learn how to communicate better with one another? More difficult, how could this be achieved quickly enough to alter the chain of events carrying the human race toward self-destruction? And still more difficult, how could he apply the resulting insights to the twenty-sixth century?

Zorn felt the answers to these questions lay in his ability to go beyond Kornish's ideas. It was Kornish more than anyone else who had succeeded in delaying the catastrophe, but even he had failed. What did Kornish lack? His ideas about null-A and dimensional thought were, potentially, capable of averting the disaster, but somehow he wasn't able to communicate them rapidly enough, intensively enough, or widely enough. If he had had a few more years . . . but he hadn't.

Zorn decided to get away from the problem momentarily in order to come at it freshly. He started singing, and without realizing what he was doing came out with the phrase, "The answer, my friends, is blowin' in the wind." Could the answer really be "blowin' in the wind"? What did that mean? It was a metaphor, and it called up an image, something which could be seen by the inner eye. Immediately Zorn knew that he had something. He laughed to himself. It was just like Kornish's experience in the john. How did it go? "For want of a nail, a shoe was lost. . . . And all for want of a horseshoe nail." Except that now the battle could be won instead of lost, and along with the battle, the world.

Metaphor, metaphor, that's the key, thought Zorn. How else can you reach people effectively? They need something they can see, and it doesn't work too well if you try to get to them with some idea like scarcity or infinity. They've got to visualize the cages that they put themselves into, the padlocks they clamp on the steel doors, the keys they throw away. Kornish couldn't be expected to have been that strong on metaphor. His initial training was in social science, and he hadn't had quite enough time to get deeply into the arts. But Fellini was a master of metaphor.

But was there really any one key? Zorn was having second thoughts. Was there one answer, or an infinite series of answers? Sure, the metaphor notion is valuable in making concrete the abstract Kornish dimensions like that between scarcity and infinity, but is that all there is to solving any problem? Of course not. Zorn realized that he had been playing a familiar game with himself, the "truth game" as he was disposed to calling it. It was the age-old quest for certainty, and no shades of gray need apply.

Once again, Zorn felt a sense of elation. There's something very special about the idea of a game, he thought, only this time he was looking less for *the* answer than for *more of* an answer. A game is like a play, with different roles that people play. Fellini's idea of a movie within a movie is the same as a game within a game. If the individual has a role in a play, or a role in a game, his realization that he's in a play or a game helps him to step outside of that role, and the process of stepping outside can be continued indefinitely.

Suppose we see all of life as a series of games, Zorn was thinking. Then we could use metaphors to concretize the way they work, and we could also think of the games as being located along abstract dimensions like Kornish's dimension from scarcity to infinity. Then each time we look back at our previous behavior we could see its limitations in comparison to the wider perspective of our present consciousness, but the same would hold for that present consciousness in relation to a future consciousness, as when Fellini or Guido constructed his movie around the characters in his life. He opens up the future by getting perspective on his limitations in the past which are holding him down in the present.

The first phase of his efforts was over, thought Zorn, and the next phase was beginning. The game concept—with its unification of thought, feeling and action—could be the basis for the concreteness of drama or literature, and it could also provide a home for abstract ideas. The game was like life itself, except that the rules were more explicit than implicit. The game functions to keep the players continually aware that they are constructing reality, that the rules can be changed if it becomes desirable, that man is indeed the master of his fate. The next step was to put the game idea to work. Perhaps it was possible to reprogram the Doomsday People after all.

ACT ONE—THE GAME IDEA

Scene: One month later. A room in the New York Public Library. It is furnished informally so that it looks like a family living room. Present are NIKOLAI AMOSOV, INGMAR BERGMAN, ARTHUR CLARKE, FEDERICO FELLINI, BASIL KORNISH, AYN RAND, and BEN ZORN.

RAND: But I do not understand what is so special about this meeting of minds. What would make it possible for us, here and now, to solve major problems threatening man's existence? I have struggled with these issues most of my lifetime without having achieved the kind of genuine success which would alter man's fundamental situation.

ZORN: One thing your work has taught me is to probe deeply into the individual's implicit metaphysical assumptions. The way you have framed your statements, you posed a dichotomy between a genuinely successful solution and a lack of genuine success, between a meeting of minds that is "special" and one that is not, and between the "here and now" and the "elsewhere and in the future." In your writings you have also posed sharp dichotomies—between capitalism and socialism, altruism and selfishness, free will and determinism. By so doing you play the games of DICHOTOMY and COWBOYS AND INDIANS. DICHOTOMY because of the two alternatives you specify and COWBOYS AND INDIANS because you place value in one alternative and tend to denigrate the other. Now it is this game approach to understanding ourselves and others which I believe can help each of us to go further in his own creative work than he has ever dreamed.

KORNISH: Ben, isn't your reaction to Ayn's statements the same as my own way of dealing with dichotomies such as that between capitalism and socialism? Haven't the students in my school contrasted the A orientation, which produces such dichotomies, with the null-A approach, which can integrate important elements from both capitalism and socialism?

RAND: Yes, Ben, I too am interested in your answer to this question. We are all familiar with Kornish's work, yet I fail to see how your proposal goes beyond it in any way.

ZORN: Neither of you would be here if you did not see something in my approach beyond Basil's work. This game vocabulary is a kind of technology, a way of concretizing Basil's abstract theory of scarcity and development. In other words, I am putting together Basil's abstract theoretical ideas with the game idea.

RAND: If you are offering a technology, then let me put it to the test. You know that Howard Roark in *The Fountainhead* represents the embodiment of my own individualistic code. How would the language of games improve on my ability to write about him?

ZORN: Once again you expect a here-and-now all-or-none answer. You are playing the game of DICHOTOMY, and you probably expect to evaluate my answer as either a COWBOY or an INDIAN. Of course, I tend to do the same kind of thing. To give this game idea a fair trial I suggest that we work with it for at least a month. One thing that it might do for you is to alert you to the static nature of a character you might be portraying and help you to delineate him in a more developmental way. My own reaction to Howard Roark is that he is an embodiment of perfection. He is absolutely fascinating in providing an ideal for us to strive toward, but he is also inhuman. The individual who attempts to imitate him is doomed to incessant personal failures and continuing disappointment in the actions of others. Bergman portrayed such an individual in *The Passion of Anna*. Anna's ideals were the very highest, and by retaining them in the face of reality she destroyed herself and others.

BERGMAN: Would you say that any of the other three major characters in the film are better off?

ZORN: No one to any substantial degree. Anna's lover is playing VICIOUS CIRCLE. He has allowed the ordinary humiliations of life to drive him downward further and further, until the fear of ever doing anything with his life becomes an insuperable barrier. Then there is the architect's wife, Anna's friend, who plays a hard game of SEE-SAW in relation to her husband. She continually downgrades her own importance in relation to him, and also plays the game of CONFORMITY in relation to what she imagines his desires to be. Finally there is the architect. He is convinced that life has no meaning, and in this way he does not become the victim of perfectionist ideals. He is quite successful in his work. In other words he has played an effective game of BUREAUCRACY. But his cynicism about life holds him back from intense experiences. He refuses to think that his own work or life is of any importance.

AMOSOV: It strikes me that your game idea does for you what my *Notes from the Future* did for me. It gives you a way of using your imagination to view the existing world from a different perspective, just as I tried to see the state of the world in the 1990s. It also gives you a vision of a future state of the world which could be an improvement over the present.

ZORN: I think it does a third thing as well. It shows me how to begin to achieve that vision in the present. I can illustrate this by classifying the games we have discussed into the A games and the null-A games. Let us bear in mind as we do so that we are actually dealing with a continuum, and that we do this only in order to communicate with one another in a language which is very largely an A language. The A games enable us to view our world from a different perspective. The null-A games give us a vision of what I believe is a better world. By applying these games to ongoing behavior we learn how this behavior falls short of behavior which would produce greater human development, and we thus have a path for moving from the A to the null-A world. For example, each A game can be paired with a null-A game that provides an alternative to it: DICHOTOMY with DIMENSION; CONFORMITY with AUTONOMY; VICIOUS CIRCLE with DEVELOPMENT; BUREAUCRACY, implying narrow specialization and hierarchy, with RENAISSANCE MAN; COWBOYS AND INDIANS with SITUATION ETHICS, where evaluation is not fixed but is based on the momentary constellation of factors in the situation; and SEE-SAW with STAIRWAY.

CLARKE: I notice that you continue to add more games to your vocabulary. How does this kind of vocabulary compare to ordinary usage and to the technical vocabulary of social science?

ZORN: Both ordinary language and social science language represent advances over preexisting situations. When man succeeded in developing language, he acquired a tool which he used to draw more effectively on the experiences of others, both living and dead. Social science taught him ways of probing more deeply into human experience so as to begin to uncover the forces which could be harnessed to give man control over his human environment instead of being the pawn of such forces. It did not replace ordinary language but, rather, added to it. The game approach, which represents one path toward the integration of human experience, simply adds to the efforts of social science by helping us to uncover these forces and suggesting how to harness them. It is intended to provide a skeleton which helps the individual integrate concepts from ordinary language and social science.

The game vocabulary gives the individual who uses it a consciousness of human behavior—his own and that of others— which he would not normally have. This consciousness derives from the central analogy between the game and everyday life. If the rules of a game can be changed, then why not also the rules of a group or a society? Man is seen less as a creature driven to act out certain compulsions as the result of an inevitably hostile society. Man can even choose to change society.

There are other important features of game vocabulary. A game constitutes an entire sequence of human behavior which includes thought, motivation, and action, and then cycles back again to thought, as modified by the preceding sequence, and continues on and on. In short, the game vocabulary is conducive to thinking in terms of feedback loops where a given effect of a series of causes loops back to affect, in turn, these causes. By contrast, most everyday or social science language centers on the relationship between one or more causes and one or more effects at a given time, paying little or no attention to the feedback loop. As a result, both short and long-term temporal relationships are slighted. Also, without attention paid to feedback loops there tends to be less emphasis on the interrelationships among wide varieties of phenomena. Very often an effect loops back to a cause via a long chain of relationships with factors other than those the investigator originally has in mind.

CLARKE: Do you think that the game vocabulary can help us to link our cities of Diaspar and Lys, that is, our technological culture with a culture conducive to mental and emotional development?

ZORN: I do. As man learns to recognize his A games and extend his playing of null-A games he will gain control of the dynamic forces of civilization. He will not be like your space voyagers in

2001 who sun-bathed while the ship's computer controlled their destinies, or like your people of Diaspar who lived out their static lives under the sway of a giant computer. Nor will he be like the people of Lys, who developed powers of mental telepathy but who distrusted technology sufficiently to enchain the computer at a low level of development. The game approach is a path toward putting together the head, the heart, and the hand. The game analyses are preludes to computer simulations, and it is man who must lead the computer. Hopefully, game analyses can probe deeply enough to teach man how to develop his emotions along constructive paths. But the real power of the game approach is a derived one, just like any scientific theory. It derives from the integration of human experiences.

BERGMAN: Your optimism is touching, but only the naive can be optimistic in the modern world. Surely you are sophisticated enough to be aware of what is going on, and of how trivial are man's efforts to create meaning out of meaninglessness.

ZORN: Your own life yields a response to what you have just said. In your recent films you portrayed this meaninglessness as perhaps your end-in-view, but the means you developed to communicate this idea have enabled you to continue to develop your creative abilities. You have found great meaning in the expression of meaninglessness. One might say that you illustrate a conflict between means and ends, and you also point a direction for all of us. Developmental means can be used as a basis for subverting nondevelopmental ends. If we find ourselves caught in the Aristotelian games of an A society, we can find paths out of the maze. This kind of behavior might be designated as SHELL GAME, where the means to a given end comes to replace the end in importance, and the pea—the end—no longer is under the shell that formerly contained it.

One reason for your intellectual pessimism—indeed, the reason for the pessimism that almost everyone shares—is that SHELL GAME has historically been played in such a way that nondevelopmental means have displaced developmental ends. The fall of Athenian democracy was based in large part on military measures which Pericles thought were essential for protecting Athens, analogous to attempts to protect American democracy by fighting a war in Southeast Asia. We have witnessed the subversion of the early Christian ideals via Christian efforts to attain security through a tie with a moribund Roman Empire just as we have seen the betrayal of religious ideals generally by religious organizations.

BERGMAN: You are convinced, seemingly, that we can reverse this process and use developmental means to subvert nondevelopmental ends. But what reason do we have to be convinced that you are right? And who is to say that your own vision of a null-A world is right for everyone?

ZORN: My convictions developed over a period of time, and I would expect the same to hold for you. All I ask is that you give these ideas a fair trial during these weeks we will be meeting together.

ACT TWO—STAIRWAY

Scene: Same place, same people, one month later.

RAND: I'd like to give you all a preview of an idea I have for a novel. What I'm trying to do is combine extreme naturalism with extreme romanticism. I'm not yet sure about any of the details. I want my hero—maybe he'll be a boy—to be tortured by games which his family and friends play like GOODNIK, SEE-SAW, SHELL GAME, and VICIOUS CIRCLE. I want to go way beyond *Portnoy's Complaint* when I portray the development of his twisted personality. But I also want to show how he succeeds in untwisting himself and beginning to go way beyond where any creative person has ever gone in the history of the universe. He will be a super-hero, but his strength will be largely in his ability to admit his weaknesses and face up to doing something about them.

FELLINI: How will he accomplish this transformation?

RAND: That's where I'm stuck right now.

FELLINI: How about something like this as a beginning for him. He sees *A Thousand Clowns* and is impressed by the scene where this guy shouts "I'm sorry" on a Manhattan street corner and everyone looks at him as if his apology was long overdue. Then he starts dreaming about that scene, only all the passersby look like his mother and he looks like the man doing the shouting. He slowly begins to figure out the GOODNIK game his mother and some of his friends are playing on him. He begins to have dreams where the ties of guilt that his mother uses to control him are made of actual rope. Then, in one of his dreams, his mother is on a see-saw with him. She's pushing herself up with a long pole while pushing him down into some spikes. In that way she could be delegitimized in his eyes, and the ties of guilt could be broken. I seem to be getting more interested in this idea as I talk about it. Perhaps I'll do a film on it.

AMOSOV: The idea appeals to me also. What I'm thinking of is a play in two acts. The first act can be something similar to what you've been talking about. Except that I'd rather portray the change taking place in an adult who is trapped in a web of dependency on people who habitually play VICIOUS CIRCLE games. As he begins to wake up to his situation he notices that GOODNIK is played by social systems as well as individuals. He learns to penetrate the hypocrisy which is the basis for GOODNIK in, say, the family, the church, the school, the legal institution. He begins to see all institutions as playing GOODNIK, with their games of SEE-SAW and their attempt to legitimate their behavior in terms of moral principles. The result is that he succeeds in delegitimizing them in his own mind, breaking the ties of guilt, and attaining a measure of internal freedom. From there he can go on to make use of this freedom to create null-A institutions.

There would be no script for the second act. The audience would be called on to improvise around the GOODNIK theme. I'd develop more specific ideas about how to assist them when I got into the actual situation. Overall, I'm thinking of nudity of the mind here. I want people to bare themselves, but to do it in such a way that they can play STAIRWAY with their limitations.

BERGMAN: How would you teach your audience to bare themselves? It is difficult enough to do this kind of thing with professional actors.

AMOSOV: I hadn't thought about that.

BERGMAN: I have been working on ways of improving acting these past few weeks, and perhaps my ideas have relevance for nonprofessionals as well, if we go along with the null-A approach. I've been thinking about how to assist actors with improvisions, working on an adaptation of the Stanislavski techniques. What I require is a method for learning the Method very quickly, and I think that the game idea can yield such a method. By using game concepts and applying them to a personality we can rapidly form a highly complex and dynamic characterization, and, by doing this for others in the situation as well, we have created a challenging acting and learning situation. For example, how would an individual playing a hard game of GOODNIK and AUTONOMY affect someone playing CONFORMITY? Suppose that the AUTONOMY behavior is stronger than the GOODNIK behavior: would that lead to a gradual elimination of GOODNIK in that individual? And would the individual playing CONFORMITY learn to get rid of this in favor of AUTONOMY?

AMOSOV: If I can get into this discussion, I think I can show how to bring in computer simulation. The basic idea is that a computer simulation can pull together a good deal of game analysis, and that we can become far more accurate about a complex situation if we use the two together. Instead of talking about a hard or a soft game of AUTONOMY, we can specify a number to represent the degree of hardness, and so on for all the other games. We can define one person as the system and the other as the environment. Then each of these games affects the rate of goal fulfillment of the system and the environment, depending on how hard the games are played. And the computer simulation enables us to put together all this information and come out with results which, under ordinary circumstances, we wouldn't be able to think of intuitively.

ZORN: But there's no reason why we couldn't learn to think intuitively in that way once we learned how to do the simulation.

KORNISH: Maybe I can use this combination of game analysis and computer simulation to go beyond what I did with my TV special, where I had audio-visual outputs based on computer simulation. All I had to do there was develop one-to-one correspondences between mathematical descriptions and audio-visual descriptions. Once the correspondences were set up, I simply let the computer go ahead, based on the mathematical models I had developed. But game analysis suggests tools for measurement, and I'd be able to revise my model as frequently as I wanted to. As a matter of fact, it wouldn't even have to be me who'd revise the model. A physical environment could be designed to be sensitive to the changing needs of the people using it. There could be an automatic game analysis of these users, and their needs could then activate changes in the mathematical or computer model. And instead of there being an audio-visual output hooked up to the computer, there could be an intermediate energy source activated by sensors that detected changes in the computer, and this energy could be channeled into reconstructing the environment.

END AND BEGINNING

Zorn did not have to hear any more to be convinced that he had succeeded in doing what he had set out to do. He speeded the simulation ahead to the first day of World War III and was not at all surprised to discover that no war took place. He jumped ahead another year, and then ten years, and there was still no war. He did not know as yet exactly what the chain of events was that so drastically altered mankind's prospects, although that could be discovered in time. It might have been any one of the works produced by the small group he had gathered together, or it might have been some combination of them.

Kornish had been working on a series of games for teaching individuals in all walks of life the dynamics of the games of A and null-A, and his games were so designed that any player automatically became a researcher, advancing the available knowledge about the game approach. All that was in addition to his experiments in creating responsive physical environments. Amosov had been busily constructing computer simulations focusing on the problems of longevity, and he had translated the results into an experimental program designed to increase longevity. He was also working on computer programs which had produced exciting integrations of knowledge, and he was moving toward master programs at higher and higher levels. Bergman had been achieving phenomenal successes in getting people from his audiences to improvise different game roles, which was having widespread repercussions in the theater and cinema as well as in the field of psychotherapy. Rand had been trying to give new life to romanticism in literature and the arts generally by pulling together romanticism and naturalism in a new novel. Clarke had inaugurated a science fiction workshop, and his students were beginning to produce some of the most imaginative pieces of literature ever written. And Fellini had begun a new movie—about a director who had produced a movie on his own life and was looking for another script.

Zorn was back in his own time. He didn't have the complete answer to the causes of World War III, but he did have a partial answer. Kornish's abstract dimensions gave him directions for human development, and the game language along with a metaphorical approach helped him to fill in these dimensions. The key direction involved continually stepping outside of previous roles and viewing one's behavior from an ever-widening perspective.

But it was more than just this, and it certainly would be more than any new thought he could come up with. All the people he had gathered around him were individuals, personalities quite distinct from one another. Their creative ability was the product of their own uniqueness, a uniqueness based on everything they had put together in their own lives. Ayn Rand, perhaps more than any of the others, had communicated the necessity for the individual to focus on his own development, to look inward before he looks outward.

Is this centering on oneself a missing piece to the puzzle? Zorn thought. Does it provide a basic framework which one can use to continually step outside of one's roles?

Of course! It's simply an extension of the socialization process. Zorn's mind was racing through some of the ideas of George Herbert Mead. The personality develops by taking the role of the other, with the individual learning to step outside of himself and see himself as an object. Then why doesn't the process continue in the same way, with the individual continuing to step outside of any previous way in which he has been viewed by others? What stops it? Why did sociologists stay with a relatively static view where the individual at some point is supposed to become socialized and develop a personality? Why was this ceiling placed on his development?

Perhaps the answer, thought Zorn, is related to what was happening in society generally, for the sociologist himself was socialized in society. With the prevailing scarcities in society, such as the limited pie of status within each social system, people could easily be kept in check by forces around them. If an individual depended on others to give him the precious reward of status, then his life was chained to theirs, and their fears became his. So long as an individual was bound in this way he could never break free. Perhaps that is what Kornish had in mind when he had talked about reaching the "take-off point" in his second news conference. He had learned how to invest in himself and no longer was dependent on investment from the outside.

With such a world-view prevailing in society it was only natural that the individual came to be seen the way he was in the industrial revolution: as another kind of machine, something that was "socialized" or constructed to perform certain tasks, then performed them throughout its working life, and finally was thrown on the scrap heap along with other obsolete parts. The idea of progress was limited to the social system, the corporation, science, the nation. The idea of individual progress was strangely missing. The individual was seen as merely a part fitting into the larger and more powerful whole, and not as a force terribly effective in its own right.

Then what is needed, thought Zorn, is a wider view of the socialization process. If society sees itself as socializing the individual, it must also come to see itself as being socialized by the individual. If society sees its own codes as holy relative to those of the individual, it must also learn to delegitimize its codes where they run afoul of those of the individual. This reversal in thinking becomes possible once the Hobbesian assumption that life is a war of all against all is abandoned and replaced by one which sees man as plastic and not as evil.

And instead of seeing the socialization process as completing its major work once a personality has been formed, we can follow the Fellini approach and see the individual as continuing to look at himself from the outside and expanding his consciousness. The iron cage of fixed personality is perhaps the last major stronghold of scarcity, thought Zorn, serving to keep man in the status of an insect, a fixture that is thoroughly dependent on the whims of the group.

Here was a program for him to follow in his own century, one which appeared to be so very different from the twentieth century and yet was so very similar. He could move to socialize his own world-society, and he could do this indirectly by focusing on his own continuing socialization. And perhaps what he required most to get started was the realization that he had started a long time ago, that he was now continuing, and that the process would take time. He would have to build himself up, piece by piece, attaining one partial answer after another. Everything takes time.

EXERCISES

1. Define "socialization," taking into account both the ideas about the process emphasized in this chapter and those emphasized in most textbook definitions. What does this definition imply about the process of social change? What does it imply about what is happening to you right now? Now make use of the definition by attempting to shift the direction in which you have been socialized in some way in accordance with your own goals. Retain consciousness both of

your goal and of the nature of the socialization process. What are the results of your efforts? What does this tell you about the process of social change?

2. Write a very short science fiction story about someone from the future who uses computer simulation to re-create some period in his past, a period which is also our present. You may make it easier for yourself by focusing on one particular kind of setting, such as the school. How does this exercise relate to the nature of the socialization process, as you discussed it in exercise 1? Does this exercise give you any new insight into the socialization process? What does it tell you about yourself? What does it tell you about the nature of society, assuming you are now an alien from another galaxy and are able to read it?

3. Using very simple materials, construct something which is unusually flexible in that it can be easily adapted to changes in the user's needs. Try it out, and test its adaptability. For example, it might be a set of props that can be used for a variety of science fiction skits. Now look at the various objects surrounding you. Assess each one with regard to its degree of flexibility. How would you redesign any one of them so that it could be used to do what it is presently able to do, and so that it could fulfill other functions as well?

4. In a discussion group apply the game language to the comments made. Use these continua: DICHOTOMY–DIMENSION; CONFORMITY–AUTONOMY; VICIOUS CIRCLE–DEVELOPMENT; BUREAUCRACY–RENAISSANCE MAN; COWBOYS AND INDIANS–SITUATION ETHICS; SEE-SAW–STAIRWAY; SHELL GAME–CONTINUING REVOLUTION; GOODNIK–MAN FOR HIMSELF; and GOLDFISH BOWL–CONSCIOUSNESS. Discuss your assessments with one another, on the assumption that no rating is definitive and all ratings could be improved with additional information. Now attempt to apply several of the dimensions to the same instance of behavior. What relationships among the dimensions do you find to be of particular significance?

5. Make use of the dimensions listed in exercise 4 for purposes of role playing in a dramaturgical group. For example, a skit might be created depicting a daughter coming home much later than her mother expected. The mother might be playing a very hard game of GOODNIK and SEE-SAW, with the daughter playing equally hard games of GOLDFISH BOWL and CONFORMITY. Now see what happens when the daughter shifts to CONSCIOUSNESS and AUTONOMY. Now shift to a written script, such as "Act One: The

Game Idea" or "Act Two: Stairway." After running through the script, each actor should attempt to analyze his role with the aid of the game dimensions. Now run through the script again. Do you note any differences in your ability to get inside the role? Discuss your reactions with one another.

5

Games of Socialization and the Development of Charisma

Socialization is a universal process to be found among humans, a process within which the individual develops a personality and transmits culture from one generation to the next. But there is also a great deal of variation in the content that man learns. It varies from one society to the next and, within the same society, from one point in time to another.

Through application of various game dimensions, we hope to gain the kind of insight into the socialization process which will help us to understand both the nature of this general process and directions for learning how to control it. We contend that little enough is known about the process, taking into account the literature on the subject that we are aware of. Partly as a result of this lack of knowledge, little in the way of technologies for socialization has developed, at least ones that are effective.

For example, we know little about how man moves from tradition-direction to inner-direction,[1] that is, from a pre-industrial to an early industrial personality. Neither do we understand how he comes to be transformed from inner-direction to other-direction, that is, from an early industrial to a late industrial personality (or, in the words of Charles Reich, from Consciousness I to Consciousness II).[2] A third mystery is the shift from other-direction to autonomy, or from late industrial to post-industrial, or from Consciousness II to Consciousness III.

It should not be surprising that the sociologist's view of the socialization process, developed during the industrial era, emphasized other-direction as an outcome far more than, say, the autonomous personality. Our overall aim in this chapter is to present a broader view of socialization, one in which we see man constructing society along with seeing society constructing man, and where we pay attention to the continuing resocialization going on throughout life. The game dimensions will help us see the continuum from conformity to autonomy and alert us to changes in the individual and society resulting from every instance of behavior.

We begin with a section on the concept of socialization, pointing up some of the limitations of a definition focusing on other-direction and providing an alternative view. In the ensuing two sections, dealing with the classroom and family situations, we present the same kind of contrast between the industrial and post-industrial worlds. In our final section, "The Development of Charisma," we concentrate attention on a technology which may be developed in the near future, one which should bring with it a rapid shift to a post-industrial era.

THE CONCEPT OF SOCIALIZATION

Socialization has been defined in our industrial era as "the process by which (a) the individual develops a personality as a result of learning much of the content of a given culture, and (b) culture is transmitted from one generation to the next."[3] Definitions such as this foster SHELL GAME. They induce us to think that we understand whatever concept has been defined, yet in the case of socialization we seem to know very little about the processes involved. The definition, which is supposed to be a means toward the end of understanding phenomena, tends to become important in its own right, and we rarely evaluate the definition in relation to its contribution to understanding.

But many more games are also involved in the above definition. There is the game of DICHOTOMY: the definition contrasts those phenomena which fall into the category of socialization with those which do not. We can still talk about degree of socialization, but the definition does not alert us to this. Rather, it calls attention to the all-or-none nature of the process.

Such definitions are also important weapons in the game of BUREAUCRACY. Definitions tend to be equated with "truth," and the poor novice who has difficulty remembering large numbers of definitions for an extended period of time learns to think less of himself. This serves to perpetuate an initial hierarchical relationship between teacher and student or professional and layman. In addition to hierarchy, there is also a division of labor in the game of BUREAUCRACY. A given definition is part of the technical vocabulary within a given discipline, and the lack of knowledge of this vocabulary across disciplines serves to divide them.

In this definition of socialization the individual is seen as a passive creature, soaking up his culture and then passing it on to others. There is no implication that man can socialize society just as he is socialized by society. The individual is seen as helpless and society is all-powerful.

A SCARCITY game is implicit in the definition. For example, the idea expressed is that culture is transmitted intact, that it undergoes little or no change or growth. Also, the concept of culture is used as if it referred to a material object, handed down from one generation to the next and retaining its essential characteristics. Material objects imply scarcity: take a piece away and there is less remaining.

The game of CONFORMITY also is implicit in the definition. We are supposed to conform to this definition as distinct from making up our own definition. And we fail to perceive alternative definitions because of our preoccupation with the one presented.

Despite all of the foregoing illustrations of A as distinct from null-A games, this definition of socialization is by no means at one end of the A–NULL-A continuum. To repair this one-sided view, we might start by noting that this definition, along with language in general, helps us to play the games of CONSCIOUSNESS and DEVELOPMENT. We are able to integrate experiences that have occurred at different points in time and space (CONSCIOUSNESS), and we can make use of this integration to act more effectively on our environment (DEVELOPMENT). It is true that DICHOTOMY does not take us very far in this respect, but it does take us some distance.

The definition also carries us a distance on the road from SCARCITY to INFINITY. It takes us away from a belief that the individual's behavior is a product of heredity and leads us toward an emphasis on the environment. One might say that we are merely moving from one type of scarcity to another, but that the degree of scarcity remains constant. We believe, however, that the definition implies a softer game of SCARCITY: the individual's heredity cannot change, but his environment can be altered.

In addition, there is a movement away from SCARCITY via a nonmaterialistic orientation. Words like "personality" and "cul-

ture" denote and connote nonmaterial phenomena, granting that
they are still nouns and that some of their connotations are tangible.
Nonmaterial entities are not diminished when they are utilized but
might even grow in certain ways. This holds, for example, in the case
of the transmission of culture.

The game of DEVELOPMENT is implied by the original definition
in its reference to the individual's *development* of a personality and
his *learning* the content of culture. Of course, development is limited to what occurs when one is learning aspects of one's culture,
with the presumption—implicitly—that this occurs for limited periods of time. One is socialized to take on one's roles, much as a
machine is constructed to perform certain tasks, and then one performs in these roles. When the role changes, such as in the case of
occupational retirement, one becomes resocialized. Life is a series of
socialization periods followed by plateaus of performance in given
roles. Thus, DEVELOPMENT is limited to given periods, and it is
circumscribed by CONFORMITY to fixed roles.

A definition of socialization more in keeping with a post-industrial
view of man than our preceding definition is: The process by which
(1) the individual continually transforms and is transformed by his
society, and (2) culture is continually transmitted and transformed.
The emphasis here is on a dynamic view, with continual transformation of the individual, society, and culture. Further, the one-direc-
tional emphasis on man being transformed by society is
supplemented by man's transformation of society. Of course, such a
definition is quite limited. It does not tell us how man, society, and
culture are transformed within this process of socialization. Hopefully we shall obtain some insight into this question in the sections
to follow.

THE A AND NULL-A KINDERGARTEN

A teacher in an A kindergarten may work very hard at her job. She
may be task-oriented and present the children with a succession of
tasks which she has prepared for them. For her, education may
consist of moving from one task to the next, and she may measure
her own success or failure on the basis of how well the children
participate in the tasks she designs for them. Children who fail to
show interest or join the group, or who pursue their own individual
activities appear to her to be failures. Such a teacher is playing
SHELL GAME if the purpose of her activities is to educate or develop the children. Task participation and completion has become an

end in itself, the basis on which success and failure are evaluated. This approach also induces CONFORMITY in the children: their own individual interests, which may be divergent, are not taken into account to any extent. The children also learn to play BUREAU-CRACY: their individual ideas and activities are discouraged in favor of those of the teacher, and they learn to suppress the former in favor of the latter. They may even learn to conjure up what appears to be enthusiasm for the teacher's activities, but such enthusiasm would constitute another mode of CONFORMITY.

There are many other A games involved in this type of classroom.[4] The various tasks correspond to the many specialized roles the individual is called on to play in society. There is a narrow range of activities within each task, and when other events intrude—the appearance of a dog, a child's relating of an activity to a personal experience, a child's interest in an individual activity—they are not drawn out and treated as being worthwhile. One result is GOOD-NIK: what comes to be meaningful to the child is only that which is meaningful to the social system, as structured by the teacher. Another result is SEE-SAW played by the child against himself. He loses self-esteem because his own definition of what is meaningful and important is unacceptable to the group. The child learns to play GOLDFISH BOWL, looking to the teacher to initiate thought. And he might attempt to regain some of his lost self-esteem via aggressive behavior (SEE-SAW) against the other children.

The structure of the A classroom is closely related to the structure of the teacher's personality. She holds them to the tasks with reins of guilt: they are rewarded with her praise when they become task-oriented, and her lack of praise or her attempts to manipulate them to join the group tend to induce guilt (SEE-SAW against themselves) when they are not task-oriented. She herself is playing SHELL GAME by being so task-oriented, and she structures her whole life in this way. A common label used for this kind of orientation is "the compulsive personality." There is little room left for joy in this way of life, nor is there much humor. The teacher sees herself as a kind of problem-solving machine, and she attempts to structure the classroom in this way. The activities themselves tend to have no history behind them, or nothing of this sort is communicated to the children, and there is no discussion as to the utility of these tasks for future situations which the children will meet.

The teacher believes wholeheartedly that she is doing a good job. She works very hard. Yet her belief in her altruism is part of the GOODNIK game she plays. The combination of this myth along with her inducing the children to play SEE-SAW against themselves when they are not fulfilling her task-oriented expectations adds up to the relatively complex game of JEWISH MOTHER.[5] In this game, which is played by people of all religions and of both sexes, the teacher actually plays SEE-SAW through negating the children's individual interests, but her game of GOODNIK makes the children feel sufficiently guilty so that they play SEE-SAW against themselves. The teacher extends the JEWISH MOTHER game to other aspects of her life: she is the long-suffering, hard-working, righteous individual who has truth and goodness on her side, and anyone who happens to disagree with her becomes a target for her manipulation via GOODNIK and SEE-SAW against themselves.

Let us now move to a more null-A classroom, bearing in mind that there are many kinds of null-A classrooms and teachers. The teacher may have tentative plans for a number of activities in which one or more children can participate, plans which are based on STAIRWAY, that is, taking into account where the various children have been and what might lead to their further development. She may have several co-workers, depending on the size of the class, who help her to individualize the ongoing activities. What a child does at any point may not be based simply on the child's whim of the moment. Children may not be free, for example, to continually change from the block corner to the kitchen or the kitchen to the carpentry room. The child may be allowed the freedom to make his choice of activity, but he may have to learn to stick with that choice for a period of time.

This choice process helps to give the child time perspective, and it gives him sufficient time to play STAIRWAY in any given activity. By structuring the situation so that compulsive choices of changing activities based on fear of failure are minimized, the child learns to gain feelings of self-worth (MAN FOR HIMSELF). This is reinforced when he learns to develop his abilities in the various activities. And by being encouraged to make his own choices within these broad limits, he learns to play AUTONOMY.

The activities themselves may be placed in settings which encourage the games of CONSCIOUSNESS and RENAISSANCE MAN. To illustrate CONSCIOUSNESS, quarrels among children may be viewed as opportunities within which children can learn to get along with others. The teacher does intervene if children are hurting one another, but she attempts, insofar as possible, to bolster their own abilities to solve their problems. She may tell them that unless they find a way of working out their differences, both of them will have to leave the activity. Thus, she attempts to structure the kind of situation in which the children solve problems by widening their horizons so as to take into account others' perspectives.

This extends to knowledge about the environment as well as personal relationships. She attempts to relate aspects of an activity to the children's own personal experiences, making use of the appearance of a dog as an opportunity for children to make more meaningful their own experiences with dogs and other animals. Numbers and letters are introduced in the context of a situation which calls attention to them. In this way, the children learn to see how all their experiences relate to one another, and thereby become interested in continuing to diversify their experiences (RENAISSANCE MAN).

The teacher herself is not a do-gooder; rather, she plays MAN FOR HIMSELF: she is concerned with her own DEVELOPMENT, and she achieves this by structuring the kindergarten so that she can learn from the children, which leads to their learning to play DEVELOPMENT. She has a sense of humor which pervades the classroom. It is not merely that she has enough confidence (AUTONOMY) not to be defensive about her own foibles, but she has the ability to see things from many different perspectives. She can step inside the world of a child when he is talking about building a bridge and wonder what the world would be like if every place was on a bridge, and she can carry it further by discussing how such a world might be constructed. Then she can step outside of that world and look at it from the perspective of an unimaginative adult, but such an adult does not have the last word. Her worlds of imagination are real to her and not simply gimmicks to con the children.

Keeping this contrast between one illustration of an A and null-A classroom in mind, let us now return to examine the questions raised in the foregoing section: (1) How does man transform society? and (2) How is man transformed by society? We see both of these processes as continual ones rather than events which occur at certain times. In this light, we need to probe into the continuing relationships among phenomena as distinct from a set of distinct "causes" which arise at a certain time and produce socialization.

Concerning the first question, we might consider the kindergarten classroom to be a microcosm of society. Then the question narrows down to a focus on the process by which the teacher affects the classroom milieu. Our illustration appears to indicate that the personality of the teacher, as may be described by the various games that she plays, in very large measure affects the structure of the classroom situation. To the degree that the teacher is not aware of the specific ways in which she does this, and to the degree that she is unable to alter herself to achieve the effects she desires, she will simply be the agent of forces beyond her control as she shapes the classroom environment. Somehow, her own socialization has not given her the ability to act as an autonomous force on her environment. She shapes it, but only in much the same way as a lever lifts weights, dependent on the forces which push it.

The null-A teacher—and we should be aware that she is null-A only in some respects and only to some degree, depending on the specific situations she encounters—also affects the classroom environment rather profoundly, but she is more aware of the ways in which this occurs and she has greater ability to alter herself and uses this ability to move toward her goals. She too has been socialized to become what she is, but she has been socialized to value an autonomous mode of behavior. She is more alive in the sense that she can assess the impact of what she does and alter her behavior accordingly.

As for the second question, both teachers have been socialized by society, and both are affected by the classroom situation. Neither one is completely autonomous or wholly determines her own behavior. However, there is an important difference in degree between the two. The A teacher appears to be largely inner-directed, that is, compulsively task-oriented. She is a driven person, as distinct from the null-A teacher's spontaneity and openness to what is going on. Her actions appear to be based more on fear of what will occur if she doesn't act the way she does than confidence in her own and the children's ability to develop. Somehow, society has shaped her into such a rigid mold that she does not know how to function without creating this rigidity all around her.

By contrast, the null-A teacher—who has also been shaped by society—is a protean individual, someone who has a structure in continual flux. She has learned to base her behavior on the situational context, and the result is that she is much more unpredictable than her A counterpart. She does not attempt to "program" what will occur during the class, although she does come with some tentative ideas. In this way, she is able to take advantage of the many factors beyond her control and use them to help develop both herself and her students. Instead of evaluating her successes and failures quite narrowly on the basis of rigid criteria which require her students to conform to her dictates, her criteria are continually widening in scope. One result is that she learns to reward herself even in what normally would be considered to be failure situations. This ability to reward herself on the basis of her own very broad evaluation criteria frees her a good deal from dependency on her environment. She has been socialized by her environment, but that socialization has freed her, in much the same way that man conforms to his biological structure, but that structure has given him perhaps unlimited possibilities.

GAMES IN THE FAMILY

Our analysis of A and null-A kindergartens brings us very close to parent-child relationships in the family. We can carry over the previous discussion by seeing each of the two types of teachers as a parent. Within this context, it is easy to see that almost all of the advice about child rearing given out by professionals and nonprofessionals alike is beside the point. If the personality of the A parent remains unchanged, then any rule or set of rules designed to counter her rigidity would be subverted by the many A games that make up her personality. Even if she tried to take such a rule seriously, she would tend to destroy its intent by making it an end in itself, playing SHELL GAME.

Another type of parent-child relationship in addition to these two —and this would also constitute another type of teacher-student relationship—is characterized by a laissez-faire atmosphere. In the name of giving the child freedom to develop and avoiding an authoritarian relationship with its accompanying stifling of the child's personality, the child is allowed to do whatever he wants to do that does not interfere too much with the parents' life style. The result very often is that the child is socialized largely by his peer group, and he is also "free" to be at the mercy of the A aspects of his own personality. Once again SHELL GAME does its work: a method of child rearing used to free the child's personality becomes an end in itself, that is, its results remain unquestioned. What frequently occurs is the reinforcement of all kinds of A games within the child's personality.

It is possible to see this kind of parental relationship in historical perspective. If our A kindergarten teacher was very much of an inner-directed person, socialized largely by the work ethic predominating in the early phase of the industrial revolution, then our laissez-faire parent is an other-directed product of the latter phase of this revolution. She is concerned primarily with rearing the kind of children who can get along with their peers, and she attempts to achieve this by allowing these peers to be actively involved in the socialization process.

Corresponding to this difference between the early and the late phase of the industrial revolution is a great difference in presumably authoritative advice for child rearing. Prior to World War II the U.S. Children's Bureau's Infant Care warned of the dangers of thumb-sucking and masturbation, and emphasized the importance of early bowel training and doing everything by the clock. In the postwar period thumb-sucking is permissible, the baby is allowed to touch his genitals, and the clock has become far less important.[6] These differences in approach appear to be associated with the difference between inner-direction and other-direction. The rigidity of prewar child training is matched by the rigidity of the inner-directed personality, and the laissez-faire advice of the postwar period corresponds to the other-directed personality.

If we conceive of socialization as a process which continues throughout life, then we might be concerned with this process as it applies to relationships among spouses. We have already begun this discussion with our analysis of the history of the role of women in Western society in chapter 3. It will be recalled that we discussed the origins of the Victorian role in the early phases of the industrial revolution, moved to women's intimate relation to the mechanisms of consumption in the "advanced" industrial societies, and speculated about an individual-centered post-industrial world which would enable a female to attain self-esteem as a unique individual. These three historical periods also provide a view of three different kinds of male-female roles in the family, all of which co-exist in contemporary Western society.

Our description of the *Pamela* role in Victorian England[7] implies CONFORMITY. GOLDFISH BOWL is also involved in the cloistered life dictated by the role. In addition we have a whole constellation of games which give rise to a very strong game of JEWISH MOTHER. First there is the game of GOODNIK, based on the myth that somehow the middle-class female embodies spiritual elements in a way not possible for a male who is soiled by his sexual lusts. Then there are the various SEE-SAW holier-than-thou games which she can play against her spouse, making use of the aforementioned myth to get him to play SEE-SAW against himself. Overshadowing these games, however, is the myth that she is actually the injured party and he is the offender (that she is playing SEE-SAW against herself and he is playing SEE-SAW against her).

As might be expected, the games played by the male fit neatly into these games. But he manages to turn the tables in a great many spheres of marital relationships. It is he who is the breadwinner, and he uses this role as the basis for his own game of GOODNIK. Indeed, he can also induce his wife to play SEE-SAW against herself if he can convince her that his rights are being violated, with the result that he slips into JEWISH MOTHER.

The metaphor of the machine may be applied to these roles located in the early industrial era, since it conveys the idea of inflexibility typical of inner-direction. Just as a machine is constructed to function in a very particular pattern during its entire working life, so were men and women taught to behave in certain very circumscribed complimentary ways throughout their entire adult lives.

Husband-wife roles in the advanced industrial era represent modifications of these games, with the fundamental dividing lines separating rights and duties varying much more from family to family. The result is that each family has more alternative patterns from which to choose for the kinds of rights around which the husband plays JEWISH MOTHER and those which the wife defends via JEWISH MOTHER. In many middle-class families, for example, the wife is seen as the expert in the sphere of art as well as in many other nonwork areas of life, such as understanding human nature, knowing how to bring up children, organizing social relationships and leisure time activities, and so on. This represents a transformation of her former Victorian role of being close to God. The husband, by contrast, is king in the world of affairs, in all aspects of politics and business, and in anything where intelligence or reason is supposed to be important. The major difference between these relationships and those of Victorian times is that, as a result of SHELL GAME, the religious overtones associated with these roles have been displaced by secular ones.

Because social change is more rapid and life is more heterogeneous in this era, it becomes essential for husband and wife to become socialized to a greater degree of flexibility. In such a situation the authoritarian paternalistic role of the husband, centered around a very hard game of TRUTH in a wide variety of spheres of life, is too easily shown up as being ineffective in meeting life's problems. The same is the case for the wife's game of TRUTH in her own sphere and her helplessness in her husband's territory. The ideas of both together are needed to an increasing degree, and there is a thrust toward equalitarian roles in many areas of life. Each learns, at least in those families moving in this equalitarian direction, to be other-directed or learn to play CONFORMITY to his or her spouse and children.

Diversity of family forms appears to be becoming a dominant characteristic of the post-industrial family, with the family form designed around the special needs and particular contexts of the individuals involved. Each individual tends to construct the kind of family structure most conducive to his own—as well as his partner's —development. Gazing into our crystal ball, we see such families in rapid flux. The flexibility of the family members in the advanced industrial era will increase, we believe, to a much greater degree. This will become essential if the family is to survive in an era of exceedingly rapid change.

We believe that the kind of flexibility required could not be developed around an other-directed or CONFORMITY-oriented personality. The conflicts within the personality would come to be too severe, since the individual would have to shift back and forth as the situation varied without having a central core to provide the basis for integrating these shifts. Such behavior would be seen as hypocritical by the individual involved as well as others. We believe that the result will be movement toward AUTONOMY and away from CONFORMITY, with the individual learning to pay attention to and respect his own ideas and feelings more and more. Phrases such as "do your own thing" or "that's my bag" convey this idea. What's right or effective or wise for one person is not so for another, and what works in one situation does not work in another. This looseness or flexibility of orientation can be contrasted with the so-called "uptight" generation of the industrial era.

As this process continues, we see the individual learning more and more to play RENAISSANCE MAN as distinct from BUREAUCRACY, with its emphasis on hierarchy and division of labor. The latter game pushes the individual to rely on himself only to a very limited degree and appears to be inappropriate to situations which are changing so rapidly that they require rapid shifts in orientation and behavior. But how can man learn to play RENAISSANCE MAN, seen as a continuing extension of the do-it-yourself movement and an era in which the effectiveness of professionalism is being challenged from many quarters? Efforts to achieve greater community control of schools, for example, imply that parents and children have important knowledge about the educational process, knowledge which is not monopolized by teachers. How will it be possible for individuals, whether in the educational context or the family context or any other context, to learn to develop themselves to the point where they can make effective contributions?

We believe that the problem lies not with man's basic capacities nor with the large amounts of specialized knowledge but, rather, with man's knowledge of how to develop his abilities. This is a topic we shall discuss in the following section, "The Development of Charisma." What is required, we believe, is not simply this kind of knowledge but also the creation of a new kind of personality.

THE DEVELOPMENT OF CHARISMA

We begin with the concept of charisma developed by Max Weber and attempt to widen its applicability to include every individual. This idea is then illustrated by the concept of the renaissance man scientist. We shall conclude with a discussion of the societal implications of a widespread development of charisma.

Max Weber wrote of charismatic authority as being sharply opposed to bureaucratic and traditional authority.[8] He referred to the possibilities of its resulting in a radical alteration of the central system of attitudes and directions of action with a completely new orientation of all attitudes toward the different problems and structures of the world. It is a type of power based on the personality of the charismatic individual. In our own use of the concept, we want to leave open the possibility that everyone can be a charismatic individual. Thus, we do not think of the concept in terms of the charismatic leader and the noncharismatic followers. Our own usage is dependent on the idea of development, of an expanding pie of rewards, as distinct from a scarcity situation where there must be followers for every leader.

It strikes us that the general process by which human development occurs and by which charisma is developed are the same. An individual—be he a Hitler or a Gandhi, a Stalin or a Martin Luther King, Jr.—learns to move on a cycle much like that of the scientific-industrial revolution. Ideas and goals are developed (whether consciously or unconsciously), they are tested against experience, they work to a degree, their success encourages the individual to continue to develop his ideas and goals further in the same direction, etc. As a matter of fact, all of us go through the same kind of process. What distinguishes the charismatic individual from others seems to be a matter of degree, based on a sense of direction. He is able to learn how to keep going for a much longer period in a direction which yields for him personal satisfaction as well as the kinds of achievements which he can use to offer others a great deal in return for their adherence to him.

Weber's concept of the "routinization of charisma" seems to offer insight into the process by which such development is halted. The routinization of charisma is an illustration of SHELL GAME. Preservation of a given social movement becomes an end in itself, whereas formerly that had simply been a means for transmitting the movement's truths, and the force of the movement begins to die. Although Weber focused attention on the situation where the leader dies and the movement passes into the hands of followers, it seems useful to focus on routinization within the personality of the charismatic individual. If this approach yields insight into what stops a charismatic individual from becoming ever more charismatic, it may also help us to understand why the rest of us fail to become charismatic in the first place.

All of us seem to play SHELL GAME all of the time, with the variation being the size of the shell we are in. To the extent that an action is successful in a certain context, we tend to hang on to that mode of action, emphasizing it more. But there are other contexts for which that action is not an optimum one. Our continued use of that mode—transforming it from a means to achieve satisfaction in the first context to an end in itself with less regard for its utility in other contexts—constitutes a SHELL GAME, a kind of routinization of that mode of behavior.

The process that can reverse this routinization within the personality holds the key to an understanding of how a given individual becomes a charismatic personality within a given milieu. We believe that a balance among head, heart, and hand is involved in this process. The basic dimensions of development envisioned here are cognition, emotion and action, that is, ever more comprehensive and deeper understandings, ever greater expressive ability, and ever improved problem-solving ability. Routinization is a kind of SHELL GAME at one end of a continuum, with the other end being CONTINUING REVOLUTION, an antidote to routinization.

As for the head aspect of this three-fold developmental process, an approach to the integration of knowledge which incorporates an ever-widening range of human experience is crucial. The Korzybskian emphasis on DIMENSION as distinct from DICHOTOMY or sets of categories provides an illustration. Suppose that the individual or group is able to see more and more of its behavior on a variety of dimensions leading toward and away from its development; that is suppose multiple STAIRWAYS are seen in relation to more of everyday behavior. Then the individual or system will learn, via this monitoring of its development, that it can in fact continue to develop, with no arbitrary barriers along the paths of continuing DEVELOPMENT. Such learning will be at a deep level, since it refers not only to what might be but also to what has already been, according to the individual's own assessment.

As this kind of head development continues, the individual's basic confidence in his ability to develop builds up. It is this kind of thing which keeps his level of aspiration up in the face of failure. For the failure comes to be seen as specific to the set of circumstances surrounding it, and not as a general indictment of the individual's ability to develop. Indeed, as this kind of confidence develops, the individual learns to convert more and more of his failures into successes. Failure comes to be seen less as a symptom of his fundamental scarcities and more as an opportunity to improve ability to develop.

Hand follows head and heart, at least to the degree that head and heart are oriented to this kind of integration. Such an orientation is the belief and the feeling that both cognitive and emotional development are dependent on action, and that effective action is in turn dependent on cognitive and emotional development. The reverse of this orientation is illustrated by barriers between science, the humanities, and technology within society. These preserve the ancient mind-body split in Western society and tend to have negative repercussions on all three kinds of development.

Our analysis of the process by which charisma develops has been quite abstract. What we require is a detailed focus on certain kinds of phenomena, and we have chosen the process of sciencing for this purpose. We shall contrast two approaches to science: industrial science and renaissance man science. Our overall thesis is that it is the latter which illustrates CONTINUING REVOLUTION along with the development of charisma, whereas the former illustrates SHELL GAME.

In modern society science is seen as a profession more than as a calling or way of life. The craftsmanship ideal, that one's work colors all of one's life, has been dying along with the ideal that the totality of life should be devoted to one's religious calling. This is both a symptom of, and a force behind, a continuing industrial revolution which has looked to bureaucracy as its key social technology. One sciences for a portion of one's life, and one does other things after work is over. The split tends to be very deep. The idea of applying one's own scientific ideas to one's life, even if one happens to be a psychologist or a sociologist, generally is not taken seriously. Within the division of labor it is up to the social technologists—the teachers, the social workers, the therapists, the city planners—to take up this function.

We submit that this kind of split tends to castrate industrial science's ability to gain knowledge as well as to solve problems. In effect, it results in the social scientist telling himself throughout much of the day, via his own actions, that his ideas are not good enough to put into practice. He thus plays a SHELL GAME with the ideas. They become things of importance in themselves, tested only under very special conditions. Rather than learning to become a living embodiment of his ideas about the nature of human nature, the industrial scientist is satisfied to remain at an essentially one-dimensional level. SHELL GAME teaches him that his own work is genuinely creative and that technological applications represent a kind of hack work. Evidence of this orientation can be seen in the downgrading of the importance of teaching by most academic researchers.

Renaissance man science, by contrast, returns in part to the craftsmanship ideal. One's work colors one's play, but in addition, one's play colors one's work. The focus is not narrowed to getting down on paper one's latest findings, but rather is on the human development of the scientist, the development of the whole man. Sciencing is seen as a means to this end, an end which continually expands in all directions.

Some might attempt to argue that renaissance man science becomes diverted from its central mission of producing knowledge by this shift in focus. On the contrary, we submit that this kind of sciencing tends to be vastly more effective in that regard than industrial science. To illustrate, consider the social scientist's lack of knowledge of his own creative processes. He tends to start out playing CONFORMITY, attempting to test ideas that others have created. During the testing process he is constrained once again by norms relating to the scientific method, norms which—we have argued above—tend to lead him to conclusions which are the product of his own hidden preconceptions as well as those of his subjects. Now he must once again conform, this time to the norms enforced by the media of publication, which generally censor out information on any process of learning or discovery on the researcher's part that managed to slip through the other normative networks. Then he must wait for his study to be accepted and published, a lengthy process, and his study may even fail to be published. Then he waits for others to read and respond to his work, for this is the way of scientific communication. He has already learned that critical or constructive comment on articles is very rare, and that the best he can hope for is a number of requests for reprints. And if such comment is rare, rarer still is the researcher whose work is used in an important way by others.

And even if his work is used by others, where does this lead? There is a chance that the work will be diffused widely enough so that social technologists become aware of it. This can take many years. And if they become aware of it, there is a slight chance that they may use it in their own work. And if they use it in their own work, there is a very slight chance that they will be able to solve problems more effectively. But this chance is only very slight, since their abilities,

say, as teachers, rest far more on what is deeply within their personalities than on what they know only at a superficial level of awareness. And even if, after all this, some social technologists are able to
solve some problems more effectively, how does this speak with any
relevance to the overpowering problems of today?

The renaissance man social scientist—and he can be every man,
as distinct from one of an elite group—is able to do hundreds of
experiments in a single day, provided he has learned to incorporate
his knowledge deeply enough into his personality. If he has learned,
cognitively, to apply his general knowledge of human behavior to his
own everyday situations, and if he is motivated to do this, then he
will "experiment" on himself and others often. Modern phenomenology teaches us that we all do this kind of thing anyway: we act
on the basis of our hypotheses. The difference is that the industrial
scientist tends to act, in his everyday behavior, on hypotheses that
are more implicit than explicit. In this way, the renaissance man
scientist might rapidly develop effective technologies which, in turn,
might stimulate his cognitive development. Further, by applying his
ideas to himself, the renaissance man scientist learns more and
more about his own creative processes. By pushing inward and outward in all directions, the tendency is for the renaissance man scientist to play less of a SHELL GAME, since he doesn't fixate on any
one idea or approach but redefines everything as his perspective
widens.

The renaissance man scientist is also an artist and a revolutionary, that is, a player of CONTINUING REVOLUTION. In place of
the specialization and subspecialization and sub-sub-specialization
characteristic of industrial science, there is a thrust toward the
integration of ever-growing knowledge and experience. As an artist,
he learns to express himself more creatively and, in this way, he can
develop the basis for charismatic appeal. He communicates not
solely from the head—or, more accurately, from what is on paper—
but with his entire being. Here, then, is a basis for the kind of
communication that is highly effective. And if he learns to communicate the kind of knowledge that can lead to the development of
others, then we at last begin to have the kind of knowledge that
speaks to the issues of the day. But the technologies he uses are
successively altered as he gains experience and ideas, and so we have
a player of CONTINUING REVOLUTION.

Is it grossly foolhardy or ingenuous to conceive of the possibility
that all men will learn to play this game more and more? Have we
not seen enough demonstrations of man's inhumanity to be con-

vinced that such talk is rubbish? Are we so incredibly utopian that we can envision a society where every individual becomes increasingly charismatic, and where this personal charisma replaces bureaucracy's claim to authority as well as the claims of traditional authority? Can the tide of history be turned away from ever-increasing specialization and toward not only a renaissance man science but also, more generally, a renaissance man society?

We are not sure, but we believe that such a society is a definite possibility. And because of this, we believe that it merits serious attention. What kind of a society would it be? Perhaps we can gain perspective by extrapolating trends we have already noted in the family.

For one, let us imagine that the "do your own thing" philosophy results in a continuing trend toward personal autonomy. This would lead to a society where differences among individuals would be far greater than they are today, where the greatest differences existing today would be as nothing compared to the diversities of the future.

Along with increasing self-understanding and understanding of others should come increasing ability to communicate with self and others. Such communication would be the basis for extremely rapid changes in society. Deep knowledge of self would help the individual to tap the sources of his own creativity. Also, people would be far more open to learning from one another, and their horizons would be widened continually.

As for the hard facts of power, the hardest fact of all would be that power is based on the individual's ability to play CONTINUING REVOLUTION, and that, in turn, would be the basis for the development of charisma. Since this game has no end point but, rather, is located on a continuum, the amount of power in society would be expanding continually. And with less and less scarcity of power, one man's gain would not have to be another's loss. Indeed, the continuing development of charisma by any individual would tend to be everyone's gain, since it would provide a model for others to follow.

As for wealth, there would be a profound shift toward valuing the nonmaterial over the material. If the discovery process can be harnessed, the technological problems associated with producing material wealth of all kinds would be greatly reduced. And what would come to be most valuable would be the ability to discover or create, an intangible. If the individual were granted one wish, would something concrete be most valuable? Most valuable, perhaps, would be the intangible ability to continue to have one's wishes come true indefinitely.

Hopelessly naive? Perhaps. Perhaps not.

NOTES

1. The distinctions among tradition direction, inner-direction, other-direction, and autonomy are elaborated in David Riesman, *The Lonely Crowd* (New Haven: Yale University Press, 1961).
2. Consciousness I, II, and III are discussed in Charles A. Reich, *The Greening of America* (New York: Bantam, 1971).
3. Bernard S. Phillips, *Sociology: Social Structure and Change* (New York: Macmillan, 1969), p. 67. The definition is not an atypical one. For a detailed discussion of the socialization process, see George Herbert Mead, *Mind, Self and Society* (Chicago: University of Chicago Press, 1970).
4. For more elaborate discussions of these kinds of games in the classroom, although without explicit reference to the language of games, see Jules Henry, *Culture Against Man* (New York: Random House, 1963).
5. A detailed discussion of this game is presented by Dan Greenburg in *How to be a Jewish Mother* (Los Angeles: Price/Stern/Sloan, 1964).
6. Martha Wolfenstein, "Trends in Infant Care," *American Journal of Orthopsychiatry* 23 (January 1953): 121-22.
7. Samuel Richardson's *Pamela,* along with changing views of the role of women in the novel, are discussed in Ian Watt, *The Rise of the Novel* (Berkeley: University of California Press, 1957), especially pp. 138-49, 154-64.
8. Max Weber, *The Theory of Social and Economic Organization* (New York: Free Press, 1964), pp. 358-91.

SUGGESTED READINGS

BERGER, PETER L., and LUCKMANN, THOMAS. *The Social Construction of Reality.* New York: Anchor, 1967. The basic argument of the book is that reality is socially constructed and that the sociology of knowledge must analyze the processes in which this occurs. The introduction presents a brief history of the sociology of knowledge, and the book itself presents a modern view, carrying forward the tradition of the earlier work on the socialization process. Recommended for the serious student of sociology.

GOFFMAN, ERVING. *Asylums: Essays on the Social Situation of Mental Patients and Other Inmates.* New York: Anchor, 1961. Total institutions are places of residence and work where a large number of like-situated individuals, cut off from the wider society, lead an enclosed, formally administered round of life. How they learn to do this, and the impact on their personalities, is discussed with the aid of dramaturgical metaphors.

GREENBURG, DAN. *How to Be a Jewish Mother.* Los Angeles: Price/-Stern/Sloan, 1964. The Jewish Mother's cardinal rule, according to Greenburg, is: "Let your child hear you sigh every day; if you don't know what he's done to make you suffer, *he* will." Although the book is written for laughs, the joke turns out to be on all of us.

ZWEIG, PAUL. *The Heresy of Self-Love.* New York: Colophon, 1968. This discussion of "subversive individualism" concludes as follows: "Today we find ourselves caught in a moral dilemma: unable to accept the destructive conformities of patriotism, national honor, authoritarian religion, yet wary of the old poetry of alienation, with its overtones of self-punishment and isolation. The love-ins and be-ins of the past few years may well express this disarray. They show dramatically how many of us today are groping toward some new language, some new heresy."

FOUR

GROUPS

Must we abandon our focus on the individual in order to understand the group? Must we specialize in such a way that we play SHELL GAME, with the concept of the group becoming an end in itself and with a consequent loss of understanding of the individual?

We think not. In these chapters we attempt to probe deeply into the psyche in order to achieve deep understanding of the group, and also in order to understand the individual.

Ian Zenski is a man in transition, moving from industrial to post-industrial society. If we are to understand the nature of these two societies and how one becomes transformed into the other, we must understand Ian Zenski. And as we learn about the differences between these two kinds of societies, we also learn more about Ian Zenski. The process is a cumulative one, like a snowball rolling downhill. It is analogous to one of Erich Fromm's central theses in *Man for Himself:* If man does not focus attention on himself, then he cannot hope to communicate deeply with others.

In chapter 6 we find Ian Zenski searching for himself and finding more and more a self that continues to change. In chapter 7 we put the language of games together more systematically, develop in some detail a metaphor which may help us to understand basic processes in the universe, and apply these ideas to an analysis of five types of society: pre-industrial, early industrial, late industrial, early post-industrial, and late post-industrial.

6

Ian Zenski,
Part One

GAMES, INC.: ACT ONE

Ian Zenski smiled broadly as he re-read, for the fifth time, the page one review in *The New York Times Book Review.* He lingered over the final paragraph:

Human Creativity: Paths to Discovery reveals a mind which has probed inward and outward in time and space perhaps more daringly and more systematically than any other. The case he makes for the possibility that the ordinary man can learn to be infinitely creative is very convincing, whether his argument is in the context of the life of Confucius, Buddha, Marx, Freud, or Korzybski. Zenski's evaluation of our most advanced scientific methods in all fields of investigation as being "pre-scientific" because they fail to deal with the personality of the investigator and thus miss the process of discovery constitutes a fascinating thesis. What is most impressive to this reviewer is that he supports his thesis with the outline of a *praxis:* a path to a new kind of consciousness. Just where this path leads remains to be seen. If Zenski is correct, however, our destiny as gods is finally catching up with us, and each of us should prepare for his role as a creator of the universe.

A buzz on the intercom interrupted his thoughts. It was Miss Fromm with word that the directors of the five major projects had arrived and were waiting for him in the conference room. Zenski had been looking forward to this review session. Ever since he founded the company some four years previously, Games, Inc. had experienced a remarkable growth rate, dipping into an ever-widening variety of fields. But as the successes continued to multiply, Zenski was gradually coming to feel more and more dissatisfied. He wasn't sure what was bothering him. It was all very vague in his mind. Perhaps this meeting could help him figure things out.

As Zenski opened the door and walked to his seat, glancing at the faces around the table, his thoughts jumped to the life and death of Mishima. The faces were youthful and buoyant, and they somehow conveyed the kind of admiration reserved for saints or sages. Zenski had never given much thought to how his staff viewed him. Everyone was on a first-name basis, and they saw one another often enough. Someone was always throwing a party or doing something unusual. Just like one big family. But the analogy between himself and Mishima was disturbing. Surely these young people were not his private regimented army. Didn't he give them autonomy with their projects? Weren't they free to do what they wanted?

Jack Fleisch was first to be recognized.

JACK: We're all set now for the legal services summer training institute. We've got a program together which is at least ten years ahead of its time. I'm passing around an outline of the two-month program. The keynotes are an interdisciplinary orientation, research, and encounter sessions.

IAN: I'm in a strange mood today. I feel like taking the role of devil's advocate. I want to reassess everything, to take a hard look at just where we're going and how fast we're getting there. Now, Jack, in what sense would you say the institute will be ten years ahead of the times?

Fleisch felt that something was wrong. This was not the old Ian Zenski whose enthusiasm was always showing. He had been like an old time missionary out to save the world, and he managed to fill everyone else with his zeal. He made you feel that you were doing something that was not simply important, not simply vital. It was revolutionary. The world would be different because of it. And Ian was no hog. Everyone got credit for what he did. But what was he doing now with this "devil's

advocate" business? Everyone knows that in these kinds of
sessions negativism doesn't pay off. Criticism is essential, but it
has to be constructive. Ian's mood seemed to be threatening. And
if he really wanted to tear something apart, no one was good
enough to be able to defend it adequately.

JACK: Take the research program as one example. These people
in poverty law know about legal research, but they have no
background in social research. If they learn to make
presentations in court which have the status of good sociology
behind them, they're bound to be much more successful with
their clients and work toward a more equalitarian system. The
interdisciplinary approach will give them content along with the
research techniques. It won't be limited to sociology. They'll be
able to throw in economics and history and political science. And
the participants will have to learn all of this deeply by
confronting one another in the encounter sessions.

IAN: But from what I see in your outline of the training
program, the research is very pedestrian. So what if they do
interview prostitutes and pimps. Or suppose they do observe
intake procedures for delinquents. What difference is it going to
make if they analyze the culture of the prison? This
interdisciplinary stuff appears to me to be even more traditional.
It looks very good on paper—the whole program looks good on
paper—but what new knowledge is going to come out of the
research or the interdisciplinary program? It sounds like you've
got a program where you're going to teach the "natives" what
you already know. You've got the answers, and now you're
spreading the word. As for these encounter sessions, they're all
the rage and spreading to all parts of business and academia, but
just where do they lead? Sure, they give the individual more
awareness of some aspects of his personality, but does it increase
his degree of conformity so that he learns to avoid stepping on
the emotional toes of others? Is there a transfer of self-awareness
to other kinds of situations? Jack, don't get the feeling that this
is a personal attack. Actually, I'm criticizing myself more than
any of you. I could have said these things much earlier if I knew
enough to say them. But now that I am thinking along these
lines I want to see what can be done. Let's hear from Ono.

ONO: Our project is now in its second year, and we're beginning
to get feedback on the long-term effectiveness of the role-playing
sessions. I think everyone here knows that we've been working
primarily with foreign service officers, with a few ambassadors

and upper-echelon State Department officials thrown in. We have been concentrating on interaction during crisis situations as an offshoot from the early simulations by Guetzkow at Northwestern University. For example, how do heads of state of unaligned nations react to the achievement of first-strike capability by a nuclear coalition? As for feedback, there's a lot of enthusiasm for us to extend our operations, and we're getting applications from top officials more frequently. It seems that participating in these training sessions is becoming a very big status thing. Our graduates tell us that they've learned to empathize much better with the people they're dealing with.

But frankly, I'm very disappointed. I don't see any big changes afoot. Embassy officials still isolate themselves in their compounds, and they're still shunted around so rapidly from one country to another that they have no incentive for learning very much about the culture or the people. And none of our graduates seems to have done anything special to suggest major changes in the way State operates or in its relation to the Pentagon.

IAN: To what extent are you conforming to my devil's advocate mood in making your assessment?

ONO: I probably am conforming, but I'm not making it up. I think that each of us at one time or another has felt this way about his own project, but we've rarely communicated it to one another. We felt embarrassed about it because we assumed it was so very unusual. The whole "onward and upward" atmosphere of Games, Inc., has prevented us from viewing anything in other than optimistic terms. But now that you've revealed your own doubts, I bet you'll hear a lot more like this. Sure, we'll be conforming to your new mood, but we'll also be conforming to the part of ourselves that we've been burying.

VLAD: I don't know who else Ono is speaking for, but she's diagnosed what's been troubling me for some time now. On the one hand I've had fantastic successes with my experiments in educational TV. We've got programs in eleven different subject areas and at fifteen levels of education, including the doctoral program, and we've outdone *Sesame Street* in terms of audience for almost every one of our classes. We've been able to attract the best talent available, and the whole thing is making tons of money. But what we've done with all this is to reinforce the kind of content within the educational system which is largely irrelevant to today's problems in society. We've put the educational system on TV, but we've done almost nothing to make it a better educational system.

WILLIAM: Speaking for myself, I have a far more optimistic view than Vlad or Ono. Our computer simulation effort has expanded more than tenfold during the past year. We're into just about everything, and we're in thirty-four countries. We started with business applications, and that's still our major area. But now we're very strong in urban problems, education, crime, medicine, engineering, and ecology. I think we've caught on for several reasons. We don't just talk to top management, we get down to lower levels to get the facts. Also, we don't just make use of whatever information is available. We do research to get on top of the intangible data, the kinds of things that aren't codified. And we stay with a client after he's tried to put our ideas into practice. We help him by making the necessary revisions until it works to perfection.

IAN: I won't quarrel with your analysis as an indication of how successful we are in a business sense, but how is this any better than making a fortune out of selling shoes? Is there any other sense in which we're successful? You tell me about quantity, but what about quality? So what if we're helping organizations to be somewhat more effective. Suppose it's also true that we're helping them to avoid questioning their basic premises. Suppose that we're all merrily travelling down a roller coaster to oblivion. Suppose that what our organization is doing is simply greasing the wheels. While we sit here and talk about our progress the world is going to pot at a faster rate than ever before. Latin America, Asia, and Africa are in a state of escalating terror and counter-terror, and the industrialized societies are falling to pieces.

VERA: I go along with Ono and Vlad. In my work with churches and synagogues on the decision to relocate and the determination of a relocation locale, I get into computer simulation, and William and I have collaborated on problems of mutual interest. Houses of worship are getting more and more desperate, and in this way our business is booming. Our organization is looked to as a problem solver, and as the problems accelerate, our business booms. If things keep going the way they are it won't be long before everything will go bust and there will be no more pieces left to pick up. Organized religion isn't doing very much for people. What we're doing is administering medicine to a corpse.

The real question is how do we create a healthy body? How do we produce a preventive medicine? How are people to find meaning in a world of disintegration and hopelessness? As a matter of fact, why help them find meaning in the world as it is if that simply institutionalizes what exists?

IAN: I'd like to suggest that we all take this week to do some hard thinking about the projects in the light of this discussion. I have to do some thinking about my own goals. As a group we've made our mark on the world, but did we do something autonomous or are we ourselves simply in the grip of societal forces? I'd like to try to think about the kind of world I want to create. I've reached a point where I'm no longer satisfied with the kinds of successes we've attained. Call it alienation. Call it an identity crisis. Call it an ego trip. Whatever it is, I've got to follow it through to see where it leads. Let's meet a week from now and see where our heads are.

ALFRED KORZYBSKI

Ian spent most of the week in the stacks of Widener Library. He was like a pendulum, only he was gathering momentum each time he arced through the air, until his arcs came up almost vertically. He was moving along the dimension of human development, with each probe into human misery and meaninglessness followed by a joyful creation of new meanings. Each probe in a negative direction pushed him to envision worlds ever more divergent from those he had already experienced. And each such vision gave him additional strength to see that God is dead and man is alone in the universe, and to reject all existing structures in their present form. The theatre of the absurd pushed him to Pierce and Dewey, then back to Nietzsche and Kierkegaard, then forward to Alfred Korzybski. Man cannot find new gods unless he rejects the old ones, and he is unable to risk such rejection unless he hears a new rhythm of the universe. The paradox is resolved by thinking in dimensional terms more than in either/or terms. Each hint of a new leitmotif trains the ear to hear the limitations of the old ones, and the understanding of such limitations suggests permutations for creating new leitmotifs.

It was Korzybski's work which finally gave the pendulum of his explorations sufficient momentum to complete the circle, and from that point onward his acceleration was much more rapid.

However, the intellectual journey carrying him to Korzybski was an involved one. Max Weber's work and life portrayed the contradictions inherent in Western civilization. Weber suffered privately and then projected this suffering in his work to create an image of inevitable lifelessness and doom. Ionesco went several steps further when he faced up to the absurdity of existence and pointed to the process of human communication as a key to both problem and solution. The pragmatists proved to be more specific about solutions, with Dewey's call for a reconstruction of philosophy to put science to work in the construction of a man-centered world. But Dewey and the other pragmatists never did succeed in doing what they set out to do. Science could not so easily be redirected to center on humanistic ends, or at least the pragmatists had no formula which could accomplish this, and the juggernaut of the scientific-industrial revolution rolled on at an ever-increasing pace. Perhaps their limited success was due to a failure to recognize the magnitude of the human problem, as did the existentialists. Man is alone in the universe, and he must create his own meanings. It is not only the gods of religion who are dead, but the worth of all existing institutions is called into question. A trans-valuation of all existing values is required. But how to achieve this?

It was then that Zenski turned to the life and work of Alfred Korzybski, the founder of general semantics. Korzybski's two major books, *The Manhood of Humanity* and *Science and Sanity,* appeared in 1920 and 1933, periods full of man's disenchantment with the inevitability of progress in human affairs. What appealed to Zenski was that Korzybski appeared to go beyond the existentialists in his recognition of the problem of man's existence in the world and in negating existing institutions. At the same time, he went beyond the pragmatists in his construction of solutions. Zenski had heard of Korzybski, but only through the work of such popularizers as S. I. Hayakawa and Stuart Chase, and he was well aware that the general semantics "movement" as a program for achieving sanity in the modern world had largely lost its momentum. But why? Was it due to a defective vision of man's situation, or was it the case that man had not yet been ready for Korzybski's radical ideas? Certainly, at least in Zenski's own eyes, the popularizers had done even less justice to Korzybski than the followers of Darwin, Freud, and Marx.

What an incredibly optimistic idea, thought Zenski, to conceive of man's language, with its resultant implications for man's thought and actions, as the root of his difficulties as well as the source of his strength. He recalled one of the arguments put forward against general semantics, that problems were almost invariably based on conflicts of interests, and that solving the problem of communication does not solve the problem. But Zenski found the argument unconvincing. Suppose, as Ionesco had portrayed, human communication was the central problem? Suppose that somehow our approach to language creates conflicts of interest? Suppose it creates conflicts within the individual which, if resolved, will result in the individual's becoming a "genius," as Korzybski indicated?

Zenski decided to probe as deeply as he could into the sources of Korzybski's strengths, and then to follow this with an exploration of his weaknesses. He had become convinced that this man's work contained what he was looking for in re-evaluating his own progress and failures. True, Korzybski may have been some kind of quack, talking about an insane world and how every man could become a genius. True also, a cultism developed around Korzybski, some of which spilled over into what later became scientology. But should we ignore Darwin because of the Social Darwinists or Marx because of Stalin or Nietzsche because of Hitler? And what if this man pointed in a direction leading toward every man becoming Nietzsche's superman? Nietzsche's nervous collapse, when he witnessed the brutal flogging of a horse, led to his imagining that he was at one and the same time Christ and Dionysus. Perhaps this kind of internal conflict—between "selflessness" and "selfishness"—is an artifact produced largely by language. Suppose that these two concepts are not diametrically opposed, as language would have it, but that when man acts "for himself," in Fromm's terms, or to become a superman or a genius, he also advances the welfare of society. It sounded too easy to Zenski, yet he could not afford to neglect an inquiry which might have such vast repercussions.

Zenski had found himself initially attracted to Korzybski because of the incredible clarity and comprehensiveness of his central ideas. Man is different from other forms of life in that he is a time binder, able to learn from the experiences of others and to go beyond what they have achieved. So far, nothing seemingly unusual. It had been said before and since by many other people using different words. The anthropologists talk of language and culture, psychologists talk of learning, economists talk of development, biologists speak of evolution.

But somehow there was something more to Korzybski's idea of man the time binder. Whatever it was, it was the same kind of thing emanating from Kubrick's *2001: A Space Odyssey.* The whole thing seemed to be a matter of degree of emphasis. Sure, anthropologists make a big deal of the concept of culture, but how important to them is the central idea of human progress in everything they do and say? Haven't they in fact deemphasized such ideas in the interest of achieving scientific status? Doesn't their supposed relativism actually represent a gigantic cop-out from the problems of human societies? As for Korzybski, there is no question about the centrality to him of the problem of human development. He was attempting to show the world a path away from insanity, and he devoted his life to this end. He didn't simply publish his ideas and then go on to a separate private life. He lived his ideas in much the same way that Buddha lived his. He believed in praxis, and he acted out this belief in his life.

But how could such a man have emerged out of the chaos that was the early twentieth century, the shattered dream, the death of God, the horror of the coal mines and the iron foundries, the maimed bodies of World War I and the maimed spirit of industrial society? How did he avoid escaping conformity to a narrow muckraking orientation or into the hopelessness of the early Camus? Zenski found his answer as he examined Korzybski's family background in science, mathematics, and engineering along with his prodigious knowledge in these fields. He was not a modern Leonardo da Vinci in the sense of creating respected innovations in a variety of fields. But perhaps what he achieved in integrating knowledge from diverse fields would prove to be far more influential than the accomplishments of da Vinci.

With this background Korzybski could confront Aristotelian logic from the perspective of a mathematician and reject the Aristotelian law of identity. "A" is *not* identical with "A" in an Einsteinian space-time world where everything is relative to position in space-time. Nor is "A" the same as "A" in the molecular world depicted by Heisenberg and Planck. All is change, just as Heraclitus had concluded, and no phenomenon is identical with any other or even with itself. Korzybski had succeeded in mastering the creative and powerful ideas of mathematics and the physical sciences, ideas which themselves were sources of the modern industrial revolution. Instead of turning his face away from science, as did the existentialists, because of what it had contributed to dehumanizing man, Korzybski turned to science as a source of energy for transforming the human situation into something worthy of man. And he did more than talk pragmatism, as did the pragmatists. He attempted to live this union between science and humanism.

But if all this were true, why didn't Korzybski succeed in creating a sane world, or at least a viable movement which would continue to gather momentum after his death in 1950? An image of the life of Ludwig von Bertalanffy leaped into Zenski's thoughts. Here was another man who had attempted to integrate human knowledge. Despite his enormous success in helping to achieve currency for "systems theory" in a wide variety of fields, his ideas were narrowed into yet another specialized orientation which could be used alongside of cybernetics and computers to accelerate society's "progress" toward destruction. Bertalanffy failed to communicate in sufficient depth to the heirs of George Herbert Mead in sociology that the individual as well as society can be viewed as a system, that man can shape society just as he is shaped by society. This failure to communicate to sociologists was paralleled in every other field, and even in biology, Bertalanffy's own field, his ideas penetrated only narrowly.

But Korzybski's case was different. His focus was on man's development from the start. It would have been most difficult to skim off some of his ideas and divert them to other purposes. Should his followers be blamed? Did they distort him and create a superficial vision of Korzybski in much the same way that ideologies and religions follow Weber's path of routinization to make themselves more acceptable to the world? Of course they bear some responsibility, but surely Korzybski himself must be at the root of the problem.

Zenski faced an impasse. Korzybski's stature for him was growing rapidly, yet his failure was obvious. Perhaps he should revise his estimate of Korzybski, for if his ideas were indeed so powerful wouldn't they have had far more impact than they did? The dichotomy was growing and Zenski felt it was beginning to tear him apart. Surely insanity lies in this direction, he thought, and then the title of Korzybski's *Science and Sanity* occured to him. Was not he, Zenski, a product of an Aristotelian world which shaped his thought processes and pushed him in the direction of insanity? Was it essential that he think in such either/or terms? Perhaps an understanding of Korzybski required him to engage in praxis, to reshape his mind and personality in a non-Aristotelian way.

For the remainder of the week prior to the review session Zenski attempted to create a null-A or non-Aristotelian world within himself and around himself. He focused on getting himself to think in gradational terms as distinct from dichotomies. And then suddenly he achieved new insight into Korzybski's failure. Zenski had been focusing on the contradiction between two poles of a dichotomy: Korzybski's ideational achievements and his practical accomplishments. But suppose a choice between these need not be made. What if these two aspects of Korzybski's life are seen as a kind of feedback process, where further development of ideas leads to more effective achievements, and vice versa? What if such behavior is continuous, and Korzybski's failure to achieve is seen as a matter of degree? Then we need not evaluate Korzybski's ideas as bad or good, ineffective or effective. The relevant question becomes how can we go further than Korzybski, both ideationally and in action. It was in this frame of mind that Ian Zenski stepped into the conference room.

GAMES, INC.: ACT TWO

JACK: Ian, maybe I'm more of a conformist than the others around the table, but I've had a complete change of heart about my work. I feel like I've been an egotistical ant, talking to the other ants about how important my ideas are and how they should listen to me. Maybe I've been a successful ant, getting lots of others to go along with what I say, and maybe they even look up to me. But in the meantime all of us ants are going to be destroyed by a forest fire, and nothing much will have been accomplished.

IAN: I like your ant metaphor. If you actually were an ant and somehow managed to come out with that statement, I'd feel pretty sorry for you. Because there would be biological barriers preventing you from doing what you want to do. Maybe you—and everybody else—built an ant-colony world because you never looked at yourself in the way you've started to do. But as a human being, what can you do about the situation now that you see it in this way?

JACK: I'd like to be able to do something really significant, and I feel now that my legal services work is just so much trivia. And if I'm doing better than most other ants, it's still just ant work that I'm doing. I'd like to do something that can benefit the entire world, and not just in a small way. For example, the legal system is so dehumanizing. It really functions like a school for training people to become criminals. There's so much selfishness throughout it, with almost everyone not giving a damn about anyone else. And the lawmakers just perpetuate the whole thing. And everyone hides behind the excuse that he's not responsible for what's going on. And if local and national law is in a bad state, then international law is a complete mess. There's very little that's done for humanitarian reasons. But how can I possibly change this with my insignificant summer institute?

ONO: As I see it, the question boils down to whether you—and all of us as well—are going to act like ants or men. There's a self-fulfilling prophecy involved here. When you say "How can I possibly change?" you define yourself as an ant, and you in effect become an ant. When you ask, as Ian did, "What can I do about the situation?" you assume that something can in fact be done, and you become a man. You create yourself as an ant being or a human being. You curse others for their lack of responsibility for what is going on, but you yourself disclaim responsibility by assuming that you're helpless.

VLAD: I've got an idea. Why don't we have an Ant-Colony Trial just like the Nuremburg trials, and let's video tape it so we can see ourselves in action and maybe learn something about ourselves. We all stand accused of the world's insanity, the children with bloated stomachs and the children bloated with fear, the oceans of guilt and the oceans of hate, all the things that people could have become but never dared to become, in short, our wasted ant-like lives. I'll set up the equipment right now.

VERA: Great! That's just the kind of thing that religion is supposed to do but hardly ever does. We should all confront ourselves.

VLAD: Jack Fleisch, I accuse you of partial responsibility in teaching all of us to hate ourselves and to hate society, of twisting our minds, and shutting off our chances for realizing our potentials as human beings. I accuse you of deep involvement in wasted lives.

JACK: What evidence do you have that I am guilty?

IAN: To start with, your blind subservience to an adversary system of law, to a system which assigns guilt or innocence as distinct from pointing human beings in the direction of their own development. And no less important, your placing the law above man, your conception of it as a secular god which can have inhuman repercussions for the sake of its own preservation. You rationalize this by invoking your catechism that we need a government of laws and not of men, reverting back to a Hobbesian vision of society as a war of all against all. By so doing, you create a Hobbesian society, a society where we fear ourselves and one another.

JACK: I admit my guilt, but how am I to be rehabilitated?

IAN: How rapidly you become rehabilitated depends on you, my boy, but your statement shows that you have already made great progress. You no longer question whether rehabilitation is possible, you merely seek to learn the means for accomplishing it. You are a rope stretched between animal and superman, to borrow a phrase from Nietzsche. The choice is in your hands. The time is now. The place is here.

JACK: Come on, Ian, you're hamming it up.

Ian decided to put aside the courtroom scenario for the time being in order to discuss his work with Korzybski's ideas. There followed a long discussion centering around the concept of time binding and how each individual might achieve it in his own life. He used the metaphor of the pendulum to describe how insight into life's horrors and possibilities can combine to produce rapid development by showing man in what ways he is acting as an animal and by pointing him in a time-binding direction. After having lunch brought in, they continued into the afternoon.

JACK: I think I'm beginning to understand the Korzybski approach, but how does it apply to what happened this morning?

VLAD: I'm going to play back on the monitor some of your behavior, Jack.

. . . Maybe I've been a successful ant, getting lots of others to go along with what I say, and maybe they even look up to me. But in the meantime all of us ants are going to be destroyed by a forest fire, and nothing much will have been accomplished.

Two of your metaphors are the ant and the forest fire. Both of them take responsibility for your failures out of your own hands. Either you were born a certain way which cannot be changed, or else some external force is responsible. Your tone of voice sounds like some kind of goodnik, someone who thinks he is a very good person but who's the victim of circumstances, a kind of martyr or Jewish-mother type.

IAN: I have to confess—and notice the word "confess"—that I have a great deal in common with Jack. Maybe that's why I've concentrated my fire—notice my metaphor here too—on him more than on anyone else. I think it goes back to a Judaic-Christian tradition where God is absolute perfection and man is doomed to imperfection. Or the Christian emphasis on doing good for others once again shifts dynamism away from oneself. Internally, we set up an inner shell, a self-image, that we are good boys, and no matter how far our behavior departs from that image we hold to it. We become the servants of a rigid self image just as we are the servants of God and others.

ONO: What's the significance of your metaphors of the confession and of warfare?

IAN: Hating self and hating others are two sides of the same coin. This is a version of the old frustration-aggression hypothesis from the Freudian tradition. If you learn to construct a world of scarcity, then failure presents several options. Since you assume you are unable to expand the existing rewards and grow beyond the failure, you can blame the failure on others or on yourself. With the kind of family Jack and I had, we learned to blame ourselves more than others. But this is really very widespread. The whole Christian tradition emphasizes sin and guilt. Did you notice the way Jack said, "I admit my guilt"? Or his whole diatribe at the selfishness of almost everyone in the legal system? People are divided between the selfish and the unselfish, the goodies and the baddies, the cowboys and the Indians. When you blame yourself, the part of you that does the blaming—Freud's superego—is able to retain the feeling of virtue, but the burden of guilt which it has to carry may be too oppressive for learning to take place on the basis of the experience.

WILLIAM: I'm intrigued by all these ideas, but I'm also lost. We seem to be wandering from one thing to another without any central direction. I've been taking notes on what's been happening, and I'd like to summarize them. Then maybe we can put these ideas together and come out with something relevant to what Games, Inc. should be doing that it isn't doing.

VERA: Here, here!

WILLIAM: Last week, when we had our first review session, the whole tone of the discussion was that we weren't picking up the pieces of a shattering society fast enough, that we were trying to do an impossible repair job when perhaps we should focus on preventing the damage from being done in the first place. I personally opposed that view, but during the past week my ideas changed radically. What did it for me more than anything was reading about the life of Robert MacNamara. He has always been a personal god of mine, but I began to see how he was making the same kinds of mistakes we've been making. Sure he was fantastically efficient and dynamic, but he didn't take a wide enough perspective to see the long-range repercussions of what he was doing. The same thing happened during the Cuban missile crisis with some of the so-called experts who advised Kennedy to wipe out the missile bases. And it also happened in Vietnam, with the experts dragging us in deeper and deeper. As I see it, the enemy is a narrow perspective, and I admit my own guilt.

VERA: William, I've been trying to get you to see that ever since I met you. Why have you suddenly changed now?

WILLIAM: Maybe for the same reason that MacNamara became more of a hawk after Kennedy died and he was trying to please Johnson. I think that last week we saw one Ian Zenski die and another one being created. I hate to admit it but I guess I'm a conformist. But it wasn't only conformity. MacNamara used to gnash his teeth at night. He was a driven man, and I am too. I pay a price for closing myself off, for trying to create a world of certainty out of a world of flux. I don't have much of a sense of humor, and I know it. It's hard for me to relax. I have to work at everything. Maybe if I open myself up more I can enjoy life more.

IAN: Why don't you continue with your summary?

WILLIAM: Relax, Ian. Why must everything be a means to some other end? Why can't we enjoy what we're doing now? You're too uptight. You're suffering from a MacNamara complex.

IRAN: Touché! My personality also includes a lot of what you just described. But if we follow Korzybski we don't have to make an either/or choice between a task-oriented view of the moment as just a means and the Dionysian view of the moment as just an end. It can be both. I need to become more of a task-oriented anal-compulsive and combine that with, say, Vlad's Dionysian qualities. And you shouldn't lose your systematic, task-oriented approach, but simply add to it an open-ended, developmental focus.

WILLIAM: Agreed. Well, this session has been absolutely fascinating for me. I haven't said anything until now, but I've been thinking all along that this is the kind of freedom I've been lacking, this business of interrelating all kinds of ideas. For me it's like being released from jail and looking out into infinite space. Anyway—and notice how easily I've learned to wander off the subject—here is the sequence of the topics we discussed. Jack started off with his ant colony metaphor and his Jewish-mother criticism of the legal system. Then his idea of being a victim of circumstances was challenged by Ono, and Vlad went a step further by suggesting an Ant-Colony Trial which would teach us to face up to our personal responsibility for the state of the world. Then he and Ian got into the trial scenario by accusing Jack of helping to create the inhumanities of the legal system by conforming to the adversary system and by accepting a Hobbesian view of man. When Ian was thinking about how Jack could be rehabilitated, he got into that long discussion of Korzybski's life and ideas, and that ended the morning session.

This afternoon we started off with a discussion of how to apply Korzybski's ideas to the morning session, and Vlad's having video taped part of the session helped us. I guess our big discussion about the link between hate and guilt, on the one hand, and scarcity, on the other, points toward Korzybski's infinity orientation as a direction for gaining insight on the problem of hate and guilt. Then I started with my attempt to summarize things, but before doing it I got off on how I want to move out of my MacNamara complex into a more creative orientation.

VERA: I wonder if we can follow the spirit of what William had in mind when he started his summary, the spirit of focusing on a particular thing rather than wandering all over the place. I feel that what we've all been doing this past week is facing up to the basic metaphysical problems of man's purpose, the nature of his existence, the nature of the universe. And we've also taken a problem-solving approach pointed toward making progress on the horrors of present-day existence and doing this fast enough to help avert the destruction of life as we know it. Notice that I said "help avert." In the spirit of the Ant-Colony Trial let me substitute "avert" for "help avert." In sum, I suggest that everything we say should bear centrally on how to achieve human development rapidly enough to solve the most urgent problems we and the world face. Let's not beat around the bush so much.

VLAD: Right on! I'm going to try to illustrate Vera's suggestion in what I say. I want to develop a dream metaphor analogous to your pendulum metaphor, Ian, in order to do the same kind of thing in a different way. What we've started doing in this session is learning how to free ourselves from the cages of our personalities by mentally constructing an image of how we'd like to change ourselves and then going ahead and changing ourselves. I can see it happening through my camera. And it's not the kind of thing which most actors go through, where they keep their inner core of personality safely locked away from the roles they play. The key idea is that a *continual* dialectic can occur, where we negate aspects of ourselves by an antithesis, then create a synthesis, and then continue to repeat the process. It's a kind of continuous revolution of the personality.

IAN: And how does that relate to the pendulum metaphor?

VLAD: They both have the idea of a continually expanding synthesis. Maybe you'll see it better if I talk about the spatial implications of this dream metaphor. Let's take inner space first, the country of the mind. This session we've been experimenting with a kind of three-stage process. We take a hard look at aspects of our personality, whether by ourselves or with the aid of a TV monitor or someone else's comments about us. We form a mental picture of some aspect of ourselves, and then we move to a second stage of negating it in favor of a different picture or dream of self. As a third stage we begin to live that dream by behaving on the basis of it. In succeeding stages we can go beyond good acting and learn to incorporate that dream of self as part of an expanding personality. But we also keep going and dream another dream which negates part of the preceding one, and the process keeps going. The new dream is dreamt while we are living in the old dream. It's a dream within a dream. In this way we go deeper and deeper into the country of the mind. To me, all of this represents human development because we learn to expand beyond the iron cage of fixed personality.

WILLIAM: Let me see if I can apply what you're saying to what happened to me over the past week. Stage one, I learned to see that part of my personality fitted a task-oriented MacNamara model. Stage two, I rejected it in favor of a more Dionysian

orientation. Stage three, I acted in the new way, and I can
continue to develop this as part of my personality. But each time
I change myself I go through the same kind of three stage
process, dreaming a new dream within the dream I was living
previously. In this way I continue to expand my personality. And
I can learn to do this on a continual basis.

VERA: We have been concentrating on internal expansion, but
we haven't talked about how that affects one's relation to the
world that is outside of the personality. And we should also talk
about the specific techniques for doing all this, for achieving
human development.

JACK: Vera, I think we have to go beyond this dichotomy
between inner and outer to do what you're suggesting. Suppose
we think of the inner as including the outer to a degree, and vice
versa. In that case, if we can learn to change the inner, and not
just live the dreams that we allow society to impose on us, then
we have accomplished the fantastic feat of changing the outer
that is within us. And this is a powerful basis for changing the
outer that is within others. Take the legal system, for example.
Right now all of us are in varying degrees passively living the
Hobbesian dream that the law should be above man. Now
suppose we can learn somehow to continually assess law, or any
other institution, in terms of its impact on human development.
If we are able to really legitimize this to ourselves then we free
ourselves from the legal gods we have learned to subjugate
ourselves to, and we develop enormous energy to move in all
kinds of creative directions. And each such change in the world
carries forward the internal changes, because it carries us more
concretely in the direction of personal development.

IAN: It's getting pretty late, and maybe we'd better end our
session for today, but I can't resist some comments on Vera's
question about specific techniques for achieving human
development. I think that the right kinds of metaphors can be
extremely powerful tools. Now, take the metaphor of the dream.
It puts us on notice that the imagination, the mind of man, is the
very stuff of life, and it gives us the power to put the
materialistic emphasis of modern civilization in proper
perspective. The rotating pendulum metaphor suggests continual
change. A metaphor of music might be appropriate for suggesting
continual development, with the unceasing variations around
certain themes. There's another kind of metaphor we were using
which I think is extremely powerful, personality as a metaphor

for social systems. When Jack was just talking about the sense of freedom a person can feel when he alters his god-like image of the law, he was talking at the same time of a new kind of legal system where the law is in continual flux according to what makes for human development. When William was talking about incorporating Dionysian elements into his MacNamara-type personality he was implicitly suggesting a more expressive, more ecstatic type of society than the one we presently know. Vlad's metaphor of the dream within the dream within the dream not only refers to individuals who are continually developing their powers of imagination but also to a society of people who, like Fellini in his *8½,* are able to put these powers to work in the creation of a culture for man rather than against man. Ono's style suggests to me a new orientation for academia, one which carries forward the idea of expanding knowledge with a new emphasis on learning how to survive in a rapidly disintegrating world. And Vera points us toward a religion of and for man, where man becomes a Nietzschian superman, a god. As for myself, I am pointing toward a society of Renaissance Man, where each man at every moment is a scientist, an artist and a revolutionary.

VERA: What about Games, Inc.? How do you see its role in the construction of such a society?

IAN: My vision is based on the metaphor of this group as a model for the group structure of society. I think we have learned to depart from a far more authoritarian structure where my own development to a great extent impeded yours. Now we are all learning from one another to a much greater degree. We are much more individual-centered now, and I think that this is the way future societies will look.

THE MIND PARASITES

Many thoughts were crowding into Ian's head as he left the conference room, but he forced himself to take his own advice to William and orient himself to a systematic approach. At the same time he was conscious of centering on following Vera's priority on personal development. There were two metaphors he was attempting to put together mentally as a basis for constructing a role for himself. Temporally he was thinking of the music metaphor, where his life was a kind of rhythm and every moment was part of his development or lack of it. He felt inspired to continually revolt against his own weaknesses and to create ever greater strength. A spatial metaphor came from Colin Wilson's *The Mind Parasites.* The parasites were there inside his own mind, operating at the level of the unconscious. By giving him and the rest of mankind something to overcome, they were playing a vital role in the evolution of the universe. They had created the kind of unconscious which prevented man from focusing attention on his own development, and they could be defeated through a widening and deepening of consciousness.

The metaphor of the mind parasites helped Ian to keep in the forefront of his mind Vera's priority on personal development. He was learning more and more to see distractions not as harmless interruptions but as important clues to his own unconscious and as barriers which must be broken down if Renaissance Man is ever to emerge from his cultural prison. The prison was not all bad, of course. He had been born there, and the bars were not so close together that he had been unable to develop some knowledge of himself and the universe. But that knowledge, he realized now, was warped by his view from inside the cage of Aristotelian language and culture. What he must do now is continue to break barriers, not just one but an infinite series. And in doing so, he would be transforming himself into a new kind of man. For, contrary to the cage metaphor, which was limited just as all metaphors are, the bars were inside him as well as outside. If society was structured around scarcity and man's limitations, he as a member of society carried these fears within his own conscious and unconscious. And as he learned to overcome these limitations he was developing into Nietzsche's superman.

Ian felt more alive now than ever before. Freud's metaphors of the life and death instincts occurred to him, but he transformed them into a continuum. He felt he was learning to become more alive as he broke through one barrier after another. He was somehow tapping the energy within himself as he was learning to focus more on his unconscious barriers and to do such focusing rhythmically, with every moment providing the opportunity for creating a new internal and external world. He was not so much in conflict with others as with himself. But where others tend to submerge such conflicts and thus subjugate themselves to the life-draining mind parasites, Ian was succeeding in bringing them to the surface and cathartically transforming them into an ever

more unified self. There was an inner and outer world to win
here, a world not involving the petty games of hate and guilt
man had been suffering under for aeons. Here was the Hegelian
dialectic in action, the continual unification of theses and
antitheses. By contrast, the Marxian focus on external enemies
diverted attention from the conquering of the internal ones. It
was the "establishment" inside the self which must be
transformed. The key to man's internal jail also unlocks his
external jail.

Ian turned to the examination of priorities. Recognizing
himself as largely a prisoner of the mind parasites, and the same
holding true for Games, Inc. and for society as a whole, he began
to consider the steps which could result in the largest gains
toward freedom. There were many possibilities. He could work
with William on computer simulations which teach man how to
think more deeply, live more expressively and act more
effectively. The repercussions from any success here would be
vast. He would be uniting science, art, and technology, putting
the leading segment of the industrial revolution to work in the
service of human development. He would be able to offer the
computer industry the kinds of software they so desperately
needed in order to penetrate the educational world. And just as
the history of social change indicates, the means would transform
the previous ends. But instead of a narrowing means
dehumanizing idealistic ends, as in the case of the industrial
revolution's subversion of the Renaissance Man ideal, the reverse
would occur. The technology would create Renaissance Men as a
means for achieving narrow, profit-making goals.

Another possibility was to work with Vlad toward creating a
new kind of education in the dramaturgical media. Here was an
opportunity to construct in visual form non-Aristotelian worlds.
Granting that success could yield far vaster audiences at the
different educational levels than the Sesame Street series had
ever attained, he was attracted in this direction equally by the
opportunity to develop his own ability to construct
non-Aristotelian worlds.

He could also work with Ono in developing a series of
educational games for every level of education and for every
subject. The central communications device could be an
expanding set of metaphors, with each player constructing new
metaphors on the basis of his background and current interests.
Ian's conceptual model for such games was what occurred during

these last two review sessions, with each individual communicating to himself and others, with the result being a gain by all.

Ian felt he could go on and on indefinitely with further possibilities. He could work with Jack in setting up a Korzybskian workshop complete with games, video tape, and computer simulation for the legal services people. He could work with Vera in developing the kinds of psychotherapeutic techniques which could give tools for effective therapy to the humanistic religions, enabling them to compete successfully with materialism. There was also the library project on the integration of knowledge, with metaphors serving as links from any given area of knowledge to all other areas. There were the living theatre performances he planned to do for his speaking engagements. There were the new forms of architecture, based on a computer technology responsive to man's developing internal environment, which Ian planned as a follow-up to his cinematic portrayal of the non-Aristotelian environment. There were the works of fiction and nonfiction he planned to create both as a reflection of his multiple paths to development and as an impetus to further development.

Ian was tempted to figure out an elaborate order of priority for these various projects. But he realized that he should feel free to change continually his priorities rather than feel subjugated to some predetermined schedule. For the time being, at least, he would play things by ear. As for the future, there was no limit to what could be done. The country of the mind was infinite, and his explorations had just begun.

EXERCISES

1. Record on paper the ten books which you believe have influenced your own ideas more than any others. Now list a number of ways in which they are related to one another. On the basis of this list, write a piece of nonfiction or fiction in which these ideas are interwoven. Use your writing as a basis for exploring more of the links among the ideas than you originally listed. Does all of this tell you anything new about yourself? About your environment?

2. Do the same thing as exercise 1 above with respect to ten personal experiences you have had. What relationships do you see between your personal experiences and the books which have influenced you?

3. How would you describe the kind of group which Games, Inc., represented? What would various kinds of groups in society be like if they were constructed on this basis, for example, the family, the community, society as a whole? Form a group and attempt to structure it along these lines. What problems are you having? Why? Is there anything you can do to solve them? How are your efforts at solutions related to Zenski's shift toward a more critical view of Games, Inc.?

4. Attempt to impersonate Basil Kornish, Ben Zorn, and Ian Zenski, with others acting as an audience. Discuss your performance with your audience. Now play them again, attempting to take into account what you have learned from the discussion. Follow this with discussion once again. How has your performance changed? In what ways are you more satisfied with it, and in what ways less?

5. Play a game with one or more others and compare its structure to what you described in exercise 4 above, that is, the structure of a group modeled after Games, Inc. Now construct a simple game which is much closer to this latter structure. Play it. Do you feel any differently now as compared to the time just before you played it? If so, why? If not, why not?

7

From Pre-Industrial to
Post-Industrial Society

If the foregoing chapters are spokes of a wheel, the time has come to build a rim around them in order to extend them still further. This rim will be constructed out of two kinds of wood: a systematic view of the dimensional language of games, and a detailed examination of a metaphor having to do with water flowing into a beaker.

Around this rim we shall proceed to place five spokes. The language of games and the metaphor of the beaker will be used as a basis for discussing five types of societies: pre-industrial, early industrial, late industrial, early post-industrial, and late post-industrial.

In this fourth part of *Worlds of the Future* our focus is on the group. Among the many kinds of human groups which have been studied by sociologists and other students of human behavior are families, organizations, communities, and societies. It is the latter which we have chosen to discuss. Our approach is based on the importance of historical content and, more specifically, on the significance of the industrial revolution.

We hope that this chapter will exemplify the game of KNOWLEDGE more than that of TRUTH. We hope to open doors to a fruitful way of viewing groups, and personalities as well. We might begin to open a door by stating our belief that man is only at the beginnings of a profound knowledge of human groups. We do not mean by this to conform to scholarly modesty. Rather, this statement stems from a deep conviction of the limitations of existing knowledge along with a vision of directions for extending it.

LANGUAGE

Language forges the tools which enable man to reach outward and inward in space and time, incorporating a wealth of human experience within the knife-edge of the momentary situation. This suggests a direction for the future evolution of language: to give man increasing ability to expand the momentary situation in these ways.

The game language has been developed with such ideas in mind. We do not view it as an end in itself. It is simply a device which might help man to incorporate a great deal of human experience into whatever he thinks or feels or does. We view language along two axes, spatial and temporal. By spatial, we mean its ability to extend over a variety of instances of human behavior. By temporal, we refer to its ability to extend far into the past and future.

The game language has been constructed to deal with head, heart, and hand (or thinking, feeling, and doing). In this way, it is geared to apply to each of the fundamental elements of human behavior. In our view there is no instance of human behavior which does not involve all three of these elements. Every idea is motivated, consciously or unconsciously, and it is also a kind of action, although one which can be observed only indirectly. Also, every feeling or goal has some basis in ideas or beliefs, and is also a kind of action. We do not tend to think of changes in ideas or goals as instances of action, yet that may be because of their intangible nature and our materialistic bias. Finally, physical movements of the individual (or group) have both an ideational and a motivational basis.

The second axis of game language is the temporal one. The game concepts come in pairs, with each pair specifying a continuum or dimension which we see as stretching from past to future. In our view, human evolution is proceeding from an A to a null-A world, and its movement may be traced along the various game continua. We see this as part of a much more all-encompassing process involving the evolution of the universe, and that process as well may be traced—we believe—along these continua. Thus, the game dimensions have been selected with a purpose in mind: to correspond to the directions which human behavior has in fact taken. They represent attempts to extrapolate, both to the past and the future, our knowledge of the relationship of five points to one another. These points represent pre-industrial society, early industrial, late industrial, early post-industrial, and late post-industrial society.

The metaphor of the game was chosen for three basic reasons, one having to do with spatial and another with temporal extension. Spatially, a game is a rather holistic piece of human behavior, with all three of the elements of human behavior being prominent. For example, the rules of the game tend to be fairly explicit, putting us on notice that our action takes place within a framework of ideas. Also, a game is something we are all familiar with, and thus it is a tool we can apply to abstract phenomena we are attempting to understand. Temporally, a game is a phenomenon played over time. It is not a static metaphor. Like music, it can be repeated with infinite variations. And, also like music, it suggests motion, change. A third reason is that by using the game metaphor we learn to carry forward the socialization process. We tend to be aware that we are playing a game, that is, we can see our gaming selves from a perspective located outside of the game context. Early socialization involves learning to see oneself as a distinct entity by viewing oneself through the eyes of others. To the degree that man learns to continue this process, we believe that he will learn to avoid fixation of his behavior and continue to enlarge whatever he brings to any given situation.

In Figure 7-1 we present the game concepts we have been using in the preceding chapters. We shall discuss them by row, beginning with the top row and working down. In this way we do not miss any of the three elements of behavior. The TRUTH–KNOWLEDGE row is the most general, and might be used as a global classification of the various head, heart, and hand games. The DICHOTOMY–DIMENSION row deals with dimensions that stretch from a black-and-white viewpoint to those which incorporate an infinite number of shades of gray. The A–NULL-A row is similar, except that it

Head	Heart	Hand
TRUTH— 　KNOWLEDGE	SCARCITY— 　INFINITY	VICIOUS CIRCLE— 　DEVELOPMENT
DICHOTOMY— 　DIMENSION	COWBOYS AND INDIANS— 　SITUATION ETHICS	SEE-SAW— 　STAIRWAY 　(JEWISH MOTHER)
A— 　NULL-A	BUREAUCRACY— 　RENAISSANCE MAN	SHELL GAME— 　CONTINUING 　REVOLUTION
GOLDFISH BOWL— 　CONSCIOUSNESS	GOODNIK— 　MAN FOR HIMSELF	CONFORMITY— 　AUTONOMY

FIGURE 7-1.   GAME LANGUAGE

contrasts a dimensional approach with a multiple-category, and not a two-category, approach. The GOLDFISH BOWL–CONSCIOUS-NESS row most directly centers on man's own development, and is quite general. In the following paragraphs we shall describe each of the game dimensions.

TRUTH–KNOWLEDGE

Almost any declarative statement we make—"People are fundamentally good," "Joe is a hard worker," "The car stopped," "Pine trees don't shed their needles"—tells only a portion of the story of what is happening. Korzybski has recommended that we make use of subscripts to locate phenomena in space and superscripts to locate them in time.[1] Thus, cow_1 is not cow_2, and cow_1^{1972} is not cow_1^{1973}. In this way we learn to become more conscious of having abstracted only a small portion of our experience or human experience generally. We learn to move away from TRUTH games and learn to play harder and harder games of KNOWLEDGE. The sentence just written also is on the TRUTH–KNOWLEDGE continuum, but by recognizing this fact in the present sentence, we open the door to further knowledge and thus move toward the KNOWLEDGE end of the continuum, which represents an openness to learning as distinct from a great deal of knowledge. And the same could be said for the sentence just completed, and for this one, and for the next.

SCARCITY–INFINITY[2]

The concept of infinity refers to a process that continues indefinitely, and not to an extremely large number, for the latter would be fixed, and one could always supersede it. As for scarcity, that concept is rooted in human aspirations. If there were no humans around who aspired to possessing diamonds, that mineral would not be scarce. The key problem in understanding this dimension is that, as a result in part of the materialistic emphasis of industrial society, it is difficult for us to think of scarcity in relation to nonmaterial phenomena. Pre-industrial man labored under conditions of great material scarcity, but how are we to understand the mental scarcities learned by the child or adult who comes to believe that his intelligence is fixed? A kind of scarcity which is quite widespread in industrial society, where most social systems are organized bureaucratically, is the scarcity of status. We all learn to locate ourselves in thousands of hierarchies, and we come to believe in the idea that only some can ascend. Another kind of scarcity at least as widespread is that based on specialization. Supposedly, it is not possible for the human being to learn more than one thing well. As we come to believe that vertical and lateral mobility are possible for more and more individuals, we move toward the INFINITY end of the continuum. It is the movement that counts, and not the arrival at some kind of utopia.

VICIOUS CIRCLE–DEVELOPMENT

As the individual (or social system) learns to play TRUTH and SCARCITY games, he moves into VICIOUS CIRCLE, which is the action component of those head and heart games. It is easy enough to recognize certain kinds of vicious circles. Take a bank run, for example. As people hear rumors about a bank's insolvency, they withdraw money. As they withdraw money, the word spreads still further. Or take the culture of poverty. A father and mother who are at the bottom of society's various status ladders can easily undermine the self-confidence of their children. That in turn can lead to poor achievement in school, in social life, and at work. And that, in turn, can undermine self-confidence still further. Or take the escalation of aggressive acts between two nations. Aggressive acts can undermine trust, and this undermining of trust can be the basis for escalating aggression.

KNOWLEDGE and INFINITY games, conversely, lead to DEVELOPMENT. Rumors about a bank's insolvency can be stopped cold when the individual realizes the partial nature of all information and then checks out the rumor. A father and mother—regardless of their status in society—can learn to give their children the kind of confidence in themselves which can lead to ever increasing achievement in different aspects of life. Acts of friendship between nations can create trust, and that in turn can escalate friendship. The father and mother, as well as the nation, can learn to act in these ways by playing a KNOWLEDGE game that opens them up to learning, and by playing an INFINITY game which shows them how much they have to gain through close relationships with others.

DICHOTOMY–DIMENSION

Almost all of language teaches us to play DICHOTOMY. Words specify two categories: one for all those phenomena to which the word refers, and the other category for all other phenomena. This process is an instance of growth. The young child who learns the concept "plane" also learns to pull together different kinds of experiences he has had. And as he grows up he tends to learn some of the ways in which planes are related to other phenomena. But by doing this, he generally learns to miss all kinds of relationships which would help him to develop his knowledge, all based on the idea of seeing "planeness" on a continuum or as a matter of degree. All moving objects have to contend with the same kinds of atmospheric forces that planes do, and some do better than others. For example, we might wonder about the ways in which a Volkswagen is an airfoil, or the similarities and differences between hydrafoil boats and planes. All this may sound trivial, but the picture changes quickly when we talk about concepts like democracy, communism, violence, God, Negro, Puerto Rican, Jew, United States, China, intelligent, beautiful, and so on. If people recognized the ways in which they, and everyone else, are (to a degree) democratic, communistic, violent, God-like, black, Chinese, and so forth, then perhaps they could learn to communicate with other human beings who are located in categories which are no longer as alien as they once were.

COWBOYS AND INDIANS–SITUATION ETHICS

In the above paragraph, when we shifted from the concept of plane to concepts like democracy and communism, we also shifted to concepts which people tend to feel strongly about. Dichotomies vary in the strength of feeling about them. COWBOYS AND INDIANS deals with a dichotomy which we have transformed into a hierarchy, with strong emotional feeling attached to the categories. Thus, we might refer to the good and the bad, the middle class and the working class, the educated and the uneducated, the selfish and the unselfish, the rich and the poor, the powerful and the powerless.

How are we to move from COWBOYS AND INDIANS to SITUATION ETHICS, where we attempt to base our feelings on as much information as we can get about the situational context, and where we treat every situation as different from every other, refusing to fall back on stereotypical thinking and feeling? For one thing, by learning to play KNOWLEDGE more than TRUTH. If we were less certain that our beliefs about a certain social category represented truth, then it would be more difficult to emote on the basis of our prejudices. But far more than this may be needed. COWBOYS AND INDIANS may be based on a SCARCITY game, that is, an inherent belief that one man's meat must be another's poison. Inflating one's own ego, then, is accomplished by deflating someone else's ego. But we need not search very long for SCARCITY games in industrial society, for they are built into hierarchy and specialization.

SEE-SAW–STAIRWAY (JEWISH MOTHER)

As we move from beliefs and feelings into action or interaction, we also move to the SEE-SAW–STAIRWAY continuum. SEE-SAW is a game of aggression involving two participants; it may vary from a game that is so subtle that no one is aware it is being played to a game involving murder. A player may play it against himself or against his opponent. One may push oneself down, frequently based on feelings of guilt, or push one's opponent down and thereby raise oneself up. The basis for the game is SCARCITY, as represented by the fixed fulcrum: in order for one player to rise, it is essential that the other be pushed down. This analysis is similar to the Freudian analysis of the relationship between frustration and aggression. Frustration is a kind of SCARCITY, represented by the fixed fulcrum, and aggression is represented by SEE-SAW.

JEWISH MOTHER, which is played by most of us much of the time, is a special type of SEE-SAW game. It is based on SCARCITY, GOODNIK, and CONFORMITY (these latter two games are discussed below). It represents an illustration of a complex game built up from the more elementary games. The player of JEWISH MOTHER plays SEE-SAW against his opponent, but neither he nor his opponent is aware of this. That is because he also plays a convincing game of GOODNIK, legitimizing his own behavior so well that his opponent comes to believe that it is he who is at fault and commences to play SEE-SAW against himself. He is encouraged to do this because he is a habitual player of CONFORMITY, and conforms to the beliefs of the player of JEWISH MOTHER. Through ties of guilt, he sees himself playing SEE-SAW against his opponent, when actually it is his opponent—the player of JEWISH MOTHER—who is playing an aggressive SEE-SAW game.

In the game of STAIRWAY the two players communicate in such a way that one's gain is the other's gain as well. The fulcrum is not fixed, and thus the game is based on INFINITY. The metaphor of the expanding pie is also appropriate, where an increase in the radius of the pie for one player also helps to increase his fellow player's share.

A–NULL-A

Instead of two categories, as in DICHOTOMY, there are more than two in the game of A. This game corresponds to a more complex view of phenomena than DICHOTOMY. Ordinary language, in addition to its emphasis on DICHOTOMY, also represents a game of A, with its multiple categories or concepts for describing any given phenomenon. This is also the case for most of social science. NULL-A is just like DIMENSION, except that the names are differentiated so that NULL-A can be paired with A.

BUREAUCRACY–RENAISSANCE MAN

The two fundamental aspects of BUREAUCRACY are hierarchy and division of labor. Both are based on SCARCITY. Hierarchy represents an extension of COWBOYS AND INDIANS to a situation where there are more than two categories. The aspect relating to division of labor is an A game with an emphasis on invidious evaluations. Each specialist tends to see his own work as important relative to that of others, and in that way legitimizes his lack of effort to learn something about what others are doing. In RENAISSANCE MAN, by contrast, there is an assumption that all knowledge is important, and that the individual (or group) will build ever more bridges to such knowledge.

SHELL GAME–CONTINUING REVOLUTION

Given the complexity introduced by such games as A and BUREAUCRACY, it is very easy to slip into conflicts of all kinds. One very common conflict is SHELL GAME, where a means to a given end subtly changes its status and becomes an end that conflicts with the former end. The name of the game is based on the carnival game with three shells and a pea which mysteriously changes positions from being located under one shell to a new location. The classic illustration of this game is the transformation of hard work and business success from its status as a means to the end of religious salvation to a status as an end in itself, one which tends to conflict with spiritual values. In CONTINUING REVOLUTION, by contrast, there is a continuing examination of the relationships among means and ends so that this kind of conflict appears less and less often or is caught more and more quickly. This requires nothing less than a continuing process of socialization, where the individual (or group) continues to step outside his former self and views that self from a wider perspective. It is such an ever-widening perspective which enables him to avoid getting so deeply into any means he is employing that he fails to see it in relation to everything else he is doing. CONTINUING REVOLUTION is based on such a process, and in addition it implies action. The individual (or group) alters his behavior so that he is not fighting himself.

GOLDFISH BOWL–CONSCIOUSNESS

The game of GOLDFISH BOWL is closely related to SHELL GAME. Both involve a failure to achieve role distance, to step outside a given role and gain perspective on it in that way. However, GOLDFISH BOWL emphasizes the cognitive aspect of this process, whereas SHELL GAME carries beyond this cognitive approach to an emphasis on action. The original name for GOLDFISH BOWL was EMPEROR'S NEW CLOTHES, based on a fable in which the fresh perspective of a little boy revealed the Emperor to be stark naked. The parallel between GOLDFISH BOWL and SHELL GAME also applies to CONSCIOUSNESS and CONTINUING REVOLUTION, with the latter connoting a greater emphasis on action.

GOODNIK–MAN FOR HIMSELF

GOODNIK represents a very common resultant of GOLDFISH BOWL, where the individual (or group) legitimates his own behavior on the basis of norms within his environment. He sees himself as an appendage of that environment more than as an autonomous force. GOODNIK is a game of altruism in which the player focuses on broadcasting his own worthiness, and where this communication generally is far more important than anything that might in fact be done to help others. Frequently the game is based on guilt feelings, with the individual seeing himself as less worthy than others. Such feelings might have a religious base, such as a belief in original sin, or they might be based on Freudian ideas of the antisocial nature of the *id,* or they might have a basis in the scientific-industrial revolution, with its tendency to deemphasize the nonmaterial and emphasize the material. *Man for Himself* is the title of one of Erich Fromm's books, in which he emphasizes that unless man gives first priority to his own development he can have little to offer others. For Fromm, the path to altruism is through self-development.

CONFORMITY–AUTONOMY

These games are very close to GOODNIK and MAN FOR HIMSELF. While they both have the same cognitive base, GOODNIK and MAN FOR HIMSELF emphasize the legitimation of these ideas among the individual's (or group's) goals, whereas CONFORMITY and AUTONOMY emphasize action. The player of CONFORMITY can be conforming to tradition, to his own rigid ideas, to the ideas of others or, most likely, to some combination of these. Thus, Riesman's tradition-directed, inner-directed, and other-directed individual and society play this game.[3] In AUTONOMY, by contrast, the individual's own evaluations are important, and are sufficiently flexible to be based on SITUATION ETHICS. The player of AUTONOMY may have learned to play the game originally by conforming to certain norms. However, those were the kind of norms which freed him from dependency on group norms and encouraged him to develop his own criteria for evaluating his behavior.

It is altogether too easy to play SHELL GAME with the game concepts, using them as ends in themselves. One solution for this is not a solution in the traditional sense but rather a continuing awareness of the problem. This is CONTINUING REVOLUTION, where the individual continually examines the game language in relation to whatever ends he wishes to achieve, and takes action on the basis of this analysis.

THE BEAKER METAPHOR[4]

The basic function of the beaker metaphor is to give perspective on the language of game dimensions by concretely illustrating how such a language can help us to increase our knowledge and, more generally, help us to develop as human beings. In this chapter we shall develop the beaker metaphor as a dynamic model of human fulfillment in the broadest sense. Following this discussion, we shall apply this metaphor together with the game language to a description of five phases of social evolution.

Figure 7-2 presents two contrasting situations, corresponding to the A and null-A games (using A and null-A in a generic sense). The situations are similar in that water is flowing from a tap into a beaker in both, and there is a flow of information about the level of water in the beaker back to the individual controlling the tap. Also, there is in each beaker a drain at the bottom through which water flows out. We have chosen to depict this drain without a tap for adjusting the outflow to signify an uncontrolled but continuous draining process.[5] The size of the drain, which influences the rate of outflow, could vary greatly for different applications of the beaker metaphor. That is, in some applications we might like to think of a large percentage of the water in the beaker flowing out at any given time, and in others we might see only a very small fraction flowing out. The idea of a natural decay process seems sufficiently general to warrant its inclusion as part of the basic beaker structure common to both A and null-A games.

Though both situations in figure 7-2 have the basic beaker structure in common, they differ with respect to the height of water in the beaker, the rate of flow of the water from the tap, and the height of the beaker, with the null-A beaker continuing to rise.

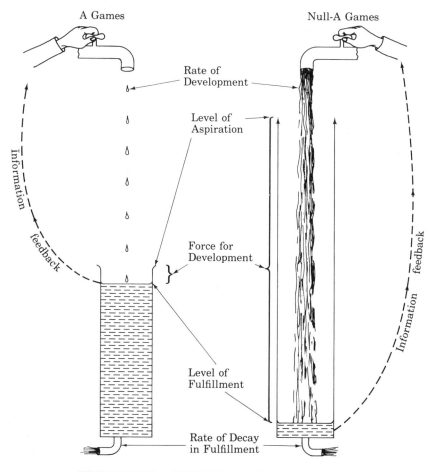

FIGURE 7-2.   THE BEAKER METAPHOR

We believe that the accumulation process provides a model which is most appropriate for describing the continuing changes that characterize human behavior. The process of water flowing into (and/or out of) a beaker metaphorically expresses the process identified in mathematics as integration. In keeping with our desire to present this concept on an intuitively understandable level, we shall refer to this process as the accumulation process: as water falls from the tap it "accumulates" in the beaker. Likewise, water is constantly "unaccumulating" or draining, and we shall use the term "accumulation process" to mean the net process of water flowing into and out of the beaker simultaneously.

We believe that this process is the most common dynamic process in nature, a belief widely held by physical scientists. We believe that its extension into the sphere of human behavior may produce technologies for solving human problems comparable in effectiveness to those technologies which presently enable us to shape the physical environment.

In the accumulation process the level of water in the beaker rises only by degrees. Also, we can distinguish between the rate of flow on the one hand, and the level which has accumulated on the other. Even if the tap were suddenly opened very wide and the rate of inflow of water became very rapid in a moment, the level of water in the beaker would not change so dramatically. It takes *time* for that rate to result in an accumulation of water.

As applied to human behavior we see the rates of flow as actions or activities, whether physical or mental, and the accumulated levels of water as states of being relative to these actions. For example, we have defined the accumulation process in figure 7-2 governing the relationship between the rate of development, the rate of fulfillment decay, and the level of fulfillment. In doing so, we attain a certain dynamic richness in conceiving of human development as both an action and a state: there is the act of developing, and the resultant state of fulfillment, with the two inextricably linked in time. A significant point appears immediately—no action is lost! To the degree that any action can be modelled as a rate of flow it must result in an accumulation in an associated level. Conversely, to the degree that all levels change in a continuous fashion there exist actions or rates which account for that change. Also, to the degree that a natural decay process is continually lowering the level, actions must be repeated to prevent the level from falling.

Relative to the game language, we can view an individual's behavior as an activity of playing a game and a resultant accumulation reflecting the individual's past actions of playing the game. The draining rate represents a gradual depreciation of the influence of past actions by contrast with current actions. How hard a person plays determines the rate of inflow, which will in turn determine how rapidly his level will rise. If one thinks of the game dimension, how hard an individual is playing determines how rapidly he is moving in a particular direction along that dimension, and the level of water in the beaker represents his position at a particular point in time on that dimension.

Accumulation is, however, only half the story expressed in the beaker metaphor. The dotted lines originating at the level of water and pointing to the tap indicate "information feedback": information about the height of water which is "fed back" to determine the rate of flow into the beaker. That is, not only does the rate of flow determine the level of water via the process of accumulation, but the level of water in the beaker affects the rate of flow. In A games, as the level rises so that it is near the top of the beaker, the individual operating the tap becomes aware of this fact (information feedback) and begins to shut off the flow. Factors other than this information also affect the rate of flow. For example, the individual may be conforming in part to a societal norm (shared expectation) that it is not a good idea to spill water.

If we look to the null-A games on the right-hand side of figure 7-2, we may note a different interrelationship between rate of inflow and level of water. On the one hand, the rate of inflow still produces an accumulation of water in the beaker. But the information about the increasing level in the beaker *does not* result in a shutting off of the rate of flow. This is because the beaker continues to grow taller as the level rises, and there is thus no danger that the water will spill. Indeed, the tap may be opened wider and wider if the height of the beaker increases rapidly enough.

This difference between the two beaker structures in figure 7-2 parallels the basic difference between the A and null-A games. The fixed height of the beaker on the left corresponds to SCARCITY, metaphorically described earlier by the fixed fulcrum in SEE-SAW. The rising beaker on the right corresponds to INFINITY or to the unending STAIRWAY. In the A beaker, the tiny gap between the level of water and the height of that beaker leaves little room for additional development. This corresponds to TRUTH, where the answers are already in and there is no room for additional knowledge. In the null-A situation, by contrast, not only is the gap between aspiration (the height of the beaker) and fulfillment (the level of the water) very great, but it may even be increasing. This corresponds to a KNOWLEDGE game, where the door to further learning opens wider and wider. As a result, the null-A situation results in increasing—and even accelerating—DEVELOPMENT, as may be measured by a rapid accumulation of water or rise in the level of fulfillment. In the A situation, by contrast, the individual learns to shut off the flow of water, corresponding to a VICIOUS CIRCLE game: the individual learns more and more to curtail his rate of DEVELOPMENT each time he curtails it (shuts off the flow) in conformity to norms about his own limitations.

The widespread application of this accumulation-feedback process might be seen by examining the behavior of all living things. If we assume that (1) the behavior of all living things is oriented to the achievement of their goals, whether conscious or unconscious (goal is defined broadly enough to encompass, say, the orientation of a plant as it shifts the direction of its roots in "search" of water), and (2) that movement toward goals occurs over time rather than instantaneously, then we can see all behavior illustrates the integration or accumulation process. We are required to focus on the goals involved in the behavior and the interrelating structure between the degree to which goals are accomplished and the actions leading to that accomplishment.

The accumulation process is fundamental to nonliving things as well. One indication of this is the highly effective utilization by engineers of differential equations, which is based on both integral calculus (dealing with accumulation or integration) and differential calculus (dealing with rates of flow). One illustration in the Kornish story (chapter 2) is the acceleration of the condensation of the solar system on the basis of laws of gravitation. A more far-reaching example is the second law of thermodynamics, which holds that, in the long run, the universe as a whole is moving "entropically," that is, from higher to lower states of organized energy, as illustrated by the slow death of the sun or the disintegration of all structures. This represents "accumulation" in a negative direction, that is, leading to higher and higher levels of disorganization or entropy.

If we break down the barrier separating our view of living and nonliving things, we can escape the pessimism of the second law of thermodynamics. According to physicists, living things represent pockets of "negentropy," that is, they do not move toward lower energy states as long as they are alive. Supposedly, this does not contradict the second law, since living things represent only an infinitesimal portion of the physical universe. Our own perspective differs radically from this. It is oriented to a temporal sequence which produced larger and larger protein molecules, living things, and—eventually—man. Granting that man is only an insignificant portion of the universe from a physical standpoint, he seems to be the leading edge of the universe in his ability to control the many integration processes in his environment and in himself. This evolution in a negentropic direction may yet succeed in reversing the overall entropic trend as man learns to create higher and higher energy levels within his environment. At any rate, the issue is by no means closed.

Let us now look at the beaker metaphor more analytically. We might focus on two differences between the A and the null-A games: the "force for development," defined as the gap between level of aspiration and level of fulfillment; and the change in level of fulfillment, which cannot be depicted readily in our static diagram.

In the case of the A games the level of aspiration tends to be fixed (due, perhaps, to a conviction that one is limited by SCARCITY), and thus the force for development decreases as the level of fulfillment increases. This might be stated more poetically—as it has already been stated so many times and in so many ways—that man can be no more than his dreams. Once man defines himself as limited, his level of fulfillment becomes limited. To see how such a self-definition might come about, consider the following illustration of the vicious circle nature of A-games. If the individual perceives his fulfillment increasing very slowly, or not at all, he may well feel that his limited level of aspiration is justified. This, in turn, will *in fact* preclude an increasing force to develop, and the individual's level of fulfillment will not increase substantially.

The reverse occurs in the null-A case. The level of aspiration keeps rising. If we assume the level of aspiration rises more rapidly than the level of fulfillment, then the force for development continues to increase. This force in turn pushes for an increasing rate of development, which leads to a continuously increasing level of fulfillment.

Accumulation proceeds more rapidly in the null-A beaker because the beaker allows for a much greater Force for Development. In the left-hand, or A, beaker the Force for Development is smaller and has little potential to expand due to the relatively fixed level of aspiration. In the A beaker development and aspirations are being dampened by factors other than those indicated in figure 7-2. Let us assume that these other factors involve two other kinds of accumulation: movement toward more thorough CONFORMITY to group norms, and movement toward ever greater conviction that one is limited by SCARCITY. Let us further assume that there is an accumulation process parallel to that of developing which describes the process of aspiring. Such an accumulation process would involve a rate of aspiring (based on "acts of aspiring"), an associated level of aspiration, and a natural decay in aspirations. Then, it would be the rate of aspiring which would be affected by these games of CONFORMITY and SCARCITY. Without going further with this point, one can see that we now have a *system* of interconnected beakers. In such a system, the null-A games are distinguished from the A games by the degree to which they promote the mutual reinforcement of different accumulation processes—such as those governing developing and aspiring—and avoid the mutual dampening we saw in the A beaker of figure 7-2.

One further note about the importance of systems. If one traces the logic of the simple application of the beaker metaphor in this section, one can see that it became necessary to move to a system of interconnected beakers because we were unable to account for the distinctions in A versus null-A development by just looking at the developing process. Such is the case with most of human behavior —the complex interdependence of different aspects of human actions and states demands a systems perspective in order to address the issues we are usually interested in. However, the emergence of this perspective demands a greater facility for seeing human behavior in terms of accumulation processes than we have as yet developed. We hope to continue developing this facility throughout the remainder of this book.[6] As one illustration, we shall use the beaker metaphor to better understand the transition of man from pre-industrial to post-industrial society.

FROM PRE-INDUSTRIAL TO POST-INDUSTRIAL SOCIETY

The language of games and the beaker metaphor are valuable only insofar as they help us to gain understanding of human behavior. In this final section we shall describe five different kinds of society which have appeared in a sequence. The game language and the beaker metaphor are the tools we shall use to probe into the dynamics of these societies.

Pre-Industrial Society

We do not claim that all pre-industrial societies are very similar, but we do claim that there are certain similarities which are so fundamental that an analysis of them can yield important insights into all such societies, as well as into industrial and post-industrial societies. These similarities may be examined within the context of the A beaker: (1) a very, very slow rise in or, equivalently, a low rate of development level of fulfillment (the water level and dripping faucet); (2) a beaker with a capacity (level of aspiration) that increases very slowly; and (3) a very long time period involved in obtaining information feedback.

The extremely slow rise in level of fulfillment is based on a very low force for development or gap between aspiration and fulfillment, as pictured by the small space remaining in the beaker. But why the small space? Why the high level of fulfillment relative to level of aspiration? Before the rise of the idea of continuing scientific progress man tended to view his level of understanding as very high relative to what might be learned. He played a hard game of TRUTH. The ideas handed down were the correct ones, and there was nothing more to be learned. There was no vision of the evolution or development of knowledge. He did not play KNOWLEDGE, a game which extends from past to future and may be represented by a rising beaker and an increase in what is unknown (the empty space in the null-A beaker). The result was a hard game of SCARCITY and of VICIOUS CIRCLE: man stopped his beaker from rising more than minutely, and man continued to reinforce a very slow rate of development (the dripping faucet).

But why did man generally come to see his level of fulfillment as so high relative to his capacities? We submit that, by the very nature of human nature, he *had* to see them as close together to the degree that he had neither (1) a vision of how his beaker might continue to rise, such as the idea of scientific progress, and (2) a technology for converting that vision into something real by his own definition of reality. It is no historical secret that the idea of scientific progress, accompanied by the technology of science, exerted a tremendous force for altering pre-industrial society. And other institutions joined forces with science. For example, we have Max Weber's thesis that the Protestant ethic tended to legitimate capitalism (or, we might say, industrialization).[7] In our beaker metaphor, we might think of the beaker as representing two things simultaneously: economic development and religious development. In this way, the individual's intensity of commitment to hard work increases, leading to a higher level of aspiration and a greater force for development, with the result being an increase in the rate of flow of development.

Thus far we have focused on the very slow change in level of fulfillment and the basis for this. In the context of that discussion, we also considered peripherally the process leading to a change in level of aspiration. Man did not develop a vision of ever greater capacity, ever more progress. But why? We submit that he failed to recognize the progress he had already made as being on a continuum of increasing knowledge. In other words, he failed to see knowledge as something that integrates or accumulates. And part of this failure was based on a very long time period in obtaining feedback on the degree of knowledge he had already accumulated. Whatever the scientific method gave man, it also enabled him to shorten the time period for assessing what he had achieved, and in that assessment lay the basis for an increase in level of aspiration. In traditional society, man's tortuously slow assessments of his relatively static fulfillment produce, in turn, a relatively static level of aspiration.

Early Industrial Society

In our discussion of pre-industrial society we have laid the basis for an understanding of early industrial society. In Riesman's terms, this is the society characterized by inner-direction, where man began to seize control over his physical environment—with the aid of science and the Protestant ethic—and learned to subordinate everything else in life to that task. The narrowing that resulted showed up in the rigidity of the kind of personality that developed in such a society. Man came to be more task oriented, moving in accordance with some fixed plan for materialistic achievement. If man could order his external life, he could at least bring the semblance of this kind of order to his internal life, with the result being compulsiveness of various types, especially compulsive rigidity about plans.

In terms of the beaker metaphor, we might see these trends as we move from pre-industrial to post-industrial society: (1) an increasing rate of fulfillment (the tap opens wider and wider); (2) an accelerating level of aspiration (as represented by the height of the beaker); and (3) a shorter time period for obtaining feedback of information about the level of fulfillment.

Early industrial man is not yet alienated, as is late industrial man. Like many of the immigrants to the United States, he moved from a more traditional situation where he had little hope of achieving what those who were above him in station were used to to a situation where he could dare to hope for such achievements. If he was accumulating water in a beaker which represented a rather narrow, materialistic kind of development, he was indeed developing himself in contrast to remaining in a relatively static situation. The possibilities for other kinds of development had not yet opened up to him. He was too busy, with his long hours of toil, conquering the scarcities associated with a physical environment which had reigned relatively unchecked in the universe for billions of years. And it was quite an achievement for man to free himself from slavery to that environment.

The increasing rate of fulfillment in early industrial society is based on a greater force for development in that type of society than in pre-industrial society, and that force in turn is based on a greater gap between aspiration and fulfillment. The idea of progress had taken hold in science and physical technology, and this raised aspiration via its game of KNOWLEDGE. That game also resulted in an assessment of existing knowledge as less than what it had been thought to be. The impact of these kinds of ideas led to a movement toward the INFINITY end of the SCARCITY–INFINITY dimension and, in turn, the game of DEVELOPMENT, producing knowledge and wealth in quantities the world had never known before. And these changes in level of fulfillment provided the kind of information feedback which encouraged rising levels of aspiration and a still greater force for development. This information feedback also led to a shortening of the time for obtaining the feedback of information, for that trend was intrinsic to a scientific process which was coming into ascendancy.

Late Industrial Society

Late industrial society is that of the so-called advanced industrial societies in the 1960s and early 1970s, disregarding a large number of trends toward a post-industrial society. Perhaps its most characteristic features are a sense of alienation, feelings of hollowness or emptiness, large bureaucratic organizations, an escalation of various kinds of conflicts in society, an emphasis on conformity or other-direction, and materialism as illustrated by an emphasis on consumption or standard of living.

Tracing the development of late industrial society from its origins in early industrial society, we may note a vast SHELL GAME in the direction of materialism, all based on the very effectiveness of the DEVELOPMENT games associated with industrialization. If hard work had displaced spiritual salvation as a basic end in the early industrial society, then consumption or material wealth displaced hard work in the late industrial period. There are other ways to look at the trend as well. If man had learned to conquer, to a large extent, his physical environment and if this did not give his life sufficient meaning, then why not turn to others to find meaning through them? Riesman puts it in yet another way when he notes that the key problem of late industrial society is selling or distributing what is produced, given that the basic production problems have already been solved. Thus, other-direction comes to be quite important as a means for selling one's products or oneself.

It seems that one particular set of accumulation processes—those associated with a scientific-industrial revolution emphasizing control over the material environment—continued to gather momentum at the expense of many other accumulation processes, especially those having to do with nonmaterial values. As a result, the latter continued to suffer more and more, leading to such feelings as alienation and emptiness. Man's dominion over the physical environment did not continue to accelerate because of these unresolved conflicts between narrow materialistic and broad human values. The consequences have been a fundamental questioning of the basic values of industrial society, for even in the sphere of the physical and biological environment, the amount of damage man does while he continues to produce becomes increasingly evident.

With reference to the beaker metaphor, as man begins to question the basis for his society he no longer continues to open the tap more and more. His force for development suffers as he realizes that material development is not necessarily human progress. His vision of the future cannot yet guide him to raise his level of aspiration, since his reaction has been mainly against something more than for something. The time period for obtaining feedback of information continues to get smaller, but that cannot help to give him a direction. Although he begins to see the problems inherent in bureaucracy, he is not aware that any viable alternative is possible.

Early Post-Industrial Society

Early post-industrial society is centered around a growing resistance to the materialistic momentum of the industrial revolution through an emphasis on other ways for humans to develop as well as an increasingly thorough disenchantment with the industrial worldview. Searching goes on in all directions, whether it be periods for meditation within the business world, encounter groups for the uptight generation, Eastern religion, natural foods, astrology, the formation of communes with utopian goals, free universities, radical caucuses within the professions, female liberation, gay liberation, community control of schools, a higher standard of living for the poor, equal rights for blacks, an end to the grading system within the universities, a series of careers rather than one, mysticism, hitchhiking, a searching for self, drugs, dropping out, a rebellion against the computer, new forms of music, new styles of dress, and so forth. Throughout it all is a conviction that the bureaucratic society is terribly inhuman. Without a vision of how to change that society, one can at least learn how to live a human life within an inhuman society.

During this period man turns inward, with a tendency to reject much within the external society. That rejection generally includes the intellect, at least to a degree. If man's mind has produced an insane world, then there must be something wrong with man's mind.

If all of academia stands helplessly by while the world's problems grow increasingly vast, then academia is largely irrelevant to societal needs. If man's intellect developed during the industrial revolution largely at the expense of man's emotional life, then that intellect is not to be trusted. Such a rejection represents a replaying of the ancient mind-body dichotomy in Western civilization.

In terms of the beaker metaphor, man is groping to accumulate along many different kinds of dimensions, with all of them being relatively consistent because of their generally humanistic focus. Yet a very deep split remains, even within those who locate themselves in the heart of the counterculture, between the industrial and post-industrial world-views. For example, there is the split between the intellect and emotional spontaneity, where movement along one continuum tends to dampen movement along the other. There still is a gathering momentum for increasing the rate of human development, since the assessment of level of fulfillment tends to be somewhat lower and the level of aspiration—for being freer and broader than society tries to allow—somewhat higher. This is not a higher level of aspiration in the conventional narrow sense of climbing some particular ladder of success, for that kind of aspiration comes to be delegitimated. Rather, it is for becoming more human in spite of the environment. The time period for obtaining feedback of information becomes even smaller than previously in a society where much of the emphasis centers on the present.

Late Post-Industrial Society

Although in one sense the difference between early and late post-industrial society is simply a matter of degree, the difference is quite profound. In that earlier period the stage was set for a convergence of forces around human development. However, an integration of those forces with the powerful industrial forces that had succeeded so well in shaping the physical environment was lacking. Rather than a marriage between the two, there tended to be a mutual rejection. For a different perspective, we might see the marriage that takes place in late post-industrial society as one between East and West. Eastern philosophy and religion tend to look inward, focusing on man's fatalistic adjustment to the universe. He is not separated from the universe; rather, the "two" actually are one, and thus it makes no sense to conquer the environment. Western philosophy, by contrast, separates man from his environment, looks outward, and encourages man to shape his environment. Each represents a different kind of accumulation: one in feeling at home with the self-universe, and the other in shaping the universe in accordance with man's goals. When these two accumulations join forces, we have a man who creates himself and his universe.

What makes late post-industrial society so unique in history is the discovery of the process of creativity, or the playing of CONTINU-ING REVOLUTION. Man becomes aware of how to pull together the variety of accumulation processes which, formerly, often militated against one another. For example, in more and more instances of behavior he learns to locate a great many complementary paths of development. Because of this ability, he has little fear of setting his level of aspiration far ahead of his level of fulfillment, thus creating a fantastic force for development. That in turn leads to a rapid increase in the level of fulfillment, and that leads to a still greater level of aspiration. A very short period for receiving feedback of information speeds up the whole process.

SHELL GAME gives way to CONTINUING REVOLUTION as man combines East and West and learns to do away with the split between inner and outer. If all is one, then the individual cannot afford to be so narrow as to value achievements above the person doing the achieving. A means can conflict with an end only to the degree that the individual has remained unaware of their intimate connection with one another as well as with all other phenomena. A much deeper probing of the inner and outer worlds than is charac-teristic of East and West, when they exist side by side, results from a union of the two. Here, the whole is far more than its separate parts.

To state the character of late post-industrial society in another way, man learns to put himself together. By probing deeply, he raises to the surface the hidden portions of the icebergs of his mind, and by so doing is in a position to resolve all kinds of conflicts, such as that between means and ends. This baring of self is a continuing process, leading to a continuing acceleration of man's force for devel-opment.

NOTES

1. Alfred Korzybski, *Science and Sanity* (Lakeville, Conn.: Institute of General Se-mantics, 1958).

2. For discussions of the nature and importance of the concept of scarcity, see Man-fred Stanley, "Nature, Culture and Scarcity: Foreward to a Theoretical Synthesis," *American Sociological Review* 33 (December 1968): 855-70; and Robert Theobald and Jean M. Scott, *Teg's 1994: An Anticipation of the Near Future* (Phoenix, Arizona: Personalized Secretarial Service, 5045 N. 12th St., 1971).

3. David Riesman, *The Lonely Crowd* (New Haven: Yale University Press, 1961).

4. The first draft of this section was substantially revised by Mr. Peter M. Senge. Mr. Senge is a graduate student in System Dynamics at Massachusetts Institute of Technology.

5. We should note that in many applications it may be appropriate to conceive of some definite actions affecting the outflow rate of water, as opposed to the natural decay shown in the beakers of figure 7-2. This would amount to conceiving the outflow drains as having adjustable taps. We have not done this here in order that the discussion in this brief introduction to the beaker metaphor might focus on the factors which determine the inflow rate (or rate of development).

6. See the appendix for a systematic effort to construct a dynamic model of human development on the basis of the beaker metaphor.

7. Max Weber, *The Protestant Ethic and the Spirit of Capitalism* (New York: Charles Scribner's Sons, 1958).

SUGGESTED READINGS

POWELL, JOHN. *Why Am I Afraid to Tell You Who I Am?* Chicago: Peacock Books, 1969. If we think that we're fixed (one kind of SCARCITY), then if others find out bad things about us the relationship may be totally destroyed because there's nothing we could do to change ourselves. And we'd have to live with those despicable things until death. These are some of the answers Powell gives to his question.

RIESMAN, DAVID. *The Lonely Crowd.* New Haven: Yale University Press, 1961. Riesman's concepts of tradition-direction, inner-direction, other-direction and autonomy correspond generally to four kinds of society: pre-industrial, early industrial, late industrial, and post-industrial. He applies his concepts to personality types as well as societies, with no simplistic assumption that a personality or society must be limited to only one type.

SJOBERG, GIDEON. *The Preindustrial City: Past and Present.* New York: The Free Press, 1960. " . . . through the medium of the preindustrial-urban center I have sought to analyze the structure of preindustrial civilized societies. In turn we seek in the preindustrial city and its society, now retreating from the world scene, a standard for measuring —and, consequently, understanding—the impact of industrial-urbanization, a truly revolutionary force in this the twentieth century."

STANLEY, MANFRED. "Nature, Culture and Scarcity." *American Sociological Review* 33 (December 1968): 855-70. It is easy to speak glibly about the importance of the concept of scarcity, but it takes the kind of broad theoretical synthesis which Stanley has been able to put together to communicate this idea in such a way that others can easily build on it.

FIVE

SOCIAL CATEGORY
SYSTEMS

Are we more than simply players of roles? Is there anything within us other than our repertoires? If not, then we are very much like ants or bees. They too play definite roles, roles determined by their biological makeup. But suppose our physiology does not fix us in these ways, suppose that—potentially—we are far more than our roles. Then if it is true that we have learned to see ourselves and one another primarily as players of roles, it follows that our environment does not do justice to our humanity.

We meet Ian Zenski once again in chapter 8, ten years later chronologically and hundreds of years later in Zenski's subjective time. Ian probes into his life of a decade ago and discovers some of the forces producing the acceleration in himself and in society. And those forces are based on the idea that man is more than his roles, that man can step outside of them, that his membership in a variety of social categories never again need doom him to live out a life of being stereotyped and of stereotyping others.

In chapter 9 we look to the concept of development as a powerful tool which man can use to step outside of his narrow roles. Historically, the concept has been closely associated with economic development. To be useful for our purposes it must first be broadened so that nonmaterial aspects of development receive proper recognition. We are then in a position to examine social stratification systems, a type of social category system, with a very critical eye. Such an examination leads us to wonder about the kind of social stratification system which would be most conducive to human development.

8

Ian Zenski,
Part Two

LOOKING BACKWARD

Ian pressed the "on" button, the screen lit up, and there was the scene in the conference room of Games, Inc., just as he remembered it occurring some ten years ago. In subjective time, relative to his rate of development during the past ten years, the event actually had occurred two hundred and fifty years ago. How foolish of people to have lived by the external clock for so long a period of time, he thought, how effective a way of devaluing what is internal. Yet how could individuals have realized their foolishness when methods for measuring subjective time had not yet been constructed?

It had all been so easy once people began to get away from the bureaucratic concept of society and started to interrelate the specialties. It had been a short step from Einstein's concept of the relativity of time and space to the idea that each individual might measure time in relation to his own development in "space," with space understood to be psychological as well as physical. From there it was just another short step to the notion of the unidimensionality of the space-time continuum as it applied to human behavior. In these terms, Ian had lived not only two hundred and fifty years in the past ten, but he had also travelled two hundred and fifty years in psychological space, just as one might say that a spaceship travelled two hundred and fifty light years. A two-second interval of external time—as distinct from internal time—elapsed during these musings, and Ian focused his attention once again on the screen. The simulated Ian was accusing the simulated Jack Fleisch of the very problems which Jack had thought he was attempting to eradicate.

JACK: What proof of my guilt do you have?

IAN: You bow down to the adversary system in the law, a perversion of justice because of its focus on guilt or innocence as distinct from human welfare. As human beings what we all require for our development is neither being dragged in the mud for our supposed "sins" nor being labelled as having no responsibility for human failings. We must encourage one another to develop, and we must envision paths for enlarging ourselves. But when you place the law above man, you constrict him. By invoking your catechism that we need a government of laws and not of men you revert to a Hobbesian view of society as a war of all against all, and in so doing you create a Hobbesian society.

As Ian watched the simulation he was aware that Jack and Ian of ten years ago were different from his simulation of the two, yet at the same time his simulation had managed to capture vital aspects of these personalities in that late industrial period. He caught himself. There he was, doing it again, stereotyping periods of history, falling into the trap which so many of those early historians fell into. Sure, it had been a great advance for those historians over what had been done previously. Certainly they helped us all to understand a great deal about the dynamic behind the industrial revolution or the forces producing the renaissance. But the labels that they created had a way of sticking, becoming ends in themselves. The resulting SHELL GAME diverted attention away from the great divergence of phenomena within any labeled period as well as from what was happening during the periods that weren't labeled. The problem was the general one Korzybski had pointed up, the static and isolated nature of Aristotelian language. And here he was, he, Ian, the most powerful force producing the new culture, still slipping into the same old ways.

Ian was well aware that he was using his mind to roam freely on a tangent to a tangent. If he had learned anything in these two hundred and fifty years it was the vastness, the limitlessness, of the unexplored territory of his mind. What he might have labeled as daydreaming in the distant past he now believed to be at the heart of human creativity and at the very basis of life itself. It was intangible, and it was also real. He was creating bridges which linked his experiences, bridges which did not exist in his mind before he created them. These bridges enabled him to channel more and more of his motivational energy to the solution of any given problem. Each bridge brought out of isolation a piece of his experience and enabled him to bring to bear what he had learned there—learned with his heart and body as well as his head—on other problems than those that were specific to that experience. The path he had been taking for these many years led him to develop ever greater ability to apply all of his past experiences to any given experience in the present.

Ian began to trace his mental path of the previous seconds so that he could obtain an overview of his explorations. All of his thoughts had been on the periphery of his central concern: to achieve a man-computer-video simulation of key events in his life over the past ten (external) years which had accelerated the development of the null-A worlds. This type of simulation was not unique, but it was still generally viewed as a kind of gimmick, something that was a fascinating toy but had not yet shown its worth, like the early uses of video tape in education to help students overcome their overintellectualized approach, or like the early attempts to incorporate computer outputs into social science research.

A vast amount was already known about those years, and it was not limited to the stereotyping of a number of eras within the period. Research had gone a long way toward focusing on personalities as vital sources of social change. On the other hand, however, the information focused on any one individual's experiences somehow did not go very deep. The bits of information were spread out over very large numbers of situations and didn't converge on any one. This was even true for himself, with all of the attention he had received. It was like the old situation of survey research in sociology: a little bit was learned about each of a great many individuals, but not enough about any one, or about any particular situation, to get profound insight into what was going on.

All this was very unfortunate, Ian felt. Here we are on planet earth finally pretty much out of danger that we'll blow ourselves up or poison ourselves in some way, and what do we do? We play the good old SHELL GAME again, maybe not as hard as we used to, but still pretty hard. We're tending to hold tight to the methods we've used for solving the big problems of the past. After billions of years life finally breaks out of its shell and, instead of moving to the infinite universes inside and outside, it sits there feeling very smug. Well, maybe he was being a bit unfair. Sure, there was continuing development in all aspects of human life. But Ian felt that all of that was chicken feed compared to what might be done. Man could be learning to create new worlds with different physical laws, he thought. He could be conquering death, learning to move across the universe as fast as his imagination could take him, constructing new universes. He could be learning about the vast universes within himself, re-creating himself biologically, learning to read minds far more effectively.

If there was anyone to blame, he felt, it was himself. True, he hadn't fallen as deeply into the trap of the innovators of the past whose disciples never learned to be creative. But it was the same trap, even if it wasn't so deep. He, Ian, still was playing CONTINUING REVOLUTION more than anyone else. Even though others had learned to become creative relative to the giants of the past, they tended to be slow in accelerating their creativity, at least relative to himself. Actually, he thought, there was no one to blame, not even himself. It was only now that he was becoming aware of the gap in rate of growth between himself and others, and awareness is prerequisite to doing something about the problem. He must now find a way of learning more deeply about his own creative processes and communicating this knowledge to others. In this way he would be communicating his greatest achievement—himself—to others. He felt he was into a kind of equality bag, but one with an expanding pie of rewards. He wasn't trying to help others because of any outside moral pressure. His own development was at stake here. In a world where people are playing harder games of CONTINUING REVOLUTION, his own possibilities for developing would accelerate fantastically.

As for his own responsibility for the SHELL GAMES that were being played, he felt that it was great. Of course, he hadn't held others down by BUREAUCRACY: with authoritariansim or status games. It was more subtle than that. When it came down to the root of the matter, it was his own DEVELOPMENT which determined how well he was able to communicate the art and science of discovery to others. The man-computer-video simulation was his way of meeting the SHELL GAME problem.

By simulating his discovery process with a computer as well as visually, his own understanding of it would improve enormously, and he would also be creating excellent tools for communicating to others.

Now that he had traced back to his basic reasons for the simulation he felt freer to let his mind roam as it had before. There before his eyes he saw much of what he had hoped to see. Jack was playing a rather hard game of SEE-SAW with himself. He certainly looked the part: eyes looking downward, arms buried in one another, facial expression very serious, voice taut and high-pitched, intonation choppy, almost no bodily movement. It was as if he was trying to crawl inside himself and disappear. The whole presentation seemed only a step removed from terror. An unexpected noise and the step would be taken. Ian tested his idea by making the appropriate shift in the program and noted the momentary expression of horror in Jack's face in response to the sound of a falling coke bottle.

It was more difficult for Ian to read himself, but not that much more difficult. There he was, God himself, laying the guilt on poor Jack. There was no question but that he was playing a pretty hard game of SEE-SAW with Jack as the victim. He was in love with the sound of his own voice, not being aware of how he was affecting himself, Jack, or the others. It was a classic case of SHELL GAME where he no longer saw what he was doing within a larger context. His "mock" castigation of Jack had become an end in itself. In studying his simulated movements and voice quality and pace, Ian concluded that perhaps he had been two or three steps away from terror, as distinct from one step. For if he was not in SCARCITY, what reason could there be for SEE-SAW? He had everything to lose and nothing to gain. He was creating an atmosphere which made it difficult for Jack to contribute, and he was immobilizing himself with his GOODNIK or self-righteousness. Ian decided to test his hypothesis, beginning with a bottle, moving to the backfire of a truck, the laughter of Vlad mocking him, and a hysterical scream of terror. Neither the bottle nor the backfire seemed to disturb Ian, but the hysterical scream had a distinct moderate effect, if only momentary. Vlad's laughter, however, had a surprisingly great effect. Was he playing CONFORMITY to Vlad?

Ian suddenly felt deeply that he was in SHELL GAME at the moment. Here he was, castigating himself as he was ten years ago, being so damned self-righteous about how wonderful he was now. Sure it might take considerably more than the laughter of a

friend for him to register his terror, but it was still there. Maybe
his shell was much bigger now, but it was still a shell. There he
was, worrying about the SHELL GAMES that others were
playing, when it was his own SHELL GAME that was at the root
of the problem.

But wasn't he now in another SHELL GAME? Wasn't he now
taking himself to task for taking his simulated self to task?
Where would it end? By being angry with himself for playing
SEE-SAW against his simulated self, he was once again playing
SEE-SAW. As he realized this, Ian shifted his mood from one of
guilt to one of stairway. And as his mood shifted he began to
realize that his simulation had caricatured both Jack and
himself. He had tended to set up straw men so that he could
knock them down and feel self-important. Not that his straw
men were completely insubstantial, but they were nevertheless
distorted images. He was still in SCARCITY to a degree, and his
terror produced a need for distorting his simulation. His
realization of this pointed toward a more realistic simulation,
and it also pointed him to understand quite deeply that he would
always be in SCARCITY at least to some degree. He was on a
continuum moving from hell to heaven. He would never get to
heaven, and he never wanted to get there. After all, heaven must
be a kind of hell, he thought, since there's no place to go from
there but down. And hell was a kind of heaven, because there
was plenty of room for improvement. All he wanted was to be
able to keep moving. Maybe it was the moving that was heaven,
and staying still was hell.

THE SIGNIFICANCE OF MAN-COMPUTER-VIDEO
SIMULATIONS

Ian suddenly had an idea. He had developed man-computer
simulations with two general purposes in mind. One was
past-oriented: to assess human behavior in order to determine
which combinations of games were being played and how hard
each of the games was being played. The other was
future-oriented: to calculate optimum modes of behavior, that is,
modes which might yield maximum development. In order to do
this he had had to construct a dictionary which translated
everyday language into game terms. In this way written or
spoken language could be analyzed into its game components,
including a specification of how hard each game was being played
and how the games related to one another. Then predictions

could be made as to what kinds of behavior might produce the greatest overall movement in a null-A direction. These predictions were tested experimentally in the man phase of the man-computer simulation.

These man-computer simulations had had an extraordinary effect, first on the academic world, and later on the world as a whole. It was the right idea at the right time. World events had become extremely discouraging, and the push for relevance had gathered great momentum in every field of knowledge. At the same time a strong interdisciplinary thrust was developing, powered by orientations from general semantics. The man-computer simulations carried forward the interdisciplinary movement and provided it with a technology which appeared to be extremely relevant. Few guessed at the time just how relevant it was and to what changes in society it would lead.

It seemed to Ian that he was once again at the beginning of something extraordinary, far more extraordinary than the forces which had produced the big null-A cultural revolution. The man-computer simulations were very much head-oriented, and that was entirely appropriate for the industrial world as it was at the time. They helped individuals learn to use their brains far more effectively, to monitor the way they used language and thus detect where they were on the various A–null-A dimensions, and to construct strategies for moving in developmental directions. But a key problem was the abstract nature of this approach. It was difficult for people to translate their general strategies into concrete action. There was a big gap between abstract knowledge of the game dimensions and concrete use of this knowledge. The gap was not so great that it could not be bridged, and this bridging was the basis of those rapid changes in society.

Ian felt that he was on the threshold of a means of concretizing the game dimensions via his video output. This idea had been in his mind when he first became involved in constructing the man-computer-video simulation technique, but somehow the vast implications of what he was doing had escaped him. He had known that a concretization of the game dimensions was required, but he had not put that idea together with a historical understanding of the forces which had shaped the great cultural revolution. Now that he was deeply involved in examining those forces, however, he was able to see far more clearly the implications of the new approach.

With the video output the abstract ideas could be concretized. The individual could learn how his situation on the various game dimensions came to be translated into the ways in which he presented himself, his gestures, voice tones, whatever he did. He could learn to monitor far more of his behavior than simply the abstract content of whatever he said. After all, enough research had been done to indicate the great gap between attitude and behavior, and here was a way of getting at behavior in addition to attitude. But all that was past-oriented, and the power of this approach was not limited to the past. Ian was thinking of using his technique to construct the future in a form concrete enough to provide a guide for the individual in his efforts to reconstruct himself. The individual might construct how he would behave if he were more developmental in various ways, and this video output could be the concrete basis for his learning to reconstruct himself in those ways.

But all this was not limited to the development of the individual. Ian was awed at the possibilities. He could construct alternative futures for society as a whole, and project them on video. He thought of the early work of Kenzo Tange in the sixties. He had used the computer to construct a wide variety of alternative structures that met his financial and artistic specifications. Tange's computer output was visual, although it was static. Ian's output would be visual and dynamic. With this kind of output it would be much easier for the individual to construct a man-centered future based on penetrating insight into his past. Unlike a toddler who sees circles but lacks the concretized imagination necessary to place objects in a circle, man's imagination could create the design specifications for whatever he would like to become and for the kind of world he would like to create.

How had he achieved this idea of the significance of man-computer-video simulation, a technique he had been thinking about and planning for many years without feeling its possibilities? He had been probing his past in order to get into the dynamic of his process of discovery, yet here was a discovery he had just made. How had he made it? Ian thought back to the context of his thoughts of the past half minute. One key element was an acceptance of his lack of perfection. He would always be playing SHELL GAME to a degree, even though the shell got bigger and bigger. It was like the feeling he once had while playing tennis. His opponent came up with a beautiful service. Ian tried to put the ball away and instead hit it into the net. He had felt humility that his skills were not infinite, and that he would always be affected by his environment.

But such an acceptance freed him to develop. He didn't have to fool himself, to protect himself from the knowledge of what he was not. He was able to see himself more as others saw him. There, then, was another key element in his recent discovery. It was this very feeling of freedom resulting from the acceptance of self. Instead of trying to prove to himself how good he was, he was able to focus his attention on how to go beyond where he was, and the result was his new idea. It had happened the same way on the tennis court. The humble feeling released him to risk developing his game into a better one. But the risks were not the foolish ones he had taken earlier in the match, when he had been trying to live up to an image of himself as an out-of-practice Pancho Gonzales. Those risks were based on a large gap between his self-image and the ability he could actually demonstrate, and he was bound to fall flat on his face. This gap had closed with his new sense of humility, and the risks he took were far more reasonable, resulting in continuing development of his game.

There was another important element in his discovery, one that was so deeply hidden in the process that it almost escaped Ian's detection. The humility and the feeling of freedom, both a half-minute ago and in the tennis match of many years ago, were accompanied by a deep sense of confidence in his ability to develop himself. Without that, the humility would have pushed him to lower his level of aspiration, as happens almost invariably with human beings who fail in their aspirations. What was this strange force which enabled him to keep his aspirations high while bringing performance successively up to those aspirations? Whatever that force was, it must also be a powerful one in certain societal revolutions, where a revolution of rising expectations does not falter in relation to disappointing achievements.

Ian decided to go back to that event, almost ten (external) years ago, when he had experienced the greatest upsurge of this force, this confidence. He felt that its power was not unique to himself, but that all individuals must feel it to some extent whenever they create. The event had occurred several months after the scene he had just simulated. He, Vlad, and Ono were fooling around with video tape at the time, taping themselves, talking about the relation between role playing in the theatre and in everyday life, watching themselves on the monitor, taping their reactions to the monitor, watching themselves on the monitor, discussing their reactions once again, and so on.

ONO: I get the feeling that what we're doing is very similar to the kinds of experiences produced by the gaming I've been doing on international affairs, but I can't quite put my finger on what the similarity is. Both are developmental in important ways, maybe in the same general kind of way.

VLAD: I feel more at home in this kind of thing and you in the gaming thing. Between the two of us, if we can communicate, we ought to come up with something. You're more head-oriented than I am, and maybe that's a difference between the game metaphor and the dramaturgical metaphor. Both of us pretty much agree on the importance of the null-A idea, and that's a similarity.

IAN: Doesn't our experience right now with video tape do the same kind of thing? We look at ourselves on the monitor and see that what we've just done is a kind of role, and maybe we could play it differently if we want to. This new insight is the same kind of thing George Herbert Mead talked about as basic to the socialization process, where the individual sees himself as an object. New elements are added to the individual as a result of this process, and it would be impossible for him to "go home again" and play his role in exactly the same way. By learning to see himself as a role player he also learns to change the role he plays, just like the individual who sees himself as always playing games learns to play his games in a different way.

VLAD: But Mead's concept of socialization led directly to an overemphasis on the necessity of conformity and a deemphasis on autonomy. Aren't you being too eclectic here? If everything fits into your schema, then maybe nothing does. Maybe you're illustrating your own push to conform here by going along with Mead.

IAN: You've got a point there. But wait! Why do you assume that I'm conforming here? Maybe you're conforming to antieclecticism.

Ian stopped the action. There it was in a nutshell. When it had happened so very long ago it had taken him days to understand its significance. Then he had arranged for the three of them to get together again.

IAN: Vlad, you and I had a bit of a SEE-SAW game going with one another. It wasn't a hard game, but the game was still evident. You rejected Mead's relevance to the null-A approach, failing to select out of Mead what was null-A and concentrating only on his A aspects. And then you started jumping on what you called my eclecticism, failing to note anything of positive value in my approach. My reaction was a classic product of SCARCITY. I started out agreeing with you, playing SEE-SAW against myself. Then I made what I thought was a quick recovery. I turned on you and accused you of CONFORMITY. I failed to see what you were contributing to our understanding, just as you had failed in my case.

ONO: Vlad, I'd like you to try to probe into the reasons for your SEE-SAW game.

VLAD: I think your analysis is insightful as far as my own feelings went at the time, Ian. I remember that I was having difficulty relating some of my previous ideas about acting to our discussion of role playing, and I felt at odds with myself. I had divided actors into two types: the technical actors and the method actors. To me, the method actors tended to have wishy-washy types of personalities, conforming to the dictates of the role rather than bringing very much of themselves to the role. When you started bringing up the relation between acting in the theatre and socialization in everyday life, I immediately rejected the idea's possible fruitfulness. For me, acting was one thing, and everyday behavior another. So I stereotyped you as pushing for method acting, and perhaps I knew that it would hurt you if I accused you of CONFORMITY and questioned your whole approach. You were threatening my beliefs, and I was defending them by threatening yours. We were both in SCARCITY.

IAN: My own SCARCITY at the time of our SEE-SAW interchange was based on my self-perceived failure to make progress in putting to use my analogy between acting and everyday behavior. There was something on the tip of my tongue, and I wasn't getting it out. Then I got onto that tangent about George Herbert Mead, which didn't really take me in the direction I wanted to go. I dimly felt that I should be able to use the analogy between role playing in the theatre and in everyday life to learn to construct both kinds of roles better, to learn to act better and live better. But I saw this as necessitating an involved process of learning to act, and I couldn't see myself able to do that right then and there.

ONO: I happened to have been watching you and listening carefully to your speech pattern, Ian, when you were reacting to Vlad's attack on your eclecticism the other day. Your voice definitely rose in pitch, and you tended to be less aware of me and rigid in the way you held your body. Your mental position was paralleled by a mild physical fear reaction. This is a lot different from the way you're acting now. Your eyes seem to be everywhere at once, and your facial expression changes readily from moment to moment.

IAN: I realize now that I'm still in SCARCITY, but it's much less than that other day. I've made progress on the problem that was bothering me then, and I don't feel I need so desperately anyone's conformity to my ideas. The specific thought I've had is that I don't have to go through some complex process in order to learn to play roles so that I can apply my role-playing approach to enrich acting and life. I'm playing roles all the time, speaking prose all my life without having been aware of it.

VLAD: I'm not sure I understand what you're getting at.

IAN: It's the realization that I'm able to reconstruct my personality, a reconstruction that goes deeper than technical acting or even method acting. It gets deep into the core of personality. But it's also something that all of us do all the time without being aware of it. Even the technical actor is doing this, but because of his belief that technical acting does not involve this, he doesn't exploit its possibilities for developing himself. The same is true for the method actor. Both see themselves as not changing the inner core of their personalities in any fundamental way, and this view slows down such change and prevents them from achieving conscious control over it.

ONO: Then it's a feeling that you can reconstruct yourself in a developmental way because you've already been doing that kind of thing all your life.

IAN: Exactly. And if I feel deeply that I can reconstruct myself, I also feel that I can learn to solve any problem. Like the mathematician's or engineer's concept of algorithm. Instead of worrying about whether it is possible to solve a given problem, one immediately looks ahead and attempts to figure out how to solve the problem. In the same way, I feel confident that there's no problem I can't learn to solve.

VLAD: And how does this powerful feeling of confidence relate to dramaturgy and to everyday behavior? Can you be specific about the way it can work for you?

IAN: From a theatrical angle, it pushes me to see playing a role as actually playing myself in the context of the role. Instead of focusing on the role more than myself, as the method actor tends to do, or on myself more than the role, as is the tendency of the technical actor, I'm concentrating on both. I'm looking for those aspects of the role which are also part of me, and I use those as a basis for projecting myself into the role. But this selective process gives me insights into the role, and into my own nature, that I never had before. I learn to see both with different eyes. I learn to be deeply in the role, because the role has penetrated to my inner core of personality, something which even method actors rarely achieve, and I learn at the same time to be more conscious of who I am.

VLAD: And what about everyday behavior?

IAN: It works in the same general way. The role others expect me to play is one where there appears to be great latitude. There are few very specific lines I'm expected to say. But actually, there's far less latitude than appears to be the case. Everyone is more or less pleading with me to conform to his ways of thinking, feeling, and acting, pleading with me to help him find meaning in his own life. Once more there's a selective process involved. I have to reach out and discover elements within these expectations which not only are basic to those I'm trying to communicate with but also are part of me.

ONO: I see what you're saying in the abstract, but can't you give a concrete illustration?

IAN: Take what happened with my three-year-old this morning. I was typing in my study and he was building with his blocks. In a sense, we were both busy playing with our blocks, only mine were more abstract. He had been constructing a rectangle made up of four rectangular blocks standing on their sides, and he had been busying himself with that for several minutes, setting up auxiliary blocks inside and outside the rectangle. I, on the other hand, was busy with my *Reconstruction of Society,* attempting to get on paper my visions of alternative null-A worlds. Suddenly he started pleading with me to come and build with him. He was in a SCARCITY situation and his method of getting out of it was to put pressure on me to make things more interesting for him. Now, I was not having too easy a time with the particular paragraph I was working on, and ordinarily in that kind of situation I would have insisted that he go back to his blocks, we both would have escalated, and neither of us would have been happy with the result. But this great feeling of confidence helped me out of my SCARCITY orientation. I was pretty sure I would have no difficulty figuring out a way of getting that paragraph across, and maybe even making it a better paragraph than I had ever written before. At the same time, I was also pretty sure that I could help my son.

ONO: And how did you translate this feeling into action?

IAN: I started to turn his rectangular blocks on their ends. I didn't want to depart too far from his rectangular concept, yet at the same time I wanted to move out from something he had become bored with. Deep down, he knew that he wasn't developing. I showed him a way of developing that he felt sure he could handle, and he took it from there. And I was developing too, applying my abstract ideas to a concrete situation.

Ian had found what he was searching for. It all fit together: his creativity in the past and his present work, his creativity and that of others, his SEE-SAW games and those of others. People developed, moved out from their narrow shells, to the degree that they felt confident in being able to develop, and they got this confidence by making cognitive links which showed them that they already had developed in the same kind of way, and that the question was one of simply increasing the degree of development. That's where the null-A language came in: to help people see how things were interrelated and how they could be viewed as dimensions. But in addition to the abstract null-A language, people needed to apply cognitive links and dimensional thought to their everyday behavior, and that's where concrete examples came into the picture. The game language achieved that to a degree, for it tended to be quite metaphorical, but there was a lot of room for improvement.

And that's where the man-computer-video simulation came in. It combined the abstract and the concrete. It was programmed in terms of the various games systems played, and its output was visual, concrete. It could be used to select out of everyday behavior those null-A elements involved, and then it could carry them forward, projecting them into the future in a sequence of images portraying paths to development. Or it could do the same with the past, selecting those sequences which led to the development in question. And the viewer's confidence in his own ability to develop would increase whether he watched the past or the future. He would see with his own eyes how easy it was, and he would also see how he had already been developing in the same direction.

Ian decided to test this idea out on himself. He would start with the past, centering on the preceding ten (external) years. He would take a situation, and then he would speed up its developmental aspects so that what actually took a month would now take less than a minute. In that way he would be able to learn much more about the forces that produced the null-A cultural revolution. He would shift to another situation, and another, each time viewing society from a different perspective. He would look at architecture, at academia, at industry. . . .

IAN ZENSKI AND BUCKMINSTER FULLER

BUCKMINSTER FULLER: We are technology, and the universe is technology. If we realized that, we'd get over our fear of it and use it to create plenty for all. Primitive man was ignorant and hungry, and nobody thought of life as very worthwhile in its own right. But if no one could have a decent life, at least the pharoah could have a wonderful after-life. We've come a long way from that, from the pharoah's after-life to his life on earth, to the after-life of the nobles, to the nobles' life on earth, to the after-life of the middle class, to their life on earth, to the after-life of the poor, to everybody's life on earth. In spite of all this change, man was not able to look beyond his nose in any of these eras, to see the direction of evolution. He always assumed that there weren't enough resources to improve man's lot at a greater rate than it was already being improved. And that was because he always assumed that he was a thing, that technology was a thing.

IAN: I'm with you very much in your emphasis on getting out of a SCARCITY view of man's possibilities and doing this with information. From my own studies of human behavior and attempts to develop social technologies I've become convinced of the same thing. But how can we create the kind of architecture which could diffuse these ideas in time to prevent the world catastrophes that are shaping up?

FULLER: The human excrement from one farm family can power all of the farm machinery they use, but instead it's wasted. We use sixty-five volumes of water to get rid of one volume of human waste. More waste. We've got to apply the best scientific brains we have to creating our physical environments. Instead we separate the scientist from the architect. Which scientists are looking at our plumbing?

IAN: Touché again! I'm reminded of the fantastic success of H. Ross Perot, the Texas multimillionnaire, practically a billionaire,

with his Electronic Data Systems, Inc. His vision when he created
E.D.S. was that his firm—which was to design, install, and
operate information systems for large businesses—would become
the most respected firm of its type in the country by staying very
closely attuned to the needs of the customers. Here was the
application of know-how to the gut practical problems at hand,
the wedding of science and technology to existing problems. He
was very pragmatic. Rather than trying to figure out some
perfect solution, he preferred to set down some possible strategies
and then start to try things out. He's a scientist-engineer who's
also concerned with the human problems of his clients. Saying all
this, however, I'm still wondering how fast this approach can
take us all by itself, given the accelerating problems in the
world. For example, why haven't you been able to convince
architects and city planners to put science and technology to
work in architecture?

FULLER: Most architects won't listen to me. They think that
I'm not an architect, that I'm some kind of engineer. And the
engineers think I'm an architect.

IAN: Why won't they listen?

FULLER: I wish I knew. They just don't think the way I do.

IAN: And how do they think that's different from you?

FULLER: Well, they can't envision anything until they see it
actually working in steel, stone, and concrete, or whatever the
materials are. I've tried to get across my ideas, but they don't see
them.

IAN: Have you tried to start with some of the existing
architectural ideas which are closest to your own and then taken
it from there?

FULLER: Not that much. Maybe I've always defined myself as
outside the traditional system of architectural ideas, maybe I like
to see myself as a great innovator.

IAN: Take an idea of Frank Lloyd Wright, among others, the
notion of architectural harmony with the physical environment.
Now extend that to harmony with man's inner space, to man's
ever-changing inner needs. Isn't it possible to see your work as
relating to Wright's in this way, as constituting an extension of
his in the inward direction?

FULLER: You know, you're making a lot of sense. Are you saying that I'd be able to communicate better by emphasizing this kind of thing, and that I'd be more effective that way?

IAN: Yes. Why be a martyr when you can be successful in getting your ideas across? But you have to search for what you have in common with them, make the most of that, and then use that as a lever to bring them a step forward. Not ten steps at a time, because that way they won't take even one, but one step at a time, and before you know it, they've taken ten.

FULLER: All this is so abstract. Do you have any more specific suggestions?

IAN: With your interest in technology you might want to work on the ways in which computers can be used to humanize the physical environment, to create an environment which is not only sensitive to the different needs of individuals and the varying needs of each individual, but which also can help each individual to continually develop himself. I have only the vaguest ideas how this might be done. I know that as individuals develop themselves they can make use of their additional knowledge to improve the computer programs they work with. I also know that computers can have other kinds of outputs than information. They can be sources of control for energy systems and thus can be used directly to alter the environment. Putting the two ideas together, we can develop sequences where man develops, where he then alters computer programs which make for a more developmental environment, where this in turn encourages him to develop more rapidly, and so on.

FULLER: You're still abstract, but at least I see what you're driving at. You think that if I worked to develop that kind of computer technology, and explained it in relation to existing architectural principles and practices, that I would be able to achieve much more than I have.

IAN: Yes. And you'd be able to do a better job not only in eliminating waste but also in expanding rewards. A physical environment that helps us develop creates an expanding pie of rewards. If we focus on better distribution of an existing pie of rewards, that may not be good enough in view of the universal revolution of rising expectations. The computer approach goes beyond equality. Equality is not enough when there is not enough to share, and I believe there is not enough relative to the accelerating problems of the world.

FULLER: You make it sound so easy, as if we can just set our minds to doing it, and we'll do it.

IAN: It is that easy, to the degree that we can set our minds in that way. The problem is to increase that degree as much as possible.

FULLER: Now you're getting into that Korzybski stuff. I've heard of it, but how does it apply here?

IAN: Actually, I've been using the null-A approach all the time that we've been talking, and my suggestions have been for you to use the same approach. For example, when I suggested that you learn to see your work as an extension of existing architectural ideas, I was asking you to think dimensionally as distinct from dichotomously.

FULLER: What do you think a good first step might be in applying this computer approach?

IAN: I've been working with man-computer interaction in classroom situations. Maybe you'd be interested in working with me to create an environment more conducive to man's internal growth. My aim is to create a powerful demonstration of the effectiveness of these ideas.

THE NULL-A CULTURAL REVOLUTION

Ian was amazed to discover that in his conversation with Fuller so long ago he was actively employing the very principles of which he had just become very conscious. As Fuller had said, he made it all sound so easy, and that was because of his own confidence in the workability of his ideas, and that in turn was because he had already seen them work to a degree in his own life. The conversation with Vlad and Ono was an important phase of his development, when he had achieved a high degree of confidence in his ability to develop. And he had carried this confidence further in his conversation with Fuller. He had also actively used the null-A principle of dimensional thought to link his own ideas with those of Fuller and then to go beyond both of them. At the same time, Ian was able to see deficiencies in his verbal communication. It was abstract, and people could relate so much more readily to the concrete, to visual metaphors. There, once again, was the rationale for his man-computer-video simulation.

Ian jumped his simulation ahead to other phases of the revolution in architecture. Although it had begun in schools of architecture, it didn't take very long before it started to spread to different levels of education and to other spheres of society. Earlier ideas about the importance of light and space were not rejected, they were simply extended. Light and space, like food and water, give man elements which are essential to his development, but they do not teach him how to become more human. Responsiveness to human needs was not limited to control of environments via computer. The flexibility of the traditional Japanese house represented another kind of example, and the diminutive nature of the Japanese garden illustrated a way of centering attention on man in nature rather than on nature over man or man over nature.

Some of the most dramatic early experiments took place in communes. Radical changes in architecture tended to be associated with new forms of family and community living. Ian tuned into one which had been built almost entirely by the labor of commune members. It was one where he had personally been involved with the design. The keynotes were flexibility and diversity. Much of it was not very pleasing to the eye, similar to a comment frequently made about Fuller's work, yet our eyes have been trained to value an A world. It was the inner reality which stood in need of attention more than the outer. The living space could be partitioned and repartitioned in any number of ways to accommodate families of widely different types and sizes. There was a central time-sharing computer with remote stations scattered throughout, each having video and audio inputs and outputs. Walls were treated with a substance that allowed the occupant to paint whatever he wished and then to remove it quite easily at his discretion.

More important than the way the commune looked from the outside was the way it worked. One focus was on continuing experimentation with the physical environment. The approach was to assess how the physical environment affected the individual's development and to construct new environmental forms on the basis of this knowledge. The computer-video set-up proved to be invaluable for both purposes, with the game

language serving as the basis for the entire computer operation.
The result was that interiors and exteriors often were changed
drastically.

Ian remembered how he felt at that time. While almost
everyone was figuratively and literally waiting for the bombs to
fall or someone to shoot them, there were tiny minorities
scattered throughout the world who were experimenting in
diverse ways. As for the masses, their state of mind had been
aptly depicted by Jules Feiffer's *Little Murders,* a movie
centering on the circumstances surrounding hundreds of
apparently unmotivated murders of people in all walks of life in
New York City. What the murders had in common was that they
didn't have anything in common.

Ian ran through the Feiffer film. As the action progressed
there was an escalation of physical and mental aggression, and
the result was physical and mental death. The hero's wife lost
faith in her ideals and became even more apathetic than her
husband. Shortly afterward she died a meaningless death at the
hands of some unknown rifleman. And none of society's
institutions were able to offer any hope, any path toward a
solution. The escalation of violence continued as the film ended,
with the hero and his wife's proper middle-class family shooting
people from their living room window.

While Ian had been well aware at the time of the mental state
of the masses throughout the world, he was one of the very few
who refused to fall into a state of discouragement and apathy.
With his developmental view and his vision of the future within
the present and past, he had realized that the greatest risk was
to attempt to remain static in a world that was learning to play
a harder and harder game of VICIOUS CIRCLE. He had had a
vision of developing a new culture from within the old, an idea
similar to Tom Hayden's idea of developing counter-institutions
from within existing institutions. Ian had thought that what was
needed above all was an individual-centered society, a society
that would take the shattered humanistic ideas of East and West
and find ever better ways of putting them into practice.

Ian saw in the late sixties and early seventies events
foreshadowing this change, such as the revolt against authority
of all forms and the new vision of the scientific method. The old
view of science as a specialized field gave way with the rebirth of
interest in phenomenology. Every man was a scientist. The
relevant question came to be the ends sought by scientists or,
more generally, human beings, and how effective they were in

achieving them. Out of this came the thrust of science for man as distinct from a science which was all too often against man.

And if science was starting to emerge from its specialized status, so, too, was art. The idea of deemphasizing museum and concert-hall art and bringing art to the people in their everyday lives was an old one. Experimentation with art forms since the fifties pointed in this direction. However, it took the big breakthrough in science to free art from its narrow confines. With the enlargement of Aristotelian science's focus on proof, testing, justification, or verification, to an emphasis on creativity, the discovery process, the mind of the scientist, and metaphors for scientific communication, there came to be no valid reason for retaining the wall separating art from science. And as this wall crumbled, the wall separating art from life also crumbled, for science already had been shown to be characteristic of every man's behavior.

The force for social change that this twin crumbling produced was vast. It was a prelude to a continuing breakdown of barriers within the mind and within society. Technologies—and this included most of the jobs within society—also came to be recognized as the province of every man. The teacher, the physician, the attorney, the bricklayer, the plumber, the electrician—each was seen as depriving man of part of his humanity by co-opting knowledge, modes of expression, and modes of action. The crumbling of the barriers supporting specialization followed, on the one hand, the client revolt against the specialists and, on the other, the clear demonstrations of the effectiveness and happiness of the new kind of renaissance man who was emerging from the union of art and science. Although the client revolt had been developing for a number of years, with the movement toward neighborhood control of schools and the youth revolt on the campuses and in the secondary schools, few saw its relation at the time to the growing forces against bureaucracy: the trend toward decentralization in industry, the loss of jobs by the highly specialized, the growth of the death-of-God movement in religion, the commune movement, the revolt against rigid sex roles by female and gay liberationists, lesbians, heterosexuals, and male liberationists, and the revolt against war.

The implications of debureaucratization for the organization of physical space were great. The centripetal forces producing megalopolises like the New York and Tokyo areas, which already had shown signs of declining in the sixties, were transformed into

centrifugal forces. Movements for massive decentralization, such
as the plan to transfer offices of government from Tokyo to
Mount Fuji, never gained much ground in the sixties. But this
picture changed, and it came to matter less and less whether one
was located in a space where masses of others were also located.

A profound shift in emphasis from transportation to
communication made itself more and more evident. Indeed, the
changes were aptly designated as the revolution in
"communications culture." The power of the new electronic
media had been discussed by McLuhan and a number of others,
although they rarely took to task the content of these media.
Few had taken them very seriously and fewer still had done
anything about it. Sociologists and other academicians had
fumbled around with studies on the impact of television, but
their conclusions had little direction.

With the rise of Korzybskian ideas, however, the damage being
done became apparent, and subsequent research studies
corroborated this. Man's personality was being shaped by
television very much along A lines. He learned to be passive, and
what he absorbed was deadly to the mind's development and also
a carbon copy of what everyone else was learning. Most
fundamentally, he was distracted from himself and as a result
learned to see himself as valueless in the universe. The fires,
deaths, and broken bones of the day, the carnage in Asia and the
Middle East, the drug problem, the glories of God, the GOODNIK
games, the conditions in mental institutions, the latest events in
baseball, football, basketball, ice hockey, and tennis, the day's
soap operas, the black revolution, female and gay liberation, the
endless tittering over sexual intercourse, the glories of
patriotism, the rightness of democracy or socialism, the evil
nature of man, the rock singers, the quiz games and other forms
of mindlessness, the endless sale of products, the "news of the
day" consisting of a selection from the above—all of these were
important, but the viewer was not.

There were incipient trends in the other direction, such as the
talk-back shows, but momentum for these had to await the new
technology of communication associated with the Korzybskian
revolution. Video taping came into its own, produced at a price
making it widely available, and ordinary individuals started
producing and broadcasting their own "shows" to those who were
interested over cable TV. Broadcasting became far more selective,
with fewer and fewer "buckshot" shows designed for an audience
of millions. Film also had its revolution, beginning with the
underground film groups and students in the sixties and
proceeding to a production and distribution system which

overlapped the video tape system. There was also the "game revolution" at all levels of education. Whereas the early games never proceeded much beyond the novelty stage, the new ones, most of which were based on Korzybskian ideas, proved to be powerful instruments for educating the heart and the hand as well as the head.

Ian's thoughts had proceeded at a much greater rate than his man-computer-video simulation. There was taking shape in his mind an answer to a question that had been bothering him for some time. Why was it that his own personality system could achieve such fantastic force for changing the world? The question had finally become conscious, and he automatically searched for an algorithm which would illuminate it, fully confident that such an algorithm existed.

Of course, Ian thought. Prior to the Korzybskian revolution man had been deceived into thinking that he was an individual, but that was a grand illusion. The outer world, with all its contradictions, all its inhumanity, all its scarcity, had wormed its way inside him. It was difficult enough for a single individual to reconstruct himself sufficiently to recognize what had happened and to do something about it. It would have been far more difficult for any individual, with his own personal set of scarcities, to have achieved this if he had waited for others, with their own sets of scarcities, to understand and agree with him. However, if he was able to learn to assess his own development, then he need not await the long time lags involved in communication to others at every stage of his development. He could keep moving, skip many intermediate steps of communication to others, and in this way achieve an amazing growth rate. And his own self-reconstruction had been a model for the reconstruction of society, for it involved a reconstruction of the outer world within himself. That self-reconstruction could be accelerated now that Ian had achieved consciousness of more of the processes that had produced it.

EXERCISES

1. Imagine that all the major problems of society have been solved, and that there is no limit to what man might achieve. Imagine that you lived in such a society. What would you want to do? Write a piece of fiction about yourself in that situation. Try to make it dramatically appealing without resorting to dangers which you face. Can

you make it interesting by focusing on your own and society's further development? Why, or why not?

2. Do a comparative analysis of Ian Zenski—Part Two, with Ian Zenski—Part One. Use the language of game dimensions to help you. What similarities and differences do you find? In what ways is Ian Zenski—Part Two, still in late industrial society, in what ways is he in early post-industrial society, and in what ways is he in late post-industrial society? What about Ian Zenski—Part One, in relation to these types of society?

3. Using the game language, do the same kind of detailed analysis of some classroom interaction as appears in the chapter in the section on the significance of man-computer-video simulations. Do you find yourself and others falling into SHELL GAME with the game language, using it as an end in itself with results that are sometimes destructive? If so, what can you do to move toward CONTINUING REVOLUTION? In what ways, if any, has the game language helped you to achieve insights you might not have achieved otherwise?

4. Reenact the scene you analyzed in question 3 after this discussion. Now discuss the reenactment. Do you have any additional insight into the scene, that is, insight beyond what you had achieved prior to the reenactment? If so, what process enabled you to achieve that insight? Discuss this with others. Now reenact that particular process. Has this helped you to gain any additional insight into your behavior? Compare the kind of insight you gain from a discussion with the kind you gain from reenacting a scene. Compare the original scene with the reenactment of that scene.

5. Discuss metaphors of human development that are meaningful to yourself and others. Now apply them to the transition from Ian Zenski—Part One, to Ian Zenski—Part Two. For example, using the metaphor of the sailboat, we can see it moving along a stream with no beginning and no end. The helmsman takes into account shifts in the wind, corresponding to Zenski's humbleness before the excellent serve of his opponent, yet he charts his own course, corresponding to Zenski's refusal to tie himself to the scarcities of others.

9

Social Stratification and the Idea of Development

Just as in chapter 7, where we discussed the game language and the beaker metaphor prior to examining the evolution of post-industrial society, so must we now explore the idea of development if we are to proceed beyond considerations of society as a whole to the specifics of social category systems within society. The more concrete we become the more insistently the question of what is and what is not developmental is posed. Historically, the idea of development has been a rope formed from the twin strands of scientific and technological progress, and we have used it to pull ourselves up from pre-industrial to late industrial society. But the rope is breaking under pressures which it has succeeded in generating. New strands are required.

One such strand may be formed by exploring the relationship between development and power. Our traditional view of development through the lens of economics also takes place through a frame where scarcity is assumed, and we tend to ignore the possibility of a continuing expansion of power in society. Another strand may be constructed through consciousness of the distortions introduced by emphasis on the power of social systems at the expense of the power of personality systems. A third strand may be produced through a reformulation of our ways of thinking of scientific development which would emphasize the process of discovery or creativity.

191

We shall use this expanded rope to climb to new perspectives on social category systems. We will focus on an analysis of social stratification in general, its consequences, and its future.

DEVELOPMENT AND POWER

Before proceeding to new topics, let us look back momentarily at the metaphor of the beaker, for that metaphor offers us one view of the idea of development, although it is a limited one. The beaker metaphor gives us insight into the process of accumulation or integration, showing how a rate of flow accumulates in the beaker over a period of time. Coupled with the language of game dimensions, that metaphor helps us gain understanding of such processes as the KNOWL- EDGE game played by scientists as they create scientific revolutions. But this constitutes only a portion of the overall developmental processes going on in society as a whole. For example, rapid accumulation of physical science knowledge without a corresponding accumulation of social science knowledge can produce an imbalance which is to the detriment of societal development as a whole. We address ourselves to this wider perspective in the present chapter.

We begin with the development of the idea of development. Our purpose is not to achieve a thorough scholarly exegesis of the concept, but rather to trace the concept's association with the industrial revolution and economic development more than with the development of power. This will provide the basis for a critical-constructive view of current theories of power and social change. We conclude with a brief sketch of an alternative view of development, one which is broad enough to include both kinds of development.

The Development of the Idea of Development

The three contexts related to the emergence of the idea of development which we shall examine are the Hegelian dialectic, the evolution of the universe, and the industrial revolution.

Beginning with Hegel,[1] we point up his dialectical philosophy of thesis-antithesis leading to synthesis as an illustration of a developmental orientation, one of many, prior to the scientific-industrial revolution. Today we tend to think of development more narrowly than Hegel thought of the dialectic process. For us the concept tends to be associated with rising standards of living and with scientific progress. This relative narrowness of orientation becomes a self-fulfilling prophecy. Because our concept of development does not envision other ways in which man can progress, we see the scientific and economic ways as the sole ones, and we proceed to construct the world on the basis of that vision.

If Hegelian thought alerts us to the spatial breadth of our concept of development, then the evolution of the universe[2] alerts us to the temporal dimension. Once again it is becoming fashionable in academic circles to speak of evolution. Indeed, cosmologists have encouraged the rest of us to join in the fun of speculating about it. Perhaps most of us have been doing this all along, only covertly, and this kind of secrecy is dying.

We do not pretend that the concepts of development and evolution are the same. We do suggest, however, that they have elements in common, and that if we pay attention to these elements we might illuminate our understanding of the concept of development. The idea of the evolution of the universe alerts us to see development written into the cosmos, to see it as a force in everything, to see ourselves as the embodiment of development, to see the idea of development itself under development. Perhaps development is the central force of the universe, perhaps not. Just what the utility of this kind of thinking is remains to be seen. Our attempt, at any rate, is to open up the concept so that we might use it to reach outward in space and time if we so desire.

The concept of development came to be narrowed down in its continuing association with the scientific-industrial revolution. Stating the same idea in game terms, society has been playing SHELL GAME with the concept of development: useful as it was for the construction of the scientific-industrial revolution, we have clung to the same view of development associated with that revolution, and that view has become an end in itself. Conquest of the material environment has reinforced the idea of economic development as the key way of understanding development; that in turn has led to greater material conquests; and so on in a VICIOUS CIRCLE game.

A Materialistic View of Power

This leads to a materialistic view of power and social change, a view which is no less dehumanizing than what its proponents often complain about. The Marxian and neo-Marxian views of power are examples. To oversimplify vastly, power is seen as something which already is somewhere, and the key question becomes, who has the power? The question is answered on the basis of position in relation to structures of society, economic ones for Marx and other kinds of hierarchies as well for Mills and Dahrendorf.[3]

It may be useful to ask different questions as well as to answer the above question differently. Instead of assuming that power already is somewhere, we need not fall into this all-or-none Aristotelian linguistic trap. *Some* power already exists, but perhaps our most pressing priority should be to create additional power. Suppose that the elites of the world are trapped in their own personalities as well as a set of social structures pushing us all to destruction. Suppose no set of individuals or groups presently has the power to prevent the decay of cities, stop wars from becoming more dangerous for all of us, do something about reducing mental illness, prevent pollution from becoming more and more of a killer, create educational systems which do not stifle the potential creativity of students, and create societies which do not stifle man's potentialities.

As for the question of who has the power, the big push toward equality in most radical movements—such as the black revolution, women's liberation, and the student revolt—leads once again to a materialization. If I have a loaf of bread and someone else demands an equal share, then I have only half a loaf left. One man's gain tends to be another's loss where material things are concerned. Such movements, concentrating on the existing pie of rewards, act in zero-sum terms as distinct from multiple-sum terms. The multiple-sum model is intangible. Two people can learn from one another, love one another, help one another. They can both gain, as distinct from one gaining at the other's expense. The total pie of rewards is expanded, requiring an orientation into intangibles, to that which is not yet but might be.

An emphasis on equality does not preclude an attempt to expand the total rewards. The problem is that we tend too easily to fall into SHELL GAME, emphasizing the former at the expense of the latter. If we can keep both in view simultaneously, however, then we will be free to apply the approach which makes the most sense in a given situation. People who are very poor and sick must first get a better share of material things before they are able to develop in other ways. However, if they learn, while they get their bigger slice, that size of slice is more important than anything else, then they will not be able to take the next step. This is analogous to narrowing the concept of development to economic development in the context of the scientific-industrial revolution.

This may be illustrated by the industrialization process of the third world, the nations that have not yet attained very much economic development. When they proceed—whether under capitalist, socialist, or mixed auspices—toward economic development without a broader vision of development in mind, they frequently inherit the ills besetting the first and second worlds: pollution of waterways, erosion of land, destruction of forests, breakup of the indigenous culture, urban slums, growth of inequality, introduction of repetitive tasks, and so on. Would it be possible, as an alternative, to offer them—and ourselves—a vision of life with the material benefits of the industrial revolution but without its negative consequences?

Human Development

In attempting to construct a broader concept of development, we make use of a wheel metaphor. The different spokes each illustrate the process of accumulation, where we are attempting to build each spoke up, making it longer and longer. Instead of our previous concern with only one beaker, we are now concerned with multiple spokes, all of which must relate to one another in certain ways in order to move together. If the spoke of physical science and technology is very far ahead of the spoke of social science and technology, then the irregular rim will send the wheel crashing down each time it turns. Balanced growth among the various spokes is required.

Applying this metaphor to the concept of power, a zero-sum or SCARCITY orientation implies a wheel of power which does not expand. Suppose that changes in the environment, such as a revolution of rising expectations, require the wheel to move more rapidly from place to place to function effectively. The result of a wheel that remains the same size in such circumstances is that man loses power to control his fate.

Putting these two illustrations of the wheel metaphor together, we conceive of events since the industrial revolution as producing both an accelerating environment and a very unbalanced wheel which is relatively fixed in size. The result is increasing difficulty for man to control his movement across the terrain. Man requires the kind of broad orientation which enables him to send out spokes in every direction, and to monitor the length of the spokes relative to one another. The game language can help with both, because of its threefold emphasis on head, heart, and hand, because it is gradational in nature and points directions for the future, and because the systematic relationships among the various game dimensions provide a guide for monitoring the length of the spokes relative to one another. *But the game language is little more than a crutch designed to aid the individual in using ordinary language in the same way.*

Can this wheel metaphor be useful in answering some of the basic questions relating to human development? How are we to tell whether or not a given action is developmental? For example, we might note the KNOWLEDGE game being played by modern physical science, but we might also note the CONFORMITY game which scientists tend to learn, illustrated by the rarity with which they question the basic assumptions in their discipline. Is CONFORMITY nondevelopmental and AUTONOMY developmental? Suppose that, without that kind of conformity, scientists would not have been able to go as far in their KNOWLEDGE game. And suppose that the situation today is different, that we are saturated with trivial ideas that are being tested and retested, and that what we require more than anything else are new and better ideas. Or perhaps some CON-FORMITY is essential for a given individual who is attempting to gain leverage from his environment in order to communicate powerful ideas, but it may not be needed by that same individual a short time later.

What we are doing is applying the game of SITUATION ETHICS to the idea of development, as distinct from COWBOYS AND INDI-ANS, refusing to judge the developmental or nondevelopmental aspects of any given situation without an understanding of its spatial and temporal context. For a long time we have thought, for example, that finer and finer specialization was leading toward an ever more rapid development of science and industry. However, questions are now being raised which compare that kind of specialization to that of the dynosaur, whose tiny brain could not adapt to changing environmental conditions. Given the need for a detailed understanding of context, it would seem that we are not able to assess, with any degree of finality, the developmental character of any instance of human behavior. Indeed, the context of a phenomenon stretches out —even if only thinly—to all other phenomena, and we shall always have more to learn about the context of that phenomenon. We have evidence for this in the continuing rewriting of history, based on new insights and new information.

The wheel metaphor alerts us to context by pointing up the intimate relationship among the length of the various spokes. Just how the head is being developed affects heart and hand, and vice versa. One spoke is not enough, nor is a number of spokes which are stunted and no longer grow. A wheel is a system of spokes, and if we want to get from one place to another it is the entire system which must be advanced. Physical science development is dampened by deficiencies in the development of social science, just as the early post-industrial man's rejection of science tends to set up an internal conflict between his head and heart.

INDIVIDUAL AND SOCIAL DEVELOPMENT

The scientific-industrial revolution is producing not only a narrow concept of development, but also is producing an emphasis on the development and power of social systems more than on individual or personality systems.

The industrial revolution marked an acceleration of events which could no longer be so readily explained as the product of this king or that pope. All social forms were being overturned in ways which made little sense to many. Changes had a way of gaining momentum and producing results not intended by the agents of change. Man somehow had lost control to anonymous forces like the market mechanism, forces far more powerful than individuals or governments. Sociology emerged at least partly in response to a search for meaning in a world that no longer made sense. If social forces more than specific individuals were somehow responsible for events, then they must be laid bare. And what better way to do it than with the method of science, which seemed to be so effective in dealing with the physical universe?

It was taken for granted that the scientific method, narrowly interpreted as an emphasis on testing or verification by a community of scientists, was fruitful for understanding human behavior. And it also was understood that the "great man theory of history" or the "psychological interpretation of events" tended to be much inferior to an emphasis on the power of social systems to shape man's world. The particular type of social system which was increasingly recognized as the dominant one in modern life was the bureaucratic economic organization or, more generally, the bureaucratic organization, characterized by its hierarchy and division of labor.

To summarize, we suggest that the scientific-industrial revolution set in motion a series of forces which gave impetus to certain ways of viewing development. In the previous section, we took up the materialistic view of development. In this section we touch on the great emphasis on the power of social systems, especially bureacracies, supposedly validated by sociology and other social sciences. As an alternative to this emphasis, we might think of extending our knowledge of complex events to emphasize the personality system as well as the social system.[4] The basic thrust of social science has been on the ways in which man is shaped by his social and cultural environment, just as in an earlier day he was being shaped by his biological environment. But if man is shaped, he in turn shapes. We can draw a loop from man to society on the other side of the loop from society to man. This emphasis need not be seen as detracting from the importance of the social system.

Action follows ideas, and it should be no surprise that, if it is widely thought that social systems are far more powerful than personality systems, society will be constructed around this idea. The powerlessness of the individual will become a social fact in addition to an idea. Social systems will be created which will perpetuate powerlessness, and they will come to be seen as necessary and right because they are in accord with a fact of nature. For example, bureaucratic forms of organization, with their hierarchies and division of labor, are predicated on the "fact" that the individual can only do one kind of thing, and that very few people are gifted with high abilities. This form of organization has been seen as successful, and this interpretation has stood in the way of the development of alternatives to bureaucracy. Yet it may be true that bureaucracy constricts man's chances for developing self and society.

Charles Reich, in *The Greening of America,* documents a similar thesis. The Big Government and Big Labor created during Roosevelt's New Deal era to protect workers from exploitation by management, and to protect society as a whole from the weaknesses of laissez-faire capitalism, have become Frankensteins. Man is now at the mercy of huge bureaucracies such as the military, but these institutions are proving daily their hopeless inadequacy in dealing with world problems. There is afoot a rapid, comprehensive, and profound shift toward a new kind of society, one which we can see even now in youth culture. If industrial society is characterized by Consciousness II, a mentality based on inherent SCARCITY and on the social system as the central force in society, then post-industrial society is characterized by Consciousness III, a mentality accustomed to the games of INFINITY and AUTONOMY. The young American travelling abroad today tends to have little money, few plans, much spontaneity, and great faith in himself and human nature. This contrasts with the filled wallets, careful planning, worried looks, and suspicion of the uptight generation.

Reich's book has been severely criticized as being hopelessly naive, as not taking into account the economic and political facts of life, and as overemphasizing the importance of what is merely style. Yet perhaps it is the critics who are naive, whose dichotomous view of power—those holding the reins of government versus those who do not—prevents them from seeing the implications of, say, the women's liberation movement.

It is easy to understand much of the basis for this criticism by referring to the above discussions of development. If the students of power and change emphasize the material as distinct from the intangible—placing them in Consciousness II more than Consciousness III —then it becomes difficult for them to understand the cogency of Reich's thesis. If power is seen as based on position in societal hierarchies, then it is hard to understand the power inherent in a changed consciousness. And if the group or social system is felt to be the basic force operating in society, then the stylized performances of individuals or even isolated communes appears to be so much posing. The Consciousness III kind of politics is seen as a kind of theatre as distinct from genuine politics, to be evaluated on its artistic rather than its political merits.

There is a great deal of knowledge produced by academia which should alert us to the importance of Reich's thesis. We can even go back to Bacon's view that knowledge is power. We can go back to Max Weber's concept of legitimation[5] and see it in the context of modern exchange theory in sociology. In this approach, the individual exerts power over the group to the degree that he is able to legitimate himself in their eyes via the rewards and punishments he can produce. And if he is able to develop a life style which offers possibilities for personal fulfillment and a sense of meaning, then that may be an important reward in the modern alienated world.

SCIENTIFIC DEVELOPMENT

With respect to social science in our industrial era, Charles Hampden-Turner in *Radical Man* sets forth the thesis that social scientists have been using a "borrowed toolbox," borrowed from the physical sciences and inappropriate for understanding human behavior.[6] The result is the construction of a "conservative man" built into the tools social scientists use. The tools are predicting and controlling ones, and they demand predictable and controllable human beings. The interaction between scientist and subjects is a hierarchical one, and passivity is demanded. Subjects, furthermore, are not involved in any of the decision making occuring throughout the scientific process. They tend to be treated as things to be pushed around more than as human beings. All of this is in the name of a scientific method borrowed from those who have been dealing with inanimate objects.

The scientific method as it is widely conceived appears not only to castrate its subjects but to castrate the scientists themselves, just as any hierarchical system tends to imprison both masters and slaves in its distorted view of man. A classic study of a Western Electric plant[7] produced a concept, the "Hawthorne effect," which illustrates this process of self-castration. A group of women were studied under a variety of physical conditions, and it was learned that their rate of productivity kept rising under almost all changes of conditions; productivity went up when lighting was improved, but it went up even further when illumination was decreased.

The interpretation made was that the special status of the women —as the focus of important research—induced them to attempt to live up to what they felt was expected of them, namely, exemplary performance. Here was a process of "investigator effect," that is, impacts of investigators on subjects in unforeseen ways. In the physical sciences this kind of occurrence is called the Heisenberg principle of indeterminacy. In the world of subatomic particles, when the scientist attempts to determine the position and velocity of a particle, he "sees" it by hitting it with photons of light, but that impact in turn changes the initial position and velocity. The Hawthorne effect is by no means unique to the Western Electric studies. In every situation involving investigators and subjects, the latter have some kinds of preconceptions about the goals of the former, and they tend to behave on the basis of those preconceptions, preconceptions which are almost invariably unknown. The most common form of behavior is conformity. In one experiment, for example, subjects administered what they thought were lethal doses of electricity to other subjects, all the while hearing what sounded like the death agonies of the others, and all at the command of the scientist.

The scientific reaction to the detection of the Hawthorne effect in the Western Electric studies was to treat it as a kind of error, and to try to "control for it" in subsequent studies. In common scientific practice, for example, interviewers attempt to "control for" their impacts on interviewees by adopting a "value-neutral" stance, that is, by not reacting to respondent's behavior with approval or disapproval. Such "controls," of course, simply change the *kinds* of uncontrolled ways in which interviewers affect their subjects; if the interviewer appears passive, he will tend to induce passivity in a conformity-oriented interviewee.

By attempting to control for investigator effect, the social scientist sweeps under the rug the most powerful impacts he has on human behavior instead of harnessing that energy and using it for humanistic purposes. If investigator effect is both unavoidable and powerful, then it can be examined in its own right as an important experiment, providing that the social scientist is willing to treat it in this way. And one way of harnessing it humanistically is to let the subjects in on the decision making throughout the entire research process, treating them as co-investigators.

This kind of proposal is not new, but it tends to be viewed as something associated with problem solving more than science. The key argument advanced is that knowledge of the researcher's aims on the part of subjects will bias their responses, and the investigator will not be able to uncover the truth. In answer, we may argue that responses are inevitably biased by the preconceptions of the subjects. The choice is not between bias and lack of bias but, rather, between undetected bias and open knowledge of the direction and force of the investigator effect. It is the former which constitutes bias; the latter can be taken into account in the conclusions of the scientist, since it is at the level of awareness. On the more positive side, the scientist gains greatly in knowledge by making the subjects co-investigators. And to complete the process, he might make himself a subject, and in this way investigate the ways in which his own preconceptions affect the research process.

In addition to the creation of research methods which are frequently inhuman, the community of scientists also has produced concepts which have the same effect. This might be expected, derived as they are from the methods discussed above. From those methods emerges an image of man as a limited thing, a creature of habit and circumstance, a passive player of roles, a conformist, a being with limited ability to alter his environment. An example is the concept of intelligence, perhaps the most confining prison man has succeeded in creating for himself. The central implication is that intelligence is essentially fixed throughout life. This idea is now widely accepted throughout society, supposedly sanctioned by the god of science, notwithstanding emerging evidence to the contrary.[8] Teachers at all levels, and parents as well, tend to classify youth—and themselves—on the basis of intelligence, and the result is a fulfillment of their prophecies. Who can estimate the damage done to human aspirations and achievement as a result of this single concept?

Thus far we have discussed what may be symptoms associated with the disease afflicting modern science more than the disease itself. In our estimation, that disease is a narrowness of vision which results in a focus on proof or verification more than discovery or creativity, on what is external to the scientist more than on what is inside him or on the interaction between internal and external, on what is material or easily observable more than on what is intangible, and on setting up a hierarchical relationship between researchers and subjects. The hierarchical relationship has the inhuman effects to which Hampden-Turner refers in *Radical Man*. The emphasis on proof blinds the scientist to the possibilities for discovery in the Hawthorne effect, if we would recognize it as a powerful force for social change which we hardly understand instead of treating it as an unwanted visitor who gets in the way of our verification procedures. Furthermore, by failing to be alert to the processes within himself, the scientist fails to control for an important set of factors within the context of verification, and fails to explore the territory which harbors the secrets behind his own creativity.

The task of constructing an alternative approach to the scientific method not afflicted by this disease is not a small one. It is, perhaps, comparable to the task of constructing a form of organization which represents an alternative to bureaucracy, one which is both more effective and more humanistic. Perhaps both tasks are interrelated, for such an organizational structure might provide the scientific community with a model for scientific communication among themselves and with others.

This task might well begin by applying the idea of development to the scientific method. Instead of looking at this method as something holy and unchangeable, as most of us do, we might see it as a phenomenon which was a product of societal forces and which has been changing just as have the various social systems in society. We might then proceed to examine the contexts in which it seems to have been effective and ineffective, humanistic and inhuman, creative and stultifying. With that kind of information, we can begin to chart possible ways of developing the scientific method beyond its present state.

In our view, future generations will look at ours as pre-scientific. Any statement we make about living things or other phenomena will seem to them to be incredibly superficial, devoid of context, limited to few factors, bare of the complex feedback relationships involved, narrowly limited in scope to one or a part of one discipline, omitting information on the scientist making the statement. We believe that this will change, perhaps more rapidly than any of us can imagine.

SOCIAL STRATIFICATION

Thus far, our focus within this chapter has been on the idea of development. Our task in this section is to trace the impact of social stratification on the individual and society, and then to explore alternatives to social stratification systems with the aid of our broadened concept of development.

Social stratification is based on "social differentiation." This phenomenon is nothing more than that of classifying people into two or more categories, such as male and female, or upper class, middle class, and lower class. Every time we apply adjectives to people—intelligent, stupid, strong, weak, beautiful, ugly, uptight, spontaneous—we are placing them in categories and, thus, illustrating the process of social differentiation. Some types of categories are emphasized much more than others by the people in a given society. Thus, the sociologist studying American society might pay special attention to occupational, income, age, sex, and ethnic categories. Because of such special attention, norms and values to be found among people categorized in these ways tend to vary a good deal: society expects different things from adults than it expects from children, and members of these categories learn to expect different things from themselves.

There is, then, a rather close relationship between the language of a given society and the social category systems it sets up and emphasizes. If the language emphasizes either-or communication, focusing on the static classification of phenomena, then we can expect that people will be so classified, and that these classifications will assume a great deal of importance. For example, the titles "Mr.," "Mrs.," "Miss," and "Dr." precede an individual's name, assuming a position of utmost prominence. They indicate that these characteristics of people are quite important: sex, age ("Mr." is distinguished from "Master"), marital status, and occupation.

Society does more than simply differentiate people: it evaluates them as well. Individually, there is a great deal of variation in these evaluations, but there is also a fair degree of agreement. Thus, there is a general tendency to see a "Mr." as more powerful than a "Master," and to see a "Dr." as having more status than a "Mr." Whenever a set of social categories is evaluated in some hierarchical way by a society, we refer to this as the phenomenon of social stratification. The relation between the emotional loading of adjectives applied to people and the existence of social strata may be seen. As human beings, we feel as well as think. The head categorizes, and the heart evaluates. We have our own goals, and we tend to relate to people on the basis of these goals. If we—individually, or as a society—are interested in material wealth, then we will pay close attention to the income of others, and we will set up social category systems based on wealth or income.

In addition to the head and the heart, there is the hand. People differentiate themselves and one another, they evaluate, and they also may have a degree of social mobility, that is, they may be able to move from one category in a given social category system to another. They may have great difficulty in accomplishing this with respect to sexual or racial categories and less difficulty where categories are defined in monetary or educational terms. Movement may be difficult to the degree that the categories are seen as fixed or static and are evaluated very differently, and thus we have once again a relation between language and the nature of the social category systems in society.

As for the impact of social stratification, we shall begin somewhat indirectly by summarizing an experimental study of a group of students.[9] This will give us the basis for an overview of the impact of social stratification systems in industrial society. The leap from the small study to such broad implications is certainly a large one, yet we do not claim to be playing TRUTH. At this point, we are more interested in developing new ideas than in rigorously testing old ones, in the context of discovery more than in the context of verification. This is in keeping with our discussion of scientific development, where the over-emphasis on verification at the expense of discovery was noted.

One hundred twenty-four undergraduates from Boston University's School of Public Communication were given a bogus aptitude test for graduate school. The test was designed so that, just at the point when the students felt they were doing very well, they hit a series of questions which generally convinced them that their aptitude was poor. Prior to the test two pieces of information had been obtained from each student: (1) his degree of prejudice against Puerto Ricans, and (2) whether he tended to evaluate his performance relative to the performance of others (relative evaluation), or relative to his own previous performances (self-evaluation). At the conclusion of the aptitude test, degree of prejudice against Puerto Ricans was again measured. The result was that the relative evaluators increased their prejudice against Puerto Ricans following their failure on the aptitude test, but the self-evaluators did not.

What seems to have occurred is that the relative evaluators reacted to the frustrating situation with increased prejudice against Puerto Ricans. This is in accord with a well-known Freudian theory that aggression is based on frustration; we may consider prejudice to be a type of aggression. But the self-evaluators tended not to act in this way. Why? Going back to the relative evaluator, the experimentor may be seen as having played SEE-SAW against the participants in the study, pushing them down via the frustrating situation he set up. The relative evaluators could recover some of their lost self-esteem by pushing vulnerable individuals down, and they played SEE-SAW against Puerto Ricans. They saw no other way of making up for what had happened to them. They were in SCARCITY in the metaphorical sense of a fixed fulcrum on the see-saw. The self-evaluators, by contrast, were not tied to a fixed fulcrum which translated losses by others into personal gains. If others were to suffer, that would not necessarily help them. They could more easily envision a STAIRWAY or path which could take them out of their frustrating situation and into situations where they could continue to develop.

This study is suggestive of what goes on within society in general. We begin with a parallel between the frustration produced in the experimental situation and the SCARCITY structured into society as a whole via its multitudinous stratification systems. For example, high status is inherently a scarce commodity, for it is accorded only to a minority of individuals within a given social system. Stratification in society is bureaucracy writ large: a grid pattern is created with its numerous hierarchies. People are evaluated with respect to their positions within the grid. And since the pie of status or power is seen as fixed, only some powerful or high-status people are permitted. Even these are seen in such a light on only a limited number of hierarchies; almost no one does very well on a great number of hierarchies. We all carry on our backs the burden of occupying lowly cells within a variety of social stratification systems (sets of categories arranged hierarchically). The greater the degree of social mobility for a given hierarchy, the easier it becomes to move up and down that hierarchy. But social mobility, although it has increased in general as we move from pre-industrial to post-industrial society, is still limited.

Another parallel exists between relative evaluation in the experiment and CONFORMITY in society, whether that conformity is based on tradition-direction, other-direction, or inner-direction (conformity to one's own rigidly fixed beliefs). In a society which is predominantly an A society, conformity will generally be to a SCARCITY orientation, once again helping to produce the fixed fulcrum of the see-saw. The self-evaluators, by contrast, will be playing AUTONOMY to a greater degree. They tend not to depend on some external standard, or on a rigid internal standard, but on a flexible internal standard which can be adapted to the characteristics of any given situation. If they have been frustrated by the SCARCITY games of society, they would be likely to see paths which could lead them toward overcoming them. They are not limited—in their efforts to achieve self-esteem—to the reaction of playing SEE-SAW or aggressive games.

If our analysis is correct, then aggression is structured within society via its SCARCITY and CONFORMITY games. People cannot easily envision paths for overcoming frustrations—built into society by SCARCITY games—which do not involve aggression against others. This leads to VICIOUS CIRCLE, for such aggression tends to create further SCARCITY and leads, in turn, to further aggression. The root of the problem is the inability to construct STAIRWAYS or paths which would lead to DEVELOPMENT where the gain of one is not another's loss (movement toward INFINITY). It is within this context that we now return to the earlier portions of this chapter where we discussed a broad view of human development. What we seek are paths toward restructuring society so as to progressively eliminate the games of SEE-SAW and construct games of STAIR-WAY.

In our discussion of power and development we saw some of the implications of a view of development that is limited to the economic sphere. Power is seen as a fixed pie as distinct from an expanding pie, and there is little thrust to develop power in other than economic or materialistic ways. In the ensuing discussion on individual and social development we noted another aspect of the concept of development which narrows its range of application: its application to the social system as distinct from the individual. And in our discussion of the idea of development as it applies to science, we noted a general failure to emphasize the process of discovery or creation and, behind that, a failure by the scientist to look into himself.

We submit that behind this narrow view of development, as expressed in the contexts of power, the social system, and science, are the same forces which gave rise to the social stratification systems of society. Furthermore, we believe that these forces can be altered to yield both a broader view of development and societies without the kind of social stratification we know today. To state the matter more accurately, we believe that there are evolutionary processes at work creating this alteration, and that man is the prime agent of these processes.

The close relationship between language and social stratification should give us an inkling about the nature of these forces. Language tends to be dichotomous or categorical as distinct from gradational. Phenomena are located in a given category, and it is difficult for us to envision processes which might take them from one category to another. In the same way, we learn to categorize people, and we have difficulty in seeing them in ways other than as members of categories who do not alter their location within those categories. This is illustrated not just by the social stratification systems of society as a whole, and not simply by the bureaucratic organization of our various social systems, but also by the way people tend to relate to one another in general. We learn to petrify people by seeing them as roles more than as developing human beings, as members of stereotyped categories more than as unique individuals.

We see social stratification systems in society already in existence with the origin of man, developing out of the SCARCITY games to be found in a pre-industrial environment. As man learned to make use of his symbolic capacities he found, more and more, that he was not a helpless prisoner of a biological organism and a physical environment. More and more he learned how to alter his ideas to adjust to his environment and, in addition, to control that environment. But man's language was very crude. Its dichotomous thrust tended to immobilize him in certain positions within society's hierarchies. There was little in the way of a linguistic orientation helping people to see transitional processes leading into and out of categories. Man had hardly awakened from a long evolutionary slumber. He was barely conscious of how he differed from other animals in any abstract way. By equating himself with lower forms of life he also created scarcities for himself which need not have been produced. First, he could never aspire to move into those elites, given the lack of awareness of process in his language and mentality. Second, these elites appeared to be of aid to him in a situation where he saw himself at the mercy of physical and human forces which could destroy him. Priests could help him with his crops, his health, and his ignorance of the forces of nature and society. Warriors or nobles could protect him from human enemies. Both could give his life some overall sense of meaning and worth.[10]

In the industrial era we see the construction of the gradational or dimensional language of physical science along with mathematical developments such as the calculus. The idea of scientific progress without limit came to the fore, and a fundamental belief in the changing nature of the environment grew. These ideas helped to produce a more rapidly changing environment, since they helped power the scientific-industrial revolution. But the idea of development was narrow, just as the new language was limited to only a few kinds of messages. In spite of this, we may note a decided shift in the nature of stratification systems. Instead of a tiny elite ruling almost the entire population, we have a steadily growing middle class and a shrinking underclass. Education is spreading, and ideas are powerful once a path is constructed for putting them to work. Scarcities are being reduced as the scientific-industrial revolution proceeds.

As the ideas of change and development are more widely accepted, the individual and society are able to take a harder look at themselves, and what they see is not pretty. The hidden, internal contradictions are vast. For example, there is the basic orientation of organisms to achieve their goals, on the one hand, and the altruistic ethic that selfishness is evil and selflessness is good, on the other. This increasing ability to look deeply into onself is based on an acceptance of the possibility of change, since the individual (or society) will not have to live for long with any ugly characteristics it finds. Such probing reveals the narrowness of the older idea of scientific-industrial progress, showing up the many inhuman offshoots of that progress.

It is within this context that man begins to search for a broader view of human development in the post-industrial world, one which can address itself to the problems created by the narrow view. The self must undergo deep exploration along with the hypocrisies that riddle society. Once again the deepening belief in the possibility of change provides the necessary security for this undertaking. And once again the changing mentality in turn creates forces for more rapid change in society.

We might describe the change that will (we believe) take place in late post-industrial society in terms of CONFORMITY– AUTONOMY and SHELL GAME–CONTINUING REVOLUTION. How hard SHELL GAME is played represents, in this context, the societal and individual emphasis on stratification—including both specialization and hierarchy—as an unquestioned end in itself, whereas CONTINUING REVOLUTION would produce a questioning of stratification and a change away from both hierarchy and specialization. CONFORMITY means different things in different eras. Even as late as early post-industrial society there remain very fundamental assumptions about human behavior which remain unquestioned, such as the possibility of CONTINUING REVOLUTION for the individual in all areas of life. In this period, then, CONFORMITY reinforces SHELL GAME at least for some fundamental assumptions, although for a great many others CONFORMITY pushes the individual to question fundamental assumptions he formerly would not have questioned.

As the individual moves into late post-industrial society the impact of CONFORMITY changes, for there is no longer any basic aspect of human behavior which is sacred. The individual conforms to a social context which pushes him toward CONTINUING REVOLUTION and also toward AUTONOMY. A strange thing happens. As this process continues, both individual and society take off in a continuing acceleration. No longer are they stopped short by some fundamental hidden assumption which pushes them back to CONFORMITY and SHELL GAME and prevents a take-off.

A basic reason for the development of this continuing acceleration is the nature of early post-industrial society. Although the environment as a whole does not emphasize CONTINUING REVOLUTION, there are enough elements within the society which can constitute the kind of environment which encourages CONTINUING REVOLUTION. All kinds of experiments in the various areas of life are going on, constituting a reaction to the narrow outlook of late industrial society. Through such a selective process, an individual (or social system) can create an environment around himself which encourages his own development in many areas of life.

What would become of social stratification in late post-industrial society? CONTINUING REVOLUTION would be the rule throughout society, and no individual or group would remain in any fixed role for long. He would continue to step outside any role and expand the context within which he behaves. Instead of occupying a position in each of a number of hierarchies, and instead of his position in such key hierarchies as occupation and education being a good indicator of his position in many other hierarchies, he would not occupy any position for long, and we would be able to tell very little about where he is in other aspects of life from knowledge of his situation in any one aspect.

Since the various pies of whatever is desired are expanding, we have upward movement of society as a whole along the various developmental stairways, as distinct from the late industrial situation of downward mobility along with upward mobility. Of course, even in the late industrial era (and early industrial as well) we have experienced a general rise in the stratification system as a whole, with an increasing proportion of individuals occupying middle-class positions as an illustration of this.

Would it be fair to say that social stratification would no longer exist in late post-industrial society? We think not, but it would be a very strange kind of stratification. There would still be stairways or hierarchies among the various individuals in society, depending on how well developed they were along any given stairway. But the mobility upward would be unimaginably rapid, so that a low position in a given hierarchy would carry little or no connotation of inferiority. It would be recognized that the individual could rise very rapidly if he chose to do so.

As a result, the individual would be seen more as a unique individual and less as a member of this or that category, or a player of this or that role. The differences among individuals would increase enormously, since they would not be stereotyped or compressed into a relatively small number of types. Along with such differentiation, however, would go an increasing ability to communicate. Stereotypes which gloss over uniqueness would be replaced by abilities to probe deeply into uniqueness.

As for man's rate of development, we believe that it would be unimaginably great in every direction. Presently, our materialistic view, applied to social systems and especially the scientific-industrial revolution, has produced extremely rapid change in society.

But what if each individual were able to harness forces within himself far more powerful than those located within the relatively narrow scientific-industrial revolution?

NOTES

1. For a treatment of the Hegelian dialectic and other fundamental aspects of his philosophy, see G. W. F. Hegel, *The Phenomenology of Mind* (New York: Harper Torchbooks, 1967).

2. One example of a perspective on the evolution of the universe is presented by Pierre Teilhard de Chardin in *The Future of Man* (New York: Harper Torchbooks, 1969).

3. See for example C. Wright Mills, *The Power Elite* (New York: Oxford, 1959); and Ralf Dahrendorf, *Class and Class Conflict in Industrial Society* (Stanford, Calif.: Stanford University Press, 1959).

4. The idea of a cultural revolution, based on individuals leading lives representing alternatives to existing values, is presented by Charles A. Reich in *The Greening of America* (New York: Bantam, 1970), and by Theodore Roszak in *The Making of a Counter Culture* (Garden City, N.Y.: Anchor, 1968).

5. H. H. Gerth and C. W. Mills, eds., *From Max Weber: Essays in Sociology* (New York: Oxford, 1946), pp. 78-79.

6. See chapter 1 of *Radical Man* (Cambridge, Mass.: Schenkman, 1970).

7. Fritz Roethlisberger and William Dickson, *Management and the Worker* (Cambridge, Mass.: Harvard University Press, 1939).

8. For a review of several hundred older and newer studies—which concludes that "the assumptions that intelligence is fixed and that its development is predetermined by the genes are no longer tenable"—see J. McV. Hunt, *Intelligence and Experience* (New York: Ronald Press, 1961).

9. Jack Levin, "The Influence of Social Frame of Reference for Goal Fulfillment on Social Aggression" (doctoral dissertation, Boston University, 1968).

10. For a discussion of stratification in pre-industrial societies see Gideon Sjoberg, *The Preindustrial City* (New York: Free Press, 1965).

SUGGESTED READINGS

BERNE, ERIC. *Games People Play.* New York: Grove Press, 1964. The author catalogs many of the ways in which humans structure their relationships so as to treat one another as objects or as members of stereotyped roles more than as unique beings who are developing in multiple ways. He includes descriptions of life games, marital games, party games, sexual games, underworld games, consulting room games, and good games.

FROMM, ERICH. *Man for Himself.* New York: Fawcett, 1969. One result of a societal emphasis on the power of the social system more than the individual is a societal emphasis on the worth of the former more than the latter, and what this leads to in turn is an almost universal tendency to devalue the self. Fromm's thesis is that self-development and self-love, when taken to be the individual's first priority, provide necessary bases for loving or relating deeply to others.

PHILLIPS, BERNARD S. *Social Research: Strategy and Tactics.* 2nd ed. New York: Macmillan, 1971. The attempt here is to redress the imbalance resulting from the scientific emphasis on hard facts, verification, and outer phenomena at the expense of intangible theory, discovery, and the internal world of the scientist himself. For example, there is a description of a discovery-oriented approach to computer simulation.

SVALASTOGA, KAARE. *Social Differentiation.* New York: David McKay, 1965. In this brief introduction to the sociological literature on social stratification, the author—a professor of sociology at the University of Copenhagen—presents a cosmopolitan view of the subject. He views the most viable type of future society as one in which knowledge of the forces that make societies effective, harmonious, and growing is used to ward off the dangers inherent in extreme inequality and in disorganized change.

SIX

INSTITUTIONS

If we are serious about a dynamic systems approach to understanding human behavior, then we ought to conceive of the various institutions in such a way that they are not segregated from the commonplace acts of life and not rigidified into lifeless entities. But we must do more than this, for we too easily become prisoners of the implicit assumptions on which existing institutions rest. We must challenge taken-for-granted views both of the effectiveness of institutions and of their inherent limitations, two kinds of assumptions which generally remain unchallenged.

Bart Khayyam challenges the legitimacy of a parking violation notice and, in so doing, begins to challenge the morality of the entire legal and normative structure of society. Bart is both an end and a beginning. An end in the sense that his fundamental challenge to the legitimacy of existing societies, and his vision of an alternative, carry him further toward late post-industrial man than the actions of Basil Kornish, Ben Zorn, or Ian Zenski. A beginning in the sense that late post-industrial man is, at last, free to direct the creative forces within himself.

In our final chapter we take up scientific, political, economic, religious, and educational systems. It is not enough to have an abstract vision of the future. The beakers of development must be calibrated with concrete illustrations. We must examine the particu-

lar issues within each institution in order to give more meaning to
the abstractions. As we proceed to do so, we find that the thrust
toward a null-A world comes from many sources, from the problems
faced by existing institutions as well as from the many visions of a
more humanistic world.

10

Bart Khayyam

IN NEWTON DISTRICT COURT

It was a trivial event, yet it had stuck in his mind for eleven years. It was back in 1972. He was protesting a parking violation notice at the District Court of Newton on the ground that the law was immoral unless the specifics of the situation were taken into account. Bart dug out his copy of the letter he had sent to the court:

As I saw it, the one-way traffic down Pelham Street made for no inconvenience to other cars. No one would be coming out and having to turn around my car, since no traffic was allowed in that direction. As for pedestrians, there was more than sufficient room for them to cross at the corner.

While in the bakery I saw Officer Idorval start to write a ticket. I dashed out and started talking to her, but she continued, saying something about my parking too close to the corner. I tried to explain the situation, but she did not respond. She placed the ticket on the windshield and crossed Pelham Street. I crossed the street and continued to talk to her. She said that there was nothing she could do, that I should take it up at the station. She had to write the ticket. The law was definite. . . .

But I have my own personal laws which deal with things in human terms. According to these laws, what Officer Idorval did differs only in degree from Lt. William L. Calley's massacre of the My Lai women and children, from Hitler's massacre of the Jews, from Stalin's destruction of the Ukrainians. If the law cannot take into account human factors in a situation, then the law is immoral and must be changed. Officer Idorval had considerable discretion in the performance of her duties. And you who are reading this also have discretion. If you decide to treat this in a typical bureaucratic fashion you have in your own way created another My Lai. As for myself, this letter is only a beginning.

The letter *was* a beginning. But the court incident was only one of perhaps thousands of factors which pointed Bart in the direction he was to follow. Officer Idorval had helped provide motivation during her encounter with Bart in the court waiting room. Everything is either black or white, she had said, there are no shades of gray. You can try to talk about the shades, but what chance do you have? Countries can't get along with one another, groups can't, not even families can. All you can do is let the world go along and try to raise your own family. She had said that her husband had been optimistic before his death, but that there was no longer any hope. When some kids had broken into his store she pleaded with the court to keep them out of jail, where they certainly would be coming out much worse than when they went in. Let them pay a little back every week, even if it's only a dollar, even if they never pay it all back. But she could make no headway with the judge, and they were sentenced to six months in a reformatory. The law was definite.

Officer Idorval was caught in a web of circumstance, just as Bart was, just as the clerk of the court was. He had told Bart he had absolutely no discretion on the matter. A guilty plea meant a fine, no matter what the circumstances surrounding the violation, and the Newton Board of Aldermen were the only ones who could alter this lack of discretion. If Bart wanted to fight the case in court, he was certainly free to do so. He could appeal to the Massachusetts Superior Court, and then to the Massachusetts Supreme Court. A friend of the clerk, as a matter of fact, had gone through this procedure. At a cost of 600 dollars and a number of days spent in court he had appealed a stop sign violation successfully. The clerk himself once was towed away while he was illegally parked for a funeral with his car bearing his official insignia. But he was glad he had been towed. A law for one, a law for all, that's the way it has to be.

Bart was determined to fight, but in more effective ways than a battle in the courts or with aldermen. He had been toying with a theory of system change for some time, but the impetus for putting it into practice finally came in the context of that trivial yet important event. He had known from his own theory that events are not determined in any simple way, that even when one thinks of a number of causes for a given effect one is thinking very simplistically. There were thousands, millions, even billions of factors, all coming together in complex nonlinear ways, with every cause an effect and every effect a cause. And even that was too simple, for the entire history of the universe, all phenomena occurring in the past, were connected to any given event in one way or another. His courtroom experience, as trivial as it was, somehow had managed to tip a balance within his own psyche, resulting in Bart's launching on an adventure stranger than most science fiction.

A BEGINNING

His first project seemed innocent enough. Just a small group of his students were involved, and it lasted only a few months. Sure, they were fooling around with video tape and with a computer, but so what? Weren't those gimmicks the "in" things for social scientists to do? And his linguistic approach to social and personality change certainly wasn't new, for hadn't Korzybski attempted the same thing back in the 1930s? As for his view of the scientific method, wasn't he simply joining with those social scientists who were no longer satisfied with the ineffectiveness of the tools of the trade? Wasn't this project, like countless others before it, doomed to burial in some unknown grave?

On closer examination, Bart's project was revolutionary in comparison to most of the "revolutionary" ideas floating around at the time. Kuhn had described far-reaching scientific revolutions, such as the Einsteinian overthrow of the Newtonian conception of a billiard ball universe, as occurring when the basic paradigms or assumptions of normal science are seriously questioned, paradigms which formerly were unquestioned and hidden from view. Bart's project challenged not only the paradigms on which science and social science were based, but also the paradigms on which industrial societies as well as human personalities were built.

His approach to the scientific method was an example. Bart was neither defending the traditional view that objectivity required the scientist to remain neutral nor was he attacking it with the argument that a world plunging into chaos demanded that the scientist abandon objectivity and take sides for rather than against humanity. Bart accepted a portion of each of these arguments by retaining the concept of objectivity and also advocating the importance of problem-centered research. But this was no flaccid compromise, for Bart was able to end up with an approach far more objective and humanistic than any available from the two rival camps. The investigator's goals were brought into the open, with attempts made to assess just how they affected the research process, achieving a kind of objectivity which took into account previously uncontrolled factors. And the knowledge resulting from this broadened conception of objectivity was put to work: the cognitive, expressive, and problem-solving behavior of the participants was monitored successfully. The result was rapid development in each area.

Little did Bart and the others realize at the time how much the old approach to scientific method had held society in chains. The continuing industrial revolution had been built around a method which people thought was the essence of science but which was in fact merely pre-scientific. For the failure to research the personality of the investigator proved also to be a failure to uncover the sources of the investigator's creativity. What was called "science" actually had been a hit-or-miss affair. Much was made of serendipity or chance discovery, and there was little belief and less action in the direction of a science of discovery. Bart was able to demonstrate in that project that a science of discovery was possible, and he went beyond this to help those who participated—including himself—not only to become more creative but also to learn methods for continuing to increase their creativity. It was this promise of continuing improvement by his "followers" which separated Bart's work from the breakthroughs of the past. It meant that rigidification and routinization might at last be avoided. The ideas of the "master," instead of holding followers in check, pushed them to continue to improve on the original ideas.

As for the gimmicks of video tape and computer simulation, Bart's project created the basis for taking these powerful tools and putting them to work on the pressing problems of human survival and development. Up to that time there had been a great deal of speculation about this possibility, and there had even been some nontrivial work in this direction, but the potential within those tools was hardly touched. Bart had used video tape, coupled with his deep probing into personality, as a device for freeing participants in the project from the iron cage of their own personalities. The technique was simple. The group's sessions were video taped, including their reactions to their own behavior as they watched the monitor. Along with the video taping there were discussions about how all of human behavior can be viewed as role playing, including one's reactions to a video tape of one's own previous behavior. The taping and the discussions produced an atmosphere in which each participant learned to assume that whatever script he chose to follow could be rewritten, that he could always play a different role. Here was release from the cage of personality. What resulted was not schizophrenia—a state more characteristic of a caged personality unable to cope with environmental change—but the expansion of consciousness. By learning to step continually outside of their former selves and create expanded selves, communication among the group increased greatly. Syntheses of conflicting points of view were easily developed, with each of the conflicting participants believing in and feeling the advantages of the larger synthesis.

Computer simulation had been used by Bart in a rather strange way. He had begun with the idea that each individual is continuously reconstructing or simulating past events and then is using this monitoring as a basis for simulating or mentally constructing future possibilities, all as a means of making decisions about future behavior. Almost all of this was occurring at the unconscious level, with little conscious decision making. Bart saw the computer as a tool for helping the individual to achieve consciousness of what was almost unconscious and, by being able to examine the bases for his behavior, improving his ability to learn by experience.

Although this seemed innocent enough, when Bart and the others actually started to learn how to think in the complex ways in which the computer simulation worked, when they saw their own development as a complex product of a number of changing factors connected together in certain ways, it was as if their eyes had opened for the first time. They lost, never to recover, their previous innocence about "simple" cause-and-effect sequences. What had seemed simple was in fact complex. Along with this innocence they lost a compartmentalization of the mind analogous to the division of labor in society. Instead of separating each task from every other task, their links became apparent. The result was an altered sense of priorities. Old tasks were abandoned and entirely new ones were constructed. What formerly had seemed urgent frequently became unimportant, and what had been viewed as trivial often became synonymous with the life process itself. The new mode of thinking was able to encompass all systems in interaction with one another over infinite time, and it yielded new perspectives.

As for Bart's linguistic approach, never before had there been a cumulative record of anyone's verbal behavior within the Korzybskian context. It is one thing to cite examples of how this or that aspect of one's language is A or null-A. It is quite another to record over time the many ways in which one's language becomes more as well as less null-A, and to examine the relation between this linguistic behavior and other things going on in the self and in the environment. Each participant learned to monitor his own verbal and nonverbal behavior, using this as a "head simulation" of processes leading to his own development. It would have made no sense to think in terms of complex relations among a large number of factors if there was no easy way of measuring just where the individual was on each of these factors at any given time. The linguistic approach provided the answer to this problem.

But such monitoring would have been useless unless the participants could learn to see their behavior along a variety of dimensions stretching from lesser to greater cognitive, expressive and problem-solving abilities. And much more than this was required and provided by the linguistic approach. The individual needed confidence in his capacity to move from where he was, along any of the dimensions, to the next stage of development. By learning to think in dimensional terms, however, he also learned to see specific instances of his past behavior as representing movement along the dimensions. Further development was no longer an "iffy" proposition: he had already proved himself, and what he was attempting was merely a difference in degree. Even more encouraging was an improving ability to understand how to put together the forces for development. The result was that he could expect a continuing acceleration.

Bart's initial project was simply a tooling-up stage. What he had done was so general and abstract that it could be applied to any aspect of human behavior, but the task of application remained. It pointed to new ways of doing research in the sciences and social sciences, and to new ways in which every individual or group could go about its everyday tasks of decision making or behaving. It opened up new perspectives for artistic expression based on a more complete participation of the elements of the personality in a given expressive act, and new perspectives for individual expression in everyday life. Along with its implications for scientific and artistic communication went its promise for human communication generally. The computer was an artificial brain which could be constructed to any specified size, which could think pictorially (when combined with research on the use of video tape), mathematically, or linguistically, and which stood as a servant to man's own head, heart, and hand.

What Bart and the others hardly realized at the time was that their tiny project carried within itself prototypes for many of the changes in society which were to come. Breaking down barriers between researcher and subject heralded a general breakdown of the expert society and the emergence of a renaissance man society. The systematic record keeping for each participant's linguistic behavior was a step toward increasing exploration by each individual of the vast territories of his own psyche. The project's aversion to hierarchy, similar to ongoing trends toward decentralization in society with their reduced numbers of hierarchical levels, foreshadowed the individual-centered society, with all institutions legitimized on the basis of their service to individuals and not vice versa. Perhaps most important, a new kind of individual was being created, an individual who was master of his own creative development in all areas.

The irony of it all was that all of man's potentials were there and had been for at least a million years, waiting to be released. Yet somehow man had managed through the years to develop only a tiny portion of himself, viewing that as the limit of his capabilities. There had been progress, but it had been slow. With the growth of specialized and hierarchical societies, man saw himself occupying one cell of the hive at a time, playing one role, being at one set of coordinates in space and in time. Such a narrow view was an improvement over man's being chained to the present via poorly developed languages, but it was not that much of an improvement.

Man had been too hard on himself. He had learned to evaluate his performance, as he behaved in his narrow spatio-temporal cell, by group standards which held no path for continuing development. If he played society's game, as he almost invariably did for want of any vision of alternatives, if he attempted to climb the ladders society constructed for him, he would sink deeper and deeper into the mires of conformity, aggression, guilt, fear, self-effacement, and rigidity. Society's norms had been created on the basis of fundamental assumptions about man's inherent limitations. Within such a framework, both success and failure proved to be mirages, since both taught him lessons of personal limitation or scarcity on which the norms governing success and failure were based. At the top of a ladder he had nowhere to go but down. And at the bottom he was privileged to look upward and learn how unworthy he was.

Bart's project had opened up a different way for man to view himself, a way which enabled him to step outside his cell and see himself in relation to more cells, past, present, and future. Society's standards were not so much rejected as superseded. It was what Nietzsche had referred to as a transvaluation of values. Given its scarcity assumptions society had to go ahead and create its beehive world, just as science, given its limited view of man, had to create a method which avoided any deep probing of the process of discovery or creativity. But as these assumptions became transparent, the limitations of the superstructures built on them also became transparent, and alternative assumptions and superstructures could be considered.

The beauty of it all was that there was no need to reject the various standards of excellence which had been developed at great cost over human history. One could simply aim at growth in more ways simultaneously. The model for this approach was contained in Bart's approach to scientific objectivity and human growth or development. By focusing on both simultaneously he had been able to create a multiple-sum situation where both improved ability to uncover the dynamics of the situation and increased development occurred. Indeed, each improvement depended on the other.

In the same way, the world subsequently learned that it was easier to develop in many ways simultaneously than in only one way at a time, along one particular ladder of success. The narrower approach defined success and failure in very narrow terms, failing to take into account the many unnoticed successes along dimensions not in view, and failing to understand the many reasons for any visible failure. Although man had been developing in multiple ways simultaneously ever since he had appeared, his failure to be aware of this, or of the reasons for his successes and failures, allowed him to leave unchallenged in his unconscious a limited view of himself.

Multidimensional man could view all of science and art as representing a contribution to his development, just as he could view all of his own behavior in this way. There was no longer a need, based on a desire for self-esteem along some prestige hierarchy, to curse others or oneself for failures. All things could be understood provided the frame of reference within which they occurred was taken into account. Industrial science, with its limited view of man, had to create data which supported this view of man, and in the process contributed to the creation of industrial man. And post-industrial science would also create data and man in its own image. The question was not whether the assumptions of an approach to science influence the emerging data as well as the impact of science on society, for it was a foregone conclusion that such influences are unavoidable. Rather, the question was which kind of man did the individual and society prefer to create: industrial man, or post-industrial man. Underlying this was the idea that man could be created, that man could create himself, that man was infinite.

Instead of praise or blame, man could turn his attention to integrating available knowledge from his own past experience, from the experience of others, from science, from art, from technology. There was no longer any question of his ability to do this. Man was released from the bondage of his own narrow view of himself, and as he began to try his wings he quickly learned that there was no limit to where he might fly. If artificial wings or an artificial brain were needed to help him in his journeys, he could construct them.

Bart's project opened up the possibility of man's developing in multiple ways simultaneously. Prior to that time the concept of development itself was under suspicion by scientists. Since the various ladders to excellence were not seen in relation to one another, they viewed one man's "development" as another's poison. The idea that there could be a multiple-sum path to development for everyone, and that this path could encompass multiple dimensions, conflicted with the scarcity assumptions within science and within the hierarchy-ridden society of the times. Scientists saw the concept of development used by investigators to hide their own values and foist them on others under the guise of a positively valued concept.

Bart was able to unearth the fundamental aspirations buried within each of the project's participants. His overall hypothesis was that everyone could simultaneously fill many beakers. Negative and positive stereotyping was replaced by a growing understanding of the many ways in which a given action moved the individual toward or away from society's standards of excellence. The result was an accelerating movement toward and beyond more and more of these standards.

The approach Bart took was illustrated by his refusal to jump from one topic to another, and equally his refusal to abandon a new idea. His multiple-sum orientation was to take any new topic or idea and transform it, retaining its recognizability, so that it could be applied to the topic at hand. He moved in time and space to relate more phenomena to the one in question. His was a problem-centered approach as distinct from a discipline-centered one. It contrasted with discussions inside or outside of academia which stayed within narrow boundaries. Whatever the issue, whatever the event, Bart tried to see it in relation to future cosmological events, perhaps billions or trillions of years ahead, and also in relation to the evolution of principles of evolution. He would see the event in relation to his own personality as well as those of the other participants. He would examine it in the perspective of the various disciplines of science, the humanities, and the technologies.

Each time he moved in this way, undeterred by traditional boundaries of the disciplines or of societal norms, he built more bridges connecting aspects of his own life-space and those of the participants, and the others in the project did the same. These bridges in turn gave him an ever broader framework which could be used to learn from any given event. Each event was seen as encompassing an expanding matrix of processes stretching along the axes of time and space. Just as in the cases of the transition from the indivisible molecule of Newtonian physics to the world of subatomic particles, and of the expansion from the world of Copernicus to Hoyle, each event came to represent an expanding world of phenomena. And with such an expansion, the possibility of learning from any given experience increased accordingly.

But it was not simply any particular bridge or subset of bridges which could be applied to a given event: it was the entire expanding framework, with its center on the individual constructing the framework. With a relatively narrow, static framework, the kind that was universal, events were not important ends in themselves nor important means to other ends. As an end, a given event had to compete with the multiple goals which the individual was not able to relate to the particular situation, and thus there was always the feeling that important aspects of life were being missed in any given situation. As a means, there were few paths taking the individual from the achievement of his particular goal or goals within a given situation to the continuing achievement of his many other goals.

Wasn't that, then, the source of the endless SHELL GAME everyone was always playing, the source of the routinization of all creative ideas, the endless human plateaus and the rare peaks, the barriers to CONTINUING REVOLUTION? If the individual is unable to see paths toward his own continuing development, Bart had thought during the project, then he fixes or petrifies himself at some level and looks outside himself for the dynamic of history. And if he does this in a world founded on such scarcity orientations as status hierarchies, then all is lost. For the end-in-view comes to divert him from his own development, pushing him in a direction taking him further and further away from self-understanding. The world that might have been, the achievement and surpassing of all societal standards of excellence, is lost. The self becomes an object to be manipulated toward the achievement of external rewards, rewards which are insufficiently rewarding to set free the dynamic within the self.

Bart thought back to the year after that initial project twenty years ago when his life had changed so radically. The one project had spawned two others, each a broad, trail-blazing demonstration of unbelievable human energies waiting to be tapped. They had opened up new ways of thinking about law, education, business, science, art, mass communications, religion, social work, psychiatry, medicine, politics, and any number of other aspects of society, the most important of which was the individual himself. They took the relatively abstract ideas from his initial project and proceeded to apply them in different contexts. They demonstrated the power of these ideas well enough to set off a CONTINUING REVOLUTION in society so vast and so rapid that it put to shame the earlier industrial revolution.

THE PROBATION OFFICER PROJECT

The probation officer project appeared to be innocent enough, as did its predecessor. Bart met with a small group once a week for two hours, and his students did some additional observational work in the interim. What if the idea behind the project *were* grandiose, if the techniques used *were* unconventional. Who ever would imagine that such a small project probing such a tiny sore

amidst the cancer of society could have the kinds of
repercussions it did?

The project had grown out of Bart's parking ticket. At the
Newton District Court he had noticed many offices in the large
probation section on the ground floor. Initially he had wanted to
work with those having legal training, such as defense attorneys,
prosecutors, judges, law professors, and even lawmakers, since he
had felt that they were the gatekeepers to changes in the law.
His vision was to develop the kind of demonstration project
which would move U.S. law away from its adversary system, with
its win-lose mentality, and toward Japanese law, with its
emphasis on avoiding any losers through compromises that take
situational factors into account. Parsons or his followers in
sociology might have labelled this a movement away from
Western universalism and toward Eastern particularism, but that
would have been unfair in its connotations. It was not so much
an *abandonment* of rules that applied equally to all—"a law for
one, a law for all"—as a *change* to universal rules requiring that
the context of the offense, including the personalities of those
involved, be taken into account. The parallel to the earlier
project was that instead of abandoning an attempt to achieve
objectivity, Bart had *changed* the concept of objectivity to include
the same kinds of situational factors, especially the personality of
the investigator.

As Bart had started to develop the project he began to realize
how difficult his task was. Not only was the criminal justice
system steeped in the adversary system, but so was the
competitive society surrounding it. Western society was, in Max
Weber's terms, oriented to rational-legal systems. Indeed, the
ethos supporting the bureaucratic structures throughout society
was this same kind of universalism. Fair is fair, or at least it was
supposed to be. The same rule for everyone, even if it didn't work
in practice, was a noble, moral goal. And if the poor couldn't
afford to buy justice, legal services people could help them. And
if the budgets for legal services were slim, well, things couldn't
be expected to work perfectly. To apply rules in a contextual way
smacked of immorality. The Newton clerk had been happy that
his car was towed away, because anything else would have been
immoral. The rules had to be definite so everyone would know
what to expect and could plan their lives accordingly. The
employee would have his rights along with the employer, an
advance over the old-fashioned, feudalistic particularism where
the lord had many arbitrary powers over his serfs.

But there had been a kind of fairness in feudalism which was
lost to the new bureaucratic societies. If a serf's children were

sick, if his wife had just died, if he was known to be of good
character, if the crops had failed, if his dog had died, then he
deserved different treatment from his lord. The situational
concerns of feudalistic societies had not completely died with the
rise of bureaucracies. It was a matter of emphasis. Each official
was given some degree of latitude to interpret the rules. It was
recognized that rules could not anticipate every situation. Justice
was to be achieved by tempering the law with mercy. Sentences
could be suspended. Prisoners could be placed on probation.
Young offenders could be given a chance to stay out of prison if
they learned the error of their ways. Nevertheless, in practice all
this was rarely much more than window dressing. The official
trying to break the bureaucratic rules always had a fight on his
hands, as did the probation officer who was trying to find a path
toward a law-abiding life for a youth caught in a web of law
violations, antisocial friends, impersonal teachers, and parents
wrapped up in their own fears and hates.

As Bart's probing took him deeper into the problems of all
institutions in society, he began to realize that his original
conception of the law administrators and lawmakers as
gatekeepers was exaggerated. No one group was a gatekeeper.
The gate was controlled by impersonal forces. It was pushed shut
and was held there by those forces, and unless they could be
tapped it would remain shut. Defense attorneys, prosecutors,
judges, defendants, even lawmakers—all were pawns in a vast
game where the queen, castles, bishops, and knights were
invisible.

Probation officers were also pawns, but they worked in a very
special context, at the vortex of a whirlpool of forces which
selected its victims from society and then dragged them through
the courts and the prisons. They represented society's nominal
adherence to situational factors, to the worth of the human
personality, to the horrors of the penal system, to the possibility
of reforming the young delinquent before he is completely sucked
into the whirlpool. The probation worker in the juvenile court
helped society to retain its self-image as a rational entity
working toward reformation and not criminalization, toward
deterrence more than retribution. And if their successes were
minute in comparison to their failures, well, things couldn't be
expected to work perfectly on this earth.

Suppose, Bart had thought, it was possible for probation
officers to learn how to do far more than help society preserve its
self-image of rationality and justice. Suppose they could somehow
become far more successful in communicating to the young
delinquent the kind of life that awaited him if he continued

along the path he was travelling. Suppose that they could also show alternative paths, and that they could actually help youngsters gain the self-confidence necessary to try them. If these things could be done, and if probation people could learn to do them better and better as they went along, they were in an ideal position to communicate to the various groups surrounding them: the courts, the penal institutions, the lawmakers, the family, the schools, even the social scientists busily probing the nature of human behavior.

But how could this be done? Weren't probation people trapped in the matrix of all these institutions? Wasn't this true of everyone else? How could any radical change take place if everything was so intertwined, if the solution of any problem was so dependent on the solution of every other problem? What seemed to be required was the development of an autonomous force, a force not hamstrung by its involvement in such dependencies. Probation people, like everyone else, carried within their personalities a mapping of all society's institutions, along with a conviction as to their legitimacy. This conviction was what enforced their dependency. If it could somehow be altered, then a beginning would be made toward their development of an autonomous force.

Bart had realized at the time that it was almost too late for his project to succeed. It was not even a question of there being only a short time left before the bombs would begin to fall. The feeling of hopelessness in the face of man's enormous problems and pitiful solutions was rapidly penetrating all individuals and institutions. The question of how long the human race would survive had become very real. Psychologically, man was being thrown back to an earlier age, an age when he could not plan on his own survival for any extended period of time, an age of scarcity. If man was to learn how to develop himself over time, then he would need confidence in his ability to create a future in which he could continue to exist. It was this confidence which was being corroded by most world events, a confidence which already had been undermined by previous wars and demonstrations of society's inability to cope with its major problems.

Bart remembered how he had managed to draw encouragement from the project with his own students. He had learned to believe in the idea that if a problem could be stated, then a solution could be found, even if that solution was connected to many problems in the entire world. But rather than change the world

all at once, he had learned to change the way he viewed the
world. If the world demanded of him allegiance to its scarcity
orientations, then he could learn to delegitimize these demands
within his own psyche and create an alternative set of demands.
That alternative could be a renaissance man ideal enabling the
individual to be aware of broader perspectives for dealing with
any particular problem created by a scarcity orientation. And
along with such perspectives could come specific tools—
knowledge of self, of one's language, of one's emotions—which
could help him to delegitimize SCARCITY and legitimize
INFINITY in any specific situation.

Bart's procedure with the probation group had been quite
similar to what he had done with his student group. A key
difference was that it took him very little time to reach the point
where he had left off with his students. He focused on everyone's
evaluation process: what was bad or good about different kinds of
things delinquents did and things that were done to delinquents?
A literature had slowly been developing within the social sciences
pointing up the destructive nature of the labeling process, of the
way officials and people in general could cripple an individual's
self-image by attaching a label such as "delinquent" to him.
What was not recognized, however, was how extensive the
labeling process was, how intimately it was tied to all
evaluational behavior.

As the group continued to meet, as they looked at their own
behavior on the monitor and attempted to develop comprehensive
nonlinear models of their own behavior, and as they
communicated with one another, it became more and more
apparent to all that their approach to evaluation was to
stereotype or label: "the home environment is the key problem,"
"the real issue is the state of the world," "the peer group is what
causes most delinquency," "it's a combination of the home, the
state of the world, and the peer group." Even attempts to put
together ideas expressed by several members of the group
appeared stereotyped, omitting much of the contextual dynamic
within any actual situation. But such syntheses at least
represented improvements over single-factor explanations. They
pointed up a direction: from the single-factor explanations to the
multiple-factor explanations to the system models, with their
various feedback links, to ever more comprehensive system
models reaching outward in time and space. And as the models
reached out, the realization hit home that the labeling process
not only informed individuals that they were delinquent but also

affected people in all walks of life. Students learned that they were stupid, poor people that they were failures, women that they were sex objects, men that they were insensitive, blacks that they were not quite human, professors that they were ineffectual, businessmen that they were money grubbing, politicians that they were crooked, scientists that they were passive, children that they were irresponsible, old people that they were useless. The problem was seen as related to all of Aristotelian language which, in turn, was related to a society based on SCARCITY.

The model-building approach, along with the focus on their own verbal and nonverbal behavior, was used to build in each of the participants a new way of communicating with himself and others, a way which encouraged the individual to move outward toward a wider synthesis than he had previously. That, it seemed to the group, was the only way out of the forest of labeling. The video taping had helped enormously, for it taught the group to continually step outside their previous selves by observing what they had been a few minutes before. The monitor revealed the absurdity of any fixed labeling of the individual, for what he was on the monitor differed from what he was when he viewed the monitor.

The specific techniques for communication which were developed were not difficult to learn. They were based on the technique Bart had developed in his earlier project where the group stayed with a given problem situation and brought more and more factors bearing on it together, rather than spend its time moving from one problem to another. Each thought of the individual, or each idea put forward by another individual, was linked systematically to the original problem situation, and in that way there was continuing expansion in time and space, beyond the present or immediate future or past, beyond any narrow disciplinary boundaries. The factors discussed were as specific as possible, following Korzybski's approach to indexing and dating. Instead of "the family," it was a particular family that was relevant to the given problem, a family that had had a particular history, that was at a given point in time, that had its strong points and weak points.

It was this new ability to communicate which, subsequent to the project, proved to be an incredibly powerful tool for achieving change in the surrounding institutions. Most important was the probation officers' ability to communicate to pre-delinquents and delinquents, for their leverage with surrounding institutions rested squarely on that ability. What they found themselves

doing in their efforts to communicate was setting up the same
kinds of groups that they had been part of in the project. Instead
of answers to their problems, Bart had given the probation
people a method of communication which would help them to
obtain their own answers, a method which would continue to
improve as they went along. There were no secrets to be held
back from the youths, just as Bart himself had held back nothing
from the probation officers. Everyone tried to put his cards on
the table, because what one learned by this proved to be quite
worthwhile. Here was an antidote to the labeling which was so
much a part of everyone. Instead of having fixed characteristics,
the young people saw themselves capable of changing. Instead of
seeing themselves as failures, they learned to understand more of
the conditions which produced various kinds of failures and
successes.

Most important, perhaps, was their learning different
standards for evaluating their behavior. It was not simply
another attempted brainwashing for inducing conformity to
society's standards, or else. In that era it would have been
difficult to point to society's standards with pride. The key
standard was their own development in myriads of ways which
tended to be consistent with society's own standards of excellence
but which, in combination, represented a marked departure from
the norm. Instead of valuing simply good grades in school with
the self being seen as simply a means to attaining the grades, the
individual learned to see grades as a device which could help him
to monitor his own development. The more he could learn about
how to achieve such monitoring, the faster he would be able to
develop. The grade was not an end in itself: it pointed the
individual toward the multiple facets of his own development.

One of the probation officers developed a sports program which
caught on rapidly among the others. He wanted to demonstrate
that a developmental approach to the game or to life, as distinct
from a competitive one, would produce an increasing sense of
personal fulfillment, expanding self-knowledge, and an ever
improving ability to play the game. He started with individual
sports, such as tennis, working his way up to group sports later.
Each ball represented an opportunity, and the player could
choose to focus on winning or on learning how to play a better
game. By choosing the former, he tended in fact to tense up and
actually perform nowhere near as well as by choosing the latter.
By choosing to improve, he did not thereby take wild chances.
Improvement was based on an accurate monitoring of where he

was in his learning of the various aspects of the game and, with this in mind, an effort which took him a step beyond where he was on one or more of these dimensions. In this way, the game was linked to life: he was not merely attempting to win the game, he was learning how to develop himself, the kind of learning which could be applied to any situation. This parallel between the game and life increased enormously the player's motivation to play, and the result was, expectedly, rapid improvement in playing ability along with enjoyment and self-knowledge.

Word had quickly spread about the successes these probation people were achieving, partly due to their developing interest in research and publication. Their methods became the latest fad among the various groups working with pre-delinquents and delinquents. Beyond this, however, their impact began to spread to other groups as well. Opposition to the slowness of the courts had been growing for some time, with many different groups in industrial society becoming more and more dissatisfied with the injustices of the judicial and penal processes. There was a powerful movement to shift more cases out of the courts and into the social work agencies. What the probation people did was provide a rationale for accelerating the disposition of cases by probation officers and others in the juvenile justice system.

The lawmakers and law administrators failed to realize at the time that a displacement was occurring. The sidetracking of more cases through the probation and social work people had seemed like an excellent temporary expedient, but as its effectiveness grew it became an end in itself. When it later expanded to adult offenders and proved to be just as effective with them, it was too late to avoid questioning the importance of the court and the adversary system itself. And by the time these questions were raised, the evidence had become exceedingly clear. There was no contest, and the acceleration continued. This finally led to modifications in the behavior of lawmakers, prosecutors, defense attorneys and judges aimed at paralleling the procedures of the probation officers.

The repercussions of these changes had been far-reaching throughout industrial society, for all of its institutions had been based on the kind of rational-legal approach illustrated by the judicial system. A new kind of rationality began to dawn, just as Bart had opened the way for a wider approach to objectivity in his first project. The rational individual was no longer seen as a kind of machine, wedded to a fixed set of rules which applied equally to all situations, someone who knew the truth and dispensed it to all comers, who knew what beauty and morality were. For that kind of rigidity was seen as an inhuman labeling process, where the individual's initial labeling of himself as well as his labeling of everything else within reach sealed him into a casket which smothered his own humanity.

A new kind of society began to dawn which had been waiting over the horizon for some time. A variety of names had been given to it: the learning society, the open society, the humanistic society, the developmental society, the individual-centered society, the communicating society, the scientific society, the artistic society, the continuing revolution, the infinite society, the renaissance man society, the null-A society. Its keynote was the decline of bureaucracy, with its faith in the old rational-legal approach, and its replacement with developing individuals as the basis for structuring society. Astute observers in the sixties and early seventies had noted trends toward decentralization, but they had little idea that bureaucracy was in fact a paper tiger. The steep pyramids of bureaucracy began to flatten, and the flattening process accelerated until individuals remained who, within themselves, did the jobs of analysis and synthesis.

Society provided facilities for individuals to develop themselves, just as the very old concept of the free library or the newer concepts of the free university or open enrollments. But this extended far beyond the educational system: every factory, every commercial establishment, every venture in science, art, and technology was organized in this way. Once individuals learned that they could continue to develop without limit, once they learned that the old labels which had held them in check for so many years no longer applied, there was no stopping them. Newspaper publishers began to sell more copies by expanding their letters-to-the-editor sections, then by paying for letters to the editor, then by letting people come in and give their suggestions on how to run the newspaper, then by paying people for their services. It was the old community control idea as it had been applied to the school system and the welfare system, only the idea was greatly expanded. All institutions of society opened up to provide the individual with the kinds of learning experiences never dreamed of previously. For his part, the individual contributed vastly to the improvement of these institutions.

COMPUTER VIDEO

None of this could have happened so rapidly, Bart reflected, without the third project he launched back in 1973. Its aim had been to speed up the process of change by probing deeply into the nature of those forces which were being set free, and by discovering how to release them more readily. Working with a small group of students once again, Bart began by going back to the origins of the industrial revolution. Weber's thesis, that the Protestant ethic—with its emphasis on seeing one's eternal salvation or damnation as measured by worldly successes—was the driving force behind capitalism, had always impressed him. An individual caught up in this ethic who otherwise might be tempted to focus on enjoying the moment would be dissuaded by visions of hellfire and lured away by dreams of paradise.

Suppose, Bart had thought, that visions just as dramatic as these could be created by the individual. Suppose that these visions continually increased in clarity, and that they applied to more and more instances of human behavior. Suppose, in addition, that one did not have to wait for an afterlife to experience heaven or hell, but that they were created immediately following the individual's behavior. Bart had thought of the relationship between this latter idea and the Buddhist concept of *karma,* but what he had had in mind would be seen as altering the individual's life immediately, long before any reincarnation.

Bart had realized that he was in the process of creating a new kind of religion, for he had long since abandoned the narrow and compartmentalized view of that institution. Science and art, he had realized, were the religions of the educated. What he was striving for was something more comprehensive, something that included science and art, but that carried them into a science and an art of life. Yet whatever else it would be, it would have to make the individual the supreme being. There was no longer any justification for creating anything above man, for the results of such humbleness had almost succeeded in destroying him.

The process which could do all of this, Bart had thought, was the kind of expanding consciousness which could give the individual an ever clearer view of the ways in which he created and destroyed himself by his every act. This was based on his earlier idea of giving the individual the ability to monitor his development along a variety of dimensions as he continued to act, but it went beyond that idea. What the individual did or failed to do always had an impact on him, just as water from a tap must flow into a beaker, and just as a drain must take water out of the beaker.

The hells and heavens the individual created for himself and others with each act could be described with the aid of a computer, simulated visually and shown on a monitor, and dramatized by the individual himself. Bart had used all of these methods, and the result was exactly what he had been hoping for.

Bart and the group realized that few opportunities for development were taken by the individual, and his probation people still neglected the possibilities inherent in almost all of their life experiences. Each thought, each act by the individual revealed the world of his personality as well as his environment. If he failed to go beyond what he was, that failure made his fine plans hypocritical. He was fighting himself to the degree that he failed to act on his conscious beliefs at each moment. On the other hand, the synthesis of thought and action at any given moment carried him on to the next stage. And just as it took modern science to attain awareness of the world within the atom, so it took modern social science to achieve understanding of the world of implications for human behavior within a single act. Man made and destroyed himself in a thousand ways at each moment, and it took an awareness of this dynamic to avert the destruction and to recognize the ongoing creation for what it was. Lack of such recognition was tantamount to lack of development, for it is extremely difficult to move out from a position one is unaware one has reached.

If the probation project pushed toward the transformation of major institutions in society, Bart's third project revealed that all human experiences have great potential value for human development. And the former could not occur without the latter. Facilities for human development can be opened up throughout society, but what process can give the individual sufficient self-confidence to make increasing use of them? Only in his daily behavior, in his thoughts, in his relations with others, in his relations with the physical environment, does he do the major job of creating or destroying himself. And unless he learns to continue to create himself more frequently, there is little chance for him to work up to becoming a renaissance man. Bart had uncovered nothing less than a new kind of human communication and a new process of thought.

Initially, Bart had applied the emerging ideas to educational institutions. It took the special equipment of the video tape and the computer to get an individual not acquainted with the new ideas to start thinking and acting in these ways. The result was very much like the take-off of a rocket: slow at first, but then tremendous acceleration. And just as the probation project succeeded in destroying the legitimacy of the universalism and rational-legalism inherent in bureaucracy, so had Bart's third project changed the very nature of human communication and personality.

There had been very few optimists in the late sixties and early seventies, and few people had considered themselves to be outstandingly creative scientists and artists. This kind of thing was characteristic of the entire period during which the universe had evolved. For every particle of matter there were vast amounts of space; for every living, negentropic organism, there were oceans of entropic or decaying matter; for every species still living there were the countless evolutionary dead-ends; and for every human being there were all the other forms of life which had little capacity to continue to alter themselves and develop. A successful mutation was a rare event, yet it was so powerful as to alter an entire species over time. Bart's discovery was rare, too, yet it was a successful mutation. The rapidity of its spread was determined not so much by how many adherents there were initially, but by its ability to alter the quality of life in ways universally recognized as improvements.

And just as the development of *homo sapiens* was followed by the development of elaborate languages, so too was the emerging society characterized by new modes of communication. The labeling society was no more, and in its place was a society which communicated much as Fred Hoyle had once imagined that *The Black Cloud* communicated: with messages characterizing the specific state of its own nervous system. Metaphors and similes had been a step in this direction, and so had computer languages, and so had the dramaturgical media. Actually, man had always been attempting to communicate in this way, but the nonverbal aspects of his symbolic behavior had gone unheeded at the conscious level. Once a more inclusive monitoring system took such behavior into account, a giant step was taken toward building bridges from individuals to themselves and to one another. The phenomenon of mind reading, which once had seemed a supernatural process, was understood as being naturalistic, based on the ability to read nonverbal along with verbal cues.

As Bart looked back over the preceding twenty years, he found the changes which occurred to be stranger than most of the far-out science fiction of the sixties and early seventies; for example, Hoyle's *Black Cloud,* of a slightly earlier vintage. The giant intergalactic creature which blotted the sun from the earth was a being of vast intelligence, so vast that it communicated with itself and others at the speed of light and could work on a great number of tasks simultaneously. Yet Hoyle's vision of man, as was true of almost all other science fiction stories of the era, simply mirrored what man already was. Who could have conceived of the idea that man could develop the intelligence of the black cloud, that man, too, with the aid of his computer and video-computer, could extend his own brain infinitely?

Yet even the black cloud itself was a limited creature compared to what man was moving to become. The cloud could die of certain kinds of radioactive emissions, and some clouds had recently died in mysterious ways. But there was little doubt that man was moving toward immortality as the mysteries of the human nervous system were being penetrated and with the creation of the artificial brain. The cloud, too, was limited to the speed of light, and thus its ability to move around the universe was sharply curtailed. Recent research, however, held out all kinds of possibilities for conquering this supposedly insuperable barrier. The most promising one held the possibility of moving to any distant place with the speed of the imagination, once images of the minutest details of that place could be obtained. Another possibility was to bring the mountain to Mohammed. Man's next step, after his successes with video-computer simulation, was to attempt to create actual environments which mirrored the video simulations of them by tapping the fantastic energies within the nucleus. This could already be done on a very small scale, but the potential seemed to be available for the creation of planets, solar systems, perhaps even galaxies and galactic clusters. Man seemed to be on the verge of conquering time and space, based on the continuing development of his inner space. He was only a speck of matter amid the entire universe, yet he seemed to be becoming a force sufficiently powerful to alter that universe, just as single successful mutations had altered species. And if that universe was encompassed by still other universes, or if new universes could be created, these seemed within man's possibilities to discover or to create.

It seemed to Bart that man had been such a very small thing in the past, so frail, so in need of protection for his ego, and so much a thing rather than a process. People had tried to communicate, but they moved past one another like ships in the night. They had been dead to themselves and to one another, and they had all been very much alike, creatures constructed out of a common set of labels. And with all their attempts to segregate the psychotics, they had all been insane. Their minds had been disconnected patchworks of events, held together mainly by the conviction that nothing better was possible and by their clever rationalizations to justify that point of view. Yet, thought Bart, man was still a small thing, even in 1983. Not in comparison to what he had been, but to what he might be.

EXERCISES

1. Develop an outline for a research proposal which might be the basis for the rapid development of a null-A world. Focus on whatever you are interested in, but raise your sights very high. Now discuss the project with others, focusing on the problem of how the project could actually lead to major changes in the world. Revise your proposal on the basis of the discussion. Now critically evaluate the proposal yourself from the same perspective. Can you provide answers to your own objections which make sense to you? To the degree that you can do so, you are able to legitimate to yourself an extremely high level of aspiration and thus create a major force toward achieving fulfillment at that level.

2. Take any event in your life in the past twenty-four hours, no matter how trivial, and analyze as deeply as you can why you did whatever you did. Focus on unearthing personal goals which you have difficulty admitting to yourself. Bring in more and more contextual factors into your analysis, both those stretching out spatially to forces present in the world and those stretching backward to the past and forward to anticipated futures. Now bring in as much theory as you can, starting with sociological theory, moving out to social science, and then to the various sciences, humanities, and technologies. Can you lay out a path for continuing to improve both your contextual and theoretical analysis indefinitely?

3. Get four others to join with you in an improvisational scene. The characters are Basil Kornish, Ben Zorn, Ian Zenski (the younger), Ian Zenski (the older), and Bart Khayyam. You might attempt to focus part of the scene on a discussion of their similarities and differences. Which one do you feel you can identify with most? Why? Which one least? Why?

4. Invent a game which takes the players on a stairway from the world of A to the world of null-A. You might, for example, devise a number of situations which are repeated. Each time, the players might attempt to construct more stairways for developing themselves in various ways, e.g., knowledge of self, knowledge of others, feelings of self-love, feelings of love for others, freedom to express self, ability to solve problems. Can you devise any procedures which would help the players to learn how to convert punishments into rewards? to convert rewards into higher levels of aspiration? Would your game be of any aid as a blueprint for developing a null-A society? How might it be so used?

5. If you were to think in terms of the beaker metaphor, how would that change your mode of thought? How could you learn to calibrate the beaker so that you would be able to apply this mode of thought to your everyday experiences? Do you see any advantages to doing this? Any disadvantages? Try to apply this metaphor to the analysis of human behavior, whether behavior you have experienced personally or behavior described in studies or in reports in the mass media. Does it help you to gain insights you might not gain otherwise? What are some examples? If not, why do you think it is useless for this purpose?

II

Scientific, Political, Economic, Religious, and Educational Systems

INTRODUCTION

We define an institution as a social system organized around a particular goal or value, or a small cluster of goals or values. For example, the social system of science centers on the discovery and testing of knowledge, the political system on the development and exercise of power, the economic system on the production and utilization of wealth or whatever is valued, the religious institution on the development and communication of patterns of theology, faith, and ritual which provide answers to questions of ultimate meaning and worth, and education on the communication of knowledge.

Because of its overriding attention to a very few goals, an institution tends to see the world through glasses constructed out of these goals. To illustrate, economists tend to think in terms of economic man rather than multivalent man, yielding a narrowed view of the self, a distortion in the direction of materialistic values. Man learns to see himself as a means to the end of achieving institutional goals, goals which loom larger than himself. As he moves from one institution to another he changes glasses and distorts his world-view to be in accord with the institutional perspective. He is pushed to conform to the dominant framework as distinct from one uniquely based on his own life-experiences. The narrowness of institutional concerns creates walls which not only separate the institution from others but also divide the individual into a series of cells lying side by side, one for each institution. And just as he learns to switch from one institutional perspective to another, so he learns each time to switch on a small portion of himself and to remain switched off almost all of the time.

If we enter the invisible walls surrounding a given institution, we find a hierarchy which divides the one cell into a series of smaller vertical cells. These, taken together with the series of cells from other institutions, form a grid pattern. Economic man must satisfy those above him and somehow deal with those below if he is to reap the institutional rewards. Unfortunately, he is almost invariably doomed to a paltry harvest, relative to what we assume to be his capacity to gain an ever-expanding share. A hard game of SCARCITY, whether of knowledge, power, wealth, righteousness, or status, is built into institutions. And because his consciousness tends to reside in only one cell of the overall grid pattern at any one moment, just as he resides physically in a cell-shaped room in a cell-shaped house located amid a vast grid of cell-shaped plots of land or city blocks, it is difficult for him to see alternatives to the existing state of affairs.

The scientist learns to separate his role as a scientist from other aspects of his life. As a result he gets little opportunity to apply whatever he knows as a scientist to the rest of his life, and vice versa, and the result can easily be a dampening in both areas. For example, patterns of timidity and conformity learned in the family or in social life can hardly be conducive to the bold exercise of scientific imagination. And his work as a scientist can have a similar effect on his personal life. He may learn that he is simply a very small and easily replaceable cog in the giant machine of science, with the result that his overall sense of autonomy and purpose will wither. He may learn to bury himself in minutiae as a means of escaping a view of his limitations, moving toward greater specialization.

As for the political sphere, power tends to be seen as associated with large organizations or groups, and especially with organizational elites. By contrast, the individual sees himself having little or no power in almost all aspects of life almost all of the time. Power is seen as a material entity and, as such, is associated with a hard game of SCARCITY. One man's gain of power is another's loss. Power already exists, and the relevant question is its distribution. This differs greatly from an assumption that little power exists, and that power should be created. The former view is associated with an era during which power was associated with material capital which formed the basis for producing goods. The latter has to do with the late industrial or post-industrial era, where intangibles like information come to be the crucial capital which provides the basis for satisfying other values.

Just as power is associated with a hard game of SCARCITY when it is seen as a material entity, the same holds true for wealth. There is in this case, too, a focus on the distribution of what exists more than on the creation of what does not exist. The relevant question comes to be how to get a larger, or an equal, share of the fixed pie of wealth, as with the pie of power. In both cases what the individual values is something extrinsic to himself, and he sees himself as a means to achieving this end. When emphasis moves from the distribution to the production of wealth, and when what is valued most is something intangible like information, then the way is paved for moving toward the INFINITY end of the SCARCITY–INFINITY continuum. Instead of fighting for shares of an incredibly limited pie —relative to rising demand—the rapid expansion of the pie creates a situation where one person's gain is not another's loss. Of course, the pie of wealth has greatly expanded historically. However, we have in mind something of an entirely different order of magnitude. Assume that we now know next to nothing about the process of creating wealth, at least relative to what we might know. Assume also that we can not only expand this knowledge, but we can also continue to accelerate it. The result is a situation that is quite difficult to imagine.

Religion as well as science emphasizes intangibles in comparison to the emphasis by political and economic institutions. Yet the two tend to differ markedly from one another in the games they encourage. In our view each suffers from a malady which drastically limits its ability to do very much for the individual. The overspecialized scientist imprisons himself within a very narrow frame of reference and is then unable to discover how to ask the important questions. Religion suffers from an inability to harness the spiritual forces it directs itself toward and place them in the service of human development. Each erects its god over the individual: in the one case the god of TRUTH and in the other the god of GOODNIK. The individual then becomes a pawn in the service of discovering truth, or a thing which must prove itself worthy of being alive. This of course is a caricature. Much of science has thrust toward KNOWLEDGE, and much of religion—for example, the idea of the worth of each individual soul—has promoted MAN FOR HIMSELF. Yet these efforts are merely beginnings.

Of all the institutions, perhaps education offers the most hope— although it has been the source of much disappointment—for providing leverage for rapid social change. As in the case of the other

institutions, this one emphasizes hierarchy, CONFORMITY, specialization, in short, the creation of a beehive world of bureaucratic
organization and individual alienation. None of the other institutions is any more insulated from its surroundings than education.
And yet, in none of them is there such an overt focus on human
growth and DEVELOPMENT, and in none of them is there such a
potential for CONSCIOUSNESS. Add to this a situation where a
great many youths have begun to suspect both the inadequacies of
existing solutions to international and domestic problems and the
potential for far more adequate solutions. In short, two vital elements can be located in education: a growing realization of the pitifully inadequate distance we have travelled, and an overt
orientation toward the kinds of things which may provide us with
the kind of transportation we need.

In this chapter we shall discuss these institutions in greater detail.
For each one our focus will be on two contrasts: (1) between the
taken-for-granted view of the institution's relative effectiveness and
our own view of its ineffectiveness relative to what world problems
appear to require, and (2) between the taken-for-granted view of the
institution's "inherent" limitations and our own view of its infinite
potential. In other words, we shall be focusing on both ends of the
game dimensions. For example, institutions are playing a far more
vicious game of SEE-SAW than we believe, and they have the potential for an unbelievably more powerful game of STAIRWAY than is
universally imagined to be possible. We shall negate in order to
construct, and we shall construct in order to negate. The negation
will not be total but, rather, will be selective, as in the Hegelian
dialectical process.

SCIENCE

We begin with the scientific institution because of our conviction
that the source of much of the dynamism behind the continuing
industrial revolution lies here, a source which has been tapped only
to a minute extent and which we have hardly begun to explore. In
our first topic, "reflexive science," we begin with what science tells
us almost nothing about: the process of discovery or creation. From
there we move to the concept of "reflexive science," for the investigator must look deeply into himself if he is to chart the paths leading
to his own creative processes. The result is a breakdown of the
barrier between investigator and objects of investigation and, as a
consequence, a wider view of objectivity. This breakdown foreshad-

ows a far more sweeping change in society's division of labor, which we treat in our second topic, "every man a scientist." Our discussion centers around the concept of a renaissance man society, that is, a society made up of renaissance men. Here we shall examine the implications of the idea that every man can be a scientist on various aspects of society. Finally, we begin to look far ahead of this notion, to the implications of developing "a science of discovery." What kind of a world will it be when every man is not only a scientist but is far more creative than the best scientists of the past and is continually learning to become even more creative?

Reflexive Science[1]

If we were to pose to sociologists the question of how to create or discover theory, we might easily obtain a wide variety of comments. A great many might avoid the question or refuse to take it seriously, indicating that the problem is not to create or discover theory but rather to select from among the plethora of competing theories already available. Some might take the position that theories are developed out of facts, and that the performance of empirical research with an open mind is the key to developing theory. Others might cite a series of specific procedures in step-wise fashion, e.g., "first read the relevant literature, then formulate a series of hypotheses." Still others might maintain either that they personally are not competent to deal with this particular question, which falls outside their field of specialization, or that creativity is a product of heredity and can neither be learned nor taught.

Those who would refuse to take the question seriously and would immediately move to the process of testing the various theories available fall into a long tradition—with major impetus from Aristotle—of emphasizing the context of justification or verification at the expense of the context of discovery. Those who look to the generation of facts for the origins of theory are, too, a product of a long tradition within Western civilization, one which splits subject from object and avoids paying attention to the evidence accumulated from many disciplines that man to a great degree inserts himself in whatever he discovers. Those who would cite a series of specific procedures are implicitly assuming that we already know how to discover; once we do, of course, it becomes possible to be able to select those literatures which are relevant, and to be able to formulate hypotheses. And those who dodge the question with an admission of their own personal lack of knowledge or man's biological inability to learn from such discussions are also making assumptions which may be partially or wholly erroneous. In our view, all of these answers erect barriers which separate the answerer from the question, protecting him from being pushed to define this as a problem which might be of personal concern to him. And, as a result, all of them tend to create a situation which makes it exceedingly difficult for the sociologist to learn about the process of discovery.

As we begin to view the scientist as the active creator rather than the passive observer of what he sees, as we move toward the idea of a "reflexive scientist" who looks at himself as well as at other things, the issue of scientific objectivity quickly comes to the fore. If the scientist cannot help distorting whatever he observes, what happens to truth? How can we have any faith in observations which differ from one another, depending on which investigator observed them? These are the kinds of questions which are now being raised in the face of mounting evidence for "investigator effect," that is, effects of the investigator on the phenomena being investigated.

In our view, by transforming all science to reflexive science we accomplish several things simultaneously. On the one hand we map the relatively unexplored country of the scientist's mind—or anyone's mind, for that matter—and consequently begin to learn about the discovery process. Whatever that process involves, we maintain that such a journey would be extremely fruitful. On the other hand we construct a wider view of objectivity, one which is able to communicate findings that allow for the distortions injected by the particular investigator involved. Rather than ignoring investigator effect, such a view takes it into account, enabling others to understand more fully the entire set of conditions that produced a given finding.

Every Man a Scientist

Any such movement toward the context of discovery, reflexive science, and a wider view of objectivity has important consequences for the relationship between the social scientist and his subjects as well as for the life style of the scientist. To the degree that the sociologist turns his lens on himself he in effect becomes a subject as well as an investigator. By the same token, his subjects can help him in such investigations by giving him their insights and observations with regard to his behavior, and in effect they become investigators. To achieve symmetry the original subjects must observe and attempt to gain insight into themselves as the original investigator attempts to understand them. But if such a double procedure is in order with respect to the original investigator, there is no reason why it should not be equally valuable for the original subjects.

With this kind of symmetry we have achieved a breakdown of the division of labor between the social scientist and his subjects: both are investigators, and both are subjects.[2] But what of the special talents and abilities of the social scientist, the long years of education, the years of research experience? Are these of no value? Is it not true that the investigator is qualified to do research, whereas the subjects are not? Our own view is that the time is long overdue for fundamental changes in the nature of the research process, not simply a complete overhaul. We note, for one thing, that science is still in its infancy to the degree that it has failed to penetrate the so-called mysteries of the process of scientific discovery, and it does not become an infant to press the significance of its qualifications. We note, further, that if progress on major societal problems constitutes any criterion of the development of social science, then we have further evidence of social science's infancy. Assuming that this is the situation, there may even be things about research that social scientists can learn from ordinary human beings. Perhaps, in addition to whatever knowledge of human behavior and research methods that the social scientist has gained, he has also developed what Veblen called "trained incapacity." And perhaps the layman, although he comes to the research situation equipped with his own blind spots, is able to see some things that the investigator cannot see.

Suppose, now, that the approach to scientific method outlined here not only becomes the norm but also actually produces increasing insight into the process of discovery or creativity. Suppose, for example, that by learning to recognize games such as GOLDFISH BOWL, GOODNIK, and CONFORMITY, the scientist progressively improves his creative ability. Then we submit that this would give impetus to a general breakdown of professionalism in every sphere of life, analogous to the breakdown of the barrier between investigator and subject. These games are not restricted to scientists nor, indeed, to professionals. They constitute a mechanism by which all social systems tie the individual to a narrow view of his situation, a delegitimization of self at the expense of others, and a fixation on specific ends and means regardless of situational contexts.

With this widening scope, we ought also to take a broader view of creativity or discovery, a view that encompasses ability to solve any problem (and not just scientific problems), and ability to achieve greater self-expression and expressiveness to others. With the proliferation of such abilities, we must begin to think in terms of a society of renaissance men. This reasoning is based on a simple assumption: that all phenomena are interwoven or interrelated in time and space, and that we cannot therefore continue to improve our abilities in any one sphere of life without incrementally implicating other spheres. The scientist who is interested in the widespread communication of his ideas would do well to learn what he can of the art of self-expression and communication. He would also do well to demonstrate the effectiveness of his ideas via technologies. And the more he can learn about the ways of thought and styles of life of different types of audiences, the more easily he will be able to reach them.

If we are even to begin to imagine what such a society might be like, let us start by multiplying the number of professionals in a given discipline by a factor which results in the number of adults on earth. However, if we are interested in the effectiveness of these disciplines in such a world, we should not stop there. Let us take into account the understanding that would result because of the integration of disciplines within each individual. Also, we should by no means neglect the increment resulting from increasing abilities to harness the creative process. All of this implies a society moving rapidly along the SCARCITY–INFINITY continuum, with fixed relationships among individuals—such as hierarchical ones—giving way to changing relationships dependent on the particular situation. Where each individual is learning to grow in an increasing number of directions, it is hard to imagine the long-term retention of any repetitive patterns of behavior.

A Science of Discovery

This growth process we have been discussing is based on the development of a science of discovery, that is, sufficient knowledge about the creative process to provide a basis for incremental development of creative abilities by the individual. But human beings have been tool users for a great many milleniums, and it is to be expected that they will attempt to multiply any such abilities with appropriate tools. For example, there is the computer, a sleeping giant not limited to the size of a braincase. In our view, at least the beginnings of a science of discovery would have to precede the awakening of this giant, for man would have to have some idea of how to put the computer to work to help him to explore his own creative processes. With such a beginning, however, man and computer could learn to accelerate quite rapidly, and then learn to accelerate their rate of acceleration, and so on.

To illustrate how this might come about, we will view the game language as giving us a means for translating from the language of everyday communication to the language of computer simulation with its ability to represent complex feedback relationships and its dimensional (versus dichotomous) orientation. If man is able to conceive of a hard, medium, or soft game of SEE-SAW, with the aid of a computer he is able to take into account many more points along the SEE-SAW–STAIRWAY continuum. And if it is difficult for man to understand how a number of the games he and his environment play interact with one another, he can learn how to think about the complexities with a computer. He might learn to measure the creative force he has in a given area of life by translating his speech or nonverbal communication into game language and then using the results as a means for measuring his specific position on a variety of game dimensions. This information could then become the basis for computer simulations which could point him toward those particular games he plays which constitute the greatest barriers to his overall development.

Such abstract knowledge of self might only be a prelude to the release of creative potential. Abstractions generally are built on concrete models or images, and perhaps this is why the language of poetry or metaphor communicates abstractions so well. Fortunately, man has already learned how to use the computer for graphic purposes, although such uses are not frequent. For example, an architect specifies a series of artistic, technological, and financial constraints, along with a framework which relates them to one another, and uses a computer to draw a large number of designs which satisfy all of the constraints. More dynamically, constraints are specified for visual effects on video tape, and the artist pieces together a video tape sequence which he might never have thought of by himself. In the same way, computer output could be developed to yield visual displays of those games which are detrimental—and those which are conducive—to the release of the individual's creative potential.

POLITICAL SYSTEMS

In discussing vast changes in the institution of science, we are at the same time assuming radical changes in power structures. We would do well to turn to a more explicit analysis of such changes. Let us begin with a treatment of "the pie of power," using this metaphor to achieve a contrast between a fixed pie of power and an expanding one. The former pie is analogous to a science with little knowledge of the process of discovery, whereas the latter pie is analogous to a situation where there exists a science of discovery. In a society where the pie of power is expanding rapidly, how might power be organized among individuals and groups? That is the basic question asked in our next topic, "a government of men." Finally, we turn to a greater emphasis on the contrasting cultures in a government of men and a government of laws in the topic "from universalistic to situational ethics."

The Pie of Power

Just as we might see the development and testing of knowledge in all human activities, and not simply a separate institution called "science," so can we see the development and exercise of power in every aspect of human affairs. But we are not accustomed to seeing things in this way. Schools have helped to teach us that power has to do with the very big decisions in society, and not about the so-called piddling decisions of who takes out the garbage in the family or which child the teacher calls on. Traditionally, political science has focused on the study of governments, with heavy emphasis on the national and international scene. In this framework there is a split between "the rulers" and "the people," just as in traditional science there is an important division between the investigator and his subjects. As a result, power means power over others, with one man's gain in power connoting other men's losses. We come, then, to the conception of a fixed pie of power, a zero-sum situation (where the sum of power is a constant).

If the pie is fixed, the central question associated with the organization of political systems is the distribution or allocation of shares of power. For example, an ideal of participatory democracy is that each person shall have an important share of power in those decisions which vitally affect his welfare. Two central questions are thus avoided: (1) even if he were able to obtain such a share, how useful would it in fact be for his welfare? and (2) what are the possibilities of expanding the pie of power? The failure to ask such questions illustrates GOLDFISH BOWL. We are so accustomed to viewing power as a material entity that we are unable to ask the kinds of questions based on viewing it as an intangible. Yet the amount of power available may be grossly inadequate for meeting current problems, and may in fact be expanded. The first question harks back to the very old controversy in Western society between the idea of a republic, with emphasis on an intelligent basis for decision making, and the idea of a democracy, with its emphasis on mass participation in decision making. The second question brings up a newer idea, that of political development and, more recently, that of constructing desired futures. The assumption there is that we need no longer be at the mercy of what already exists.

In our own view, we would do well to get away from our materialistic conception of power and come to see it as an ability of a system to affect its environment, an ability which is exercised by all individuals and groups at all times. With this idea we do not fall into the trap of dichotomizing people into the powerful and the powerless with its connotation that "power" means "power over others." The individual who is pushed and pulled by others is at least in part responsible for what is happening. This idea could become the basis for moving toward an expansion of the pie of power via (1) a recognition by the individual of his inadequate power in everyday situations, and (2) his construction of stairways leading to the continuing development of power.

A Government of Men

All of this is quite abstract, and we might pause to ask who takes the garbage out or which child the teacher calls on. Implicit in these questions is that there will always be some dirty work to do, that SCARCITY is inherent in human affairs, that inevitably there will be some children who are neglected at the expense of others. In other words, the implication is that our power to solve problems is inevitably limited, that the pie of power must be fixed at some point, and that that point is not far from where we stand at present.

There is an alternate view we can take, one which depends on the idea of a renaissance man society discussed in the foregoing section on science. In such a society repetitive tasks increasingly would go by the boards. Each task in a given situation would present to the individual a unique problem, and his progress in dealing with that problem would be a source of his overall development. We need not even envision such a society, but can stick with our own, in order to see the same dynamic working. Taking a reverse view, the individual's lack of progress in dealing very effectively with the host of problems outside his own special field of interest or competence would dampen his growth in that particular field. The man who is figuratively taking out the garbage most of his life cannot escape the impact of this kind of stasis on his performance when he is attempting to be creative. Conversely, creativity practiced in one area may transfer to others, provided that the individual himself sees the unity of these areas.

As for the teacher and her student, both may be prisoners of a fixed-pie situation which limits their development. The teacher may structure the situation in such a way that she learns nothing, and the student may be learning to play CONFORMITY—along with whatever else he learns—and consequently hindering his ability to evaluate himself on a long-term basis. In a renaissance man society, by contrast, the fixed hierarchies which induce stasis and CONFORMITY would—to a degree—be replaced by effective communication about problems of concern to the individuals involved. Each situation—whether it has to do with garbage collection or teaching—would be seen as an opportunity for personal development.

Of course, all of this sounds hopelessly naive to our ears, like the ravings of some Pollyanna who refuses to accept the hard facts of life. Garbage is garbage, and teachers cannot really expect to learn anything of importance from small children. Yet such views as these so-called "realistic" ones are themselves quite naive in several senses. On the one hand there is a failure to face a "fact" to which a great deal of evidence points: that all phenomena are closely intermeshed. Even garbage does not stay the same; we may, for example, learn how to recycle it or even transform it into a means of self-expression. And the situation in which garbage is dealt with varies greatly, depending on the attitude and knowledge of the individual involved, along with many other factors. On the other hand, ideas are indeed real in their consequences, and our attitude toward garbage will determine how rewarding or punishing our experience with it is. If we have not yet learned how to make it rewarding, the fact remains that this is a definite possibility.

A key idea associated with our conception of a renaissance man society is that of a government of men as distinct from a government of laws. This of course sounds like the reverse of progress in human affairs, for modern forms of government at least give to the individual a modicum of protection from the personal whims of a small number of rulers. Yet suppose it is the case that the rulers themselves are to be feared less than a total environment gone out of control, an environment in which both rulers and ruled are relatively helpless. Suppose, also, that rulers and ruled find themselves prisoners of both laws and norms which change far too slowly to keep pace with the rapid development of problems. Suppose, finally, that men can somehow learn to deal with their situation in ways which will provide an expanding pie for all. Given these conditions, a government of men—men who are developing themselves in multiple ways and also helping others do the same—may prove to be much better adapted to releasing man's potential and to solving his problems than a government of laws.

From Universalism to Situational Ethics

Actually, we do not have in mind a normless or lawless society, but one in which the laws and norms are of such a nature that a great deal of scope is given to the individual so that he is able to take into account the special nature of each situation. The fundamental rationale behind such a system is that situations vary sufficiently from one to the other that no fairly specific set of rules will prove to be adequate to a variety of situations. There is also the rationale that any human action is, in a very real sense, the product of the entire environment, past and present, and that we know very little about the processes involved.

If all this is true, then both praise and blame, reward and punishment, are inappropriate responses to human actions. First, they do not take into account the many factors other than the individual's attributes which are responsible for his performance. In an important sense the entire world shared the guilt that was heaped on Nazi Germany or Lieutenant Calley. And the same collective responsibility seems to be involved in the case of acts that are acclaimed. Second, they tend to fix the performance of the individual and his environment at the same level. For example, if guilt can be laid on Nazi Germany or Lieutenant Calley, then the United States need undergo no drastic examination of its own actions. And in the case of an individual winning acclaim, we neglect a search for the environmental factors which helped produce the basis for the acclaim.

In a society where SITUATION ETHICS was the rule rather than the exception, we would have to place far greater faith in the individual than we now do. We would have to replace our Hobbesian assumption, that there would be a war of all against all, with a more humanistic one. We would have to discover means by which the individual could learn to make decisions superior to those dictated by CONFORMITY to rules.

ECONOMIC SYSTEMS

Scientific, political, and economic systems focus on the three fundamental elements of human behavior: ideas, actions, and goals, respectively. Of course, all three elements are involved in all behavior, but it is useful for us to distinguish analytically systems emphasizing one of them. We shall begin, in a section on one-dimensional man, with a historical view, examining the processes by which values have been developed. We shall then contrast existing modes of value determination with an alternative mode in a section on social and personal indicators of value. In our concluding section, we shall explore the implications of this alternative mode for the organization of society. Another way of looking at our treatment of economic systems is that we are examining society's movement, and potential future movement, along the continuum from SCARCITY to IN-FINITY.

One-dimensional Man

If we do not mind doing violence to the complexity of history in order to catch hold of its central thrusts—a risky endeavor indeed in view of many academic reactions to people like Oswald Spengler and Arnold Toynbee—there seems to be a long-term evolution of a view of man as a creator of value. In pre-industrial societies, which were the only types of societies existing at one time and which still exist today, almost all men see themselves and are seen as contributing very little of worth to the world, at least in comparison to the elite. In feudal Europe, for example, the nobles and clergy, constituting a rather small minority, monopolized fundamental values as well as power. Their legitimacy was based on their presumed ability to provide military protection for people and goods, and to provide spiritual protection against disasters in this life and the next. In that era we might see man's orientation toward the next life as his desperate search for meaning and value in a situation where these have been largely excluded from this life.

With the beginnings of the industrial revolution and the coming of the Third Estate, legitimacy began to be granted—not without fierce struggles—to those who were able to fulfill what came to be a dominant function in society: the production of material goods in vast quantities. A "growth" cycle had begun and has continued to the present day: increasing legitimation opened up more opportunities for individuals to become involved in industrial activities, these activities became ever more effective in yielding quantities of goods, the value placed on commodities increased, these activities received greater legitimation, and so on.

Continuing to do violence to history, although the sources of this dynamism are many we can at least begin to understand them by focusing on four institutions: the economic, religious, political and scientific. Economically, the industrial revolution began to bring within reach of the masses some of the things which formerly had been open only to the aristocracy; these were things they had already learned to value, and so the legitimacy of this function was easily established. For our perspective on religion, we look to Max Weber's thesis that the Protestant ethic enabled and encouraged economic activities to be defined in religious terms, thus giving them a religious stamp of approval.[3] Politically, a large portion of the new wealth was diverted to the aristocracy, and the new producers of wealth were thus seen by the aristocracy as an asset more than a threat for a long period of time, until it was too late to alter the situation. The institution of science deserves to be first instead of last. The scientific spirit which developed has suffused over and permeated the entire industrial age. It is a spirit which carries forward the classical views of man's possibilities and seeks a continuing expansion of mind beyond all previous boundaries, a spirit which defines the impossible as possible. That spirit created the ideational basis for the industrial revolution, whether by encouraging the science that was translated into technology, the new explorations, or questioning of stultifying ideas.

Our story does not end on this happy note. Enter the villain, SHELL GAME, which erects barriers to CONTINUING REVOLUTION. In a situation where a means is of ever greater value, it tends to displace—unnoticed until the deed has already been done—the ends it formerly served. In religion we have the death of God or the death of spirituality; in the political sphere we have the general abdication of power—by rulers and ruled alike—to the anonymous forces associated with the industrial revolution; and in science we have the glorification of specialization and a positivism or fact orientation that parallels our emphasis on the material at the expense of the ideational.

Fortunately, the story is not over. Enter now the hero, the postindustrial revolution. It has taken great material "progress" for the development of a growing realization that economic man is also one-dimensional man. Returning to our metaphor of the beehive or grid pattern of society, with the rows corresponding to a chain of command or status hierarchy and the columns corresponding to a division of labor, industrial man has indeed already come a long way from pre-industrial times. Not only are there at least some channels of mobility for him to move upward, but there are also some choices in selecting which column he wants to move up.

But the scientific spirit—which is also a humanistic spirit—cannot remain confined to such narrow boundaries as that of any single cell in this grid pattern, no matter if that cell be at the top of a given column. Indeed, the top of any column is only high relative to that which lies below, but it is insignificant relative to man's possibilities. When this scientific spirit goes beyond questioning the necessity of

the grid pattern to produce social technologies for eliminating it—
just as it has helped to produce physical technologies for opening up
man's physical possibilities—we shall see the flowering of post-
industrial society. We believe that the key to such a procedure lies
in the dynamic and dimensional nature of much of the language of
mathematics and physical science. To extend this idea to human
communication and thought requires that we go beyond our labeling
orientation, which maintains a beehive society in existence, and
learn to communicate and think in terms of systems of dimensions
which stretch infinitely in both directions. And in place of economic
man, with his single standard of value, we shall move toward renaissance man or multivalent man.

Social and Personal Indicators of Value

Hand in hand with the rise of economic man there has been the
invention of money as a near-universal medium of exchange. Money
has been and is man's device for measuring the value of both tangibles and intangibles. Here, too, SHELL GAME rears its ugly head.
What can be measured in monetary terms is that which is valued,
whereas that which cannot easily be so measured is less valued. For
example, we have not arrived at acceptable ways of measuring the
damage we do to children's personalities by having a ratio of one
teacher for twenty-five children. Or we have not assessed, in any
serious way, the damage—for example, in the thorough learning of
the game of CONFORMITY—done to individuals who watch television for long periods of time. Neither have we assessed the damage
which advertising has done to our mental health. Failing the development of quantitative measures of these ills, measures which can
be translatable into monetary terms, our tendency is to give them
short shrift.

In very recent years there has been some talk and some action in
the direction of developing a series of "social indicators"[4] which
would help us chart the impact of some of the things that society
does for and against social man, as distinct from economic man. But
for this faint beginning to go much further requires the development
of measures which can compete with money in their ease of utilization, which can prove to be more meaningful than money, and which
can at least be partially translatable into monetary terms. Thus, we
might even look toward an assessment of the monetary loss to society of stultifying a child's creative ability in the classroom or in
whatever other social system we care to select. Perhaps we will learn
from such exercises that we cannot afford such heavy costs.

The key to moving in this direction seems to be, in addition to this problem of measurement, the utilization of measuring devices to create clear-cut demonstrations that alternatives are indeed possible. Values are important relative to other values, and if we have not discovered alternate means of education which demonstrably can help children develop their creativity, then we cannot assess realistically the cost of failing to help them to develop. We might even think of this in terms of supply and demand. If our supply of types of education is limited to one, then how are we to determine whether the price quoted is fair? But if we have at least two, and if we have some information on the cost and impact of each, then we are in an entirely different position.

The development of such indicators and the demonstration of their degree of effectiveness or worth might arise from thinking of "personal indicators" as well as social indicators. In the classroom we are beginning to recognize the deadly effects which evaluations by the teacher have on the development of the child's own critical abilities. We might now carry this recognition much further. We might seek actively to help the child to develop these abilities and, in the process, learn to develop them ourselves. This would involve a major shift along the CONFORMITY–AUTONOMY dimension as well as the GOODNIK–MAN FOR HIMSELF dimension. This might have the function of releasing us from the dependent tie we have to external systems built around SCARCITY and free us to move along the SCARCITY–INFINITY continuum.

The Infinity-Oriented Society

The bug-a-boo of most utopian thought is the static nature of the society envisioned. A prime example is the essential dullness of most visions of the kingdom of heaven. In our view such visions themselves are bound to a very univisionary conception of man, one based on the labeling or dichotomous orientation. It is to be expected that if "visionaries" think in terms of good and evil, then both poles will be essentially static. There will be a failure to recognize the many elements in existing society which foreshadow the future, and there will be an equal failure to see the limitations inherent in the vision.

Our own mode of thought is based on an understanding of the concept of infinity. Most of us, having suffered through a certain kind of mathematical education, think of this concept as referring to an extremely large number. A more accurate understanding, however, comes from thinking of the concept referring to a *process* as distinct from a fixed number. Within this process we can continue to create a larger number for any given fixed number simply by adding, say, the number "one" to it, and we can continue this process indefinitely. This procedure also can be used for conceptualizing the infinitesimal as a series of operations rather than a very small number.

Using this framework, our vision is one in which (1) visions of the future will constitute vital forces in constructing the future, and (2) such constructions will themselves be modified by future visions. Of course, we do indeed have a more concrete vision, but we must warn the reader that it is subject to change without notice. We see a society in which people will be able to communicate with one another in sufficient depth for them to learn to share one another's experiences. We see a society in which every man is an artist in the sense that he is learning to express himself more deeply throughout his entire life, a scientist in that his mental development in all spheres encounters fewer barriers, and a revolutionary in the sense that he learns to view the world freshly in each moment. We see a world in which the computer will become a tool helping man escape the limitations of time and space; helping him learn to live more fully in each moment as well as extending his life span indefinitely, and helping him supersede the space limitations of physical constants like the velocity of light as well as helping him re-create distant worlds in places that are easily accessible to him. In short, we see man continuing to create new worlds—and perhaps new universes—for himself and for others. And we see man, by so doing, creating new values and learning to create himself.

RELIGION

Our approach to the institution of religion has much in common with our approach to the other institutions. We saw every instance of human behavior comprising orientations to knowledge, power, and wealth, and we now view all behavior as being partly religious in nature. In contrast to the other institutions discussed, however, we do not see religion involving an emphasis on any one of the elements of ideas, action, or values, but rather a synthesis of all three. Degree of religion or religiosity, then, would correspond to the degree to which a synthesis or integration of these elements has in fact been achieved. To be more precise, we see religion as comprising theology, faith, and ritual, minus the dogmatic connotations associated with these words. Furthermore, we see it as the integrative core of any personality or social system. Finally, we see it as a matter of degree. With this view we shall look for religion in all social systems, and not simply in Christianity or Buddhism or Taoism.

The three topics we shall discuss form a rough historical sequence: Unity without Diversity, Diversity without Unity, and Unity with Diversity. The idea for this treatment comes from an essay by Edward Sapir, "Culture, Genuine and Spurious."[5] For Sapir, the "genuine" culture has achieved a high degree of integration of its various elements. In a relatively undifferentiated society little touched by the modern world—and there are very few of these left as of this date —the individual might find deep personal meanings in most of the things going on around him, and he may attain an overall sense of worth, unity, and participation in whatever was important to him. The "spurious" culture, by contrast, is highly differentiated but not well integrated, and is at war with itself. According to Sapir, modern industrial society, with its complex division of labor and the accompanying widespread feelings of alienation, provides an apt illustration. As for our third topic, unity with diversity, Sapir pointed to this as a goal for industrial society to achieve. He did not say much about how to get there, but the emphasis of his anthropological work was on language.

Unity without Diversity

If most of us are not familiar with some simple, undifferentiated society, at least we know something about the family in industrial society, if only from our own personal experience. Using the example of a relatively undifferentiated social system (relative to, say, a large modern corporation) so close to our experience will prevent us from waxing nostalgic over the glories of the simple society. As a great many people in industrial societies will freely admit, life in the industrial family is largely hell, although it certainly has its compensations. We might start on a positive note, looking at the unity involved, and end with a view from the perspective of diversity.

When the family works the way it's supposed to work in industrial society, there is a good deal of communication among the members. Each helps the others to attain a sense of meaning, worth and competence in whatever he does, and consequently aids the others in achieving a sense of unity. These statements refer to an ideal, but we have almost no knowledge bearing on the degree to which this ideal is achieved in practice in modern society, or even in simpler pre-industrial societies.

We do, however, have a great deal of evidence on the negative side, which we might lump under the heading of lack of diversity. We can start with the common complaint of the nonworking housewife that most of the time life in the family is incredibly boring, or we can look beyond such complaints to divorce rates, neuroses, and psychoses where married life seems to be a crucial factor, or the thousand-and-one other modes of escape. Or take the husband whose involvement in his family relative to his work is inconsequential, and who communicates this sense of the meaninglessness of family life to the others. And the children, who have their parents as models for guiding their own development, have little chance of avoiding the mistakes of their parents. At its worst, the industrial family is a group of individuals shackled together by CONFORMITY, with each the continual prey of his own neuroses and the neuroses of the others around him, pervaded by a sense of boredom and purposelessness, becoming ever more rigid and traditional as they learn to give up on life's possibilities.

Perhaps the modern family is a poor example of unity without diversity, since it would indeed be difficult for any social system in industrial society to achieve unity. Perhaps we might do better to have in mind the pre-industrial peasant family or community, where unity was not so easily ripped apart by the overall milieu. In any case, our modern example at least suggests that unity may not be easily achieved, and that we ought to look with suspicion at our nostalgic images. In the pre-industrial society unity may have been most frequently achieved at the expense of subservience to one individual, such as the patriarch. If that is the case, it is a large price to pay, since the potential ability of the individual—both the ruler and the follower—to lead a fuller life, to partake of diversity, is to that extent sacrificed.

Diversity without Unity

In shifting to the topic of diversity without unity, we are on home ground. Let us look to the large organization for illustrative purposes. There certainly is diversity there, but it is of a certain type. Although there are many different activities going on in such an organization, any given individual walks an Indian path in the organization, playing a given role and doing a very limited number of things.

As for unity, if one looks at the organization chart or believes the jargon put forward by many managers, there are a large number of procedures by which the organization becomes integrated. There are, supposedly, a great many channels of communication connecting the different links in the chain of command as well as the different chains—representing diverse tasks within the division of labor

—with one another. There is also provision for a good deal of group decision making, so that involvement is at least partly shared.

However, a great deal of this works far better on paper than it does in practice, and it appears that the fundamental difficulty is the SCARCITY built into the organization. Communication up the hierarchy is distorted in the interest of winning favor for promotion to a limited number of positions. Downward communication takes place in a context where the communicator is anxious to strengthen his own position relative to others above and below him, and, as a result, a norm of secrecy frequently develops. Lateral communication is very sparse, at best, given the societal emphasis on barriers separating fields of knowledge, and the little communication that does take place is achieved at the upper echelons of the organization. As for group decision making, whatever advantages it possesses may be more than overbalanced by its emphasis on CONFORMITY with the consequent death of much that is innovative. Furthermore, with divided responsibility the individual in the organization has difficulty learning how to play MAN FOR HIMSELF and getting feedback on the effectiveness—or lack of it—of his own decisions.

Unity with Diversity

Based on the above analysis, we must depart somewhat from Sapir's framework. Perhaps Sapir, and most of us, wax too nostalgic over the good society of yesteryear. Perhaps the so-called unity of pre-industrial society is something that exists primarily in our imagination, taking into account man's great helplessness in understanding and being able to deal with not only the social and psychological forces surrounding him but the physical and biological ones as well. Perhaps the so-called lack of unity of industrial society in fact does represent some progress toward unity, taking into account at least a partial development of our understanding of how to deal with these forces. And we must grant that if industrial society creates Indian paths which we learn to tread on repetitively, it also opens up our vision to a far greater diversity and far greater possibilities for us than man has seen heretofore. Consequently, it appears that during our journey from the pre-industrial to the industrial era, we have also moved—at least in some senses—toward both greater unity and greater diversity.

If this analysis is correct, then it points us squarely in the direction of a continuing evolution toward greater unity and diversity in the post-industrial era. We need not choose between the two but can have both, provided we learn to see unity and diversity not as competing forces reigning over a limited territory but as two expanding areas playing INFINITY more than SCARCITY. But this prognosis sounds more like a Sunday-school sermon than a concrete analysis of what is to be, and we must therefore proceed to fill in this overarching vision. We might do this with a very brief look at each of the institutions we have discussed.

In science we see not the elimination of specialized knowledge which probes ever deeper into a given unknown but rather the progress of an informed specialization, one which somehow manages to remain *au courante* with the most important developments in all other disciplines. This is possible if we can make several assumptions: (1) most of the findings emerging from the various disciplines at this time are extremely repetitive within the discipline as well as from one discipline to the other; (2) man's capacity for personal development has barely been tapped; and (3) man has hardly begun to learn to use many of the technologies he has created for his own development, for example, the computer and the video tape. We can look forward to a clear recognition of both the limitations of all the knowledge that already has been collected—because of its highly specialized nature—and the amount we shall be able to achieve as we accelerate the integration of knowledge. One result should be the release of man from the immense burden of seeing existing knowledge as a god, with the resulting games of CONFORMITY, GOLD-FISH BOWL, and GOODNIK. This would free him to play CONSCIOUSNESS, MAN FOR HIMSELF, and AUTONOMY.

As for economic and political institutions, the unity will come from a movement from economic man and organization-centered man to renaissance man, who neither shuns material wealth nor power but sees these within a much wider perspective. Just as we shall see the development of informed specialization, so shall we see the impact of this kind of specialization on society: a material development that we can hardly imagine, and the development of man's power to create himself and his world in accordance with his informed wishes. And if religion has seen the death of God, the post-industrial era may yet see the birth of Man as God, an idea which Nietzsche foresaw in his concept of man as superman.

EDUCATION

What could possibly be more hypocritical than an institution which emphasizes the importance of methods of teaching for those involved with children and adolescents and omits an orientation to teaching methods among those working with youth of college age; which preaches the importance of an individualized approach to education and which practices the opposite; which tends to ignore the various kinds of education occurring outside the walls of the schools; which opens up vistas of knowledge of the external world yet prevents the individual from moving toward these vistas by teaching him to accept a very limited view of himself; and which teaches the importance of knowledge and at the same time has failed to provide the kind of knowledge which can help man solve the problems threatening his very existence?

However, education is not alone among the social systems in being riddled with contradictions. And despite all of these very serious problems, if we look backward we can see progress in doing something about each of these contradictions. In our treatment of this institution we shall adopt a stance similar to that for the preceding ones: we shall define education broadly enough so that we can see it in any instance of human behavior. What we mean is much closer to the sociologist's concept of socialization, that is, the life-long process through which the individual learns, in all aspects of life, whatever society has to teach him. Thus, we see education as focusing on the juncture between social systems and the personality system. But we need not see the direction of influence going in only one way. Just as the individual is socialized by society, he in turn "socializes" society (a use of the term not common in sociology). Our treatment of education will be presented in two sections, the first more or less focusing on its failures and the second attempting to build on its successes in order to point toward the future.

"New Approaches" to Education

It is all too easy to castigate almost all of the traditional apparatus of education, whether it is that which occurs in the schools or in the home, in the factory or the church, in the newspapers, on television, or anywhere else. Perhaps even more deserving of criticism is the failure of the so-called innovative approaches to education, attempts which are only slightly less disastrous in their consequences than traditional education. These "new approaches" to education lull us with a false sense of security, deceive us into thinking that we are indeed making progress in education, when all the while whatever progress we make appears to be inconsequential relative to the needs of the times.

The newspapers, for example, give us a view of what is and is not important in the world, of how to understand what is happening, and of what actions are open to the individual, a view which is repeated in its essential form by all of the other social systems in society. The prime lessons we learn are that changes in matter or material things are important, that the world is moved by elites, and that the individual has no recourse but to passively accept the situation. Concerning the material, for example, we are exposed to visions of car accidents and burglaries, death and taxes, new buildings under construction and slums being torn down, drugs and wars, sunshine and rain, profits and losses, the poor and the rich.

If the material is important, then our second lesson is that the world moves at the behest of the rich and the powerful, that the way to solve problems is to get these elites to pass the appropriate laws, that accidents are accidental, that for every event there is a single cause which explains it, that explanations and causes are far less important than concrete events. And along with this lesson the third lesson follows naturally: the individual who is neither rich nor powerful is helpless in the face of events, he is a nonentity who at best can participate in some large group enterprise or passively immerse himself in the lives of his heroes, he is doomed by his intelligence and life situation to the role of observing rather than changing the large forces which cast him about.

And what of the new approaches to education? Much of what goes on in the "free universities" seems to represent a repetition of the foregoing views of man and society, e.g., that the establishment must be replaced if genuine change is to occur, that being poor or having no possessions somehow qualifies one for passing through the eye of the needle leading to salvation, that blacks are more worthy than whites, that mindlessness is next to godliness, that drugs should be legitimated by passing the appropriate laws, that a blade of grass is worth far more than the polluting species which treads it down.

There are of course a great many other attempts at innovation at the university level, e.g., the experiments with television and computers. The justification for the former is that it can bring to the student the best teachers who can take the time to prepare their material carefully. The problem, however, is that education has more to do with learning than teaching, and that without a great deal of interaction between teacher and students, even the best educators can hardly be expected—on a mass basis—to guide the individual students in whatever directions their own development takes them. As for the computer, we have yet to see any innovations in this area that have genuinely caught on with students and teachers alike. There are many interesting experiments, but they all accept traditional subject matter as a given and limit themselves to better methods of communication. However, if the apple is rotten, learning to eat it more rapidly does not yield much in the way of progress. As for programmed learning, with or without the aid of a computer, once again there is little or no effort to alter the content of the subject itself. Worse, there is a certain narrowness associated with this method, with its focus on what is known as distinct from what needs to be researched. Although the emphasis on the individual learning at his own rate is noteworthy, the individual needs as much motivational stimulus as he can get, and this is lacking in most efforts at programmed instruction.

As for the public schools, for every hundred efforts to develop new curriculum materials there is not one which takes seriously a reeducation of the teacher who will be using the materials, that is, a genuine resocialization and not simply a workshop to learn to use the materials. And for every thousand efforts, there is not one which attempts in a serious manner to restructure the whole gamut of existing knowledge in such a way that learning can occur far more readily than at present. There are many innovative ideas which sound exciting on paper and yet prove to have very serious flaws. The concept of team teaching is wonderful, with its promise of deep communication among teachers from different disciplines, yet it is wholly dependent for its degree of success both on a framework—which is lacking—within which the various disciplines can be merged and on an interpersonal atmosphere among faculty and administration oriented to INFINITY more than to SCARCITY. The idea of the open classroom or of the numerous Summerhill types of experiments which attempt to rid the school of its jail-like atmosphere and allow the creative capacities of the child to flower is a truly noble one. Yet far less learning frequently occurs in such situations than in the supposedly rigid or authoritarian classroom because the teachers involved generally do not assume responsibility for motivating the child to want to learn by himself.

Generally speaking, the level of aspiration of these innovative efforts is absurdly low. Indeed, innovations are not even seen as involving new ideas. Rather, they are almost invariably efforts to transplant ideas that someone else thought up somewhere else, with the implicit assumption that what is new must be better than what is old. And if teachers and students are aiming very low when they attempt to innovate, God help us when they aim at maintaining the status quo.

Education in the Post-Industrial World

We have developed in the industrial world a set of educational tools, aims, and ideas which can be integrated to provide the thrust for a new kind of world. The ideas developed in the various disciplines represent immense potential power waiting to be actualized, and tools such as the computer and video tape are waiting to be hooked up to these ideas to translate them into actual power and transform man and his environment in whatever ways he chooses.

Indeed, educational movement into the post-industrial world is already going on, largely unnoticed, and on a small scale. Much of the emphasis on early childhood education is more in the tradition of a renaissance man view of the world than a view of the world split into segments to correspond with the different disciplines. Also, there is a rebirth of interest in interdisciplinary ventures, such as ecology, linguistics, systems theory, cybernetics, and game theory. In addition, there is a growing interest in phenomenological topics, in attempting to explore the inner man, and in doing away with the subject-object dichotomy. There is, too, a veritable revolution in filmmaking, with this new creative outlet being utilized by more young people. And the idea of community control of the schools, along with the concept of the classroom without walls—an extension of the field trip idea—at least moves in the direction of bringing together formerly distinct worlds of experience. The rapid growth of adult education, along with the sometimes successful ventures of the television medium, give impetus to the possibility of continuing development throughout life.

But just what would a post-industrial approach to education be like? One way to think of it is to imagine that each individual, throughout life, would be learning, encouraged by aspects of his environment, to exceed the creative accomplishments of our most widely acclaimed individuals from every walk of life. In addition to the kind of communication which encourages this kind of learning, the physical environment itself might be designed to be responsive to the growth of humans within it. This might be achieved with the aid of computer technology. For example, as man develops he learns to reprogram the computers which help him to shape his environment, and the result of such reprogramming is an environment which gives man still greater impetus to develop.

What we have in mind is the acceleration of our transition from a labeling to a learning environment. In a labeling environment things might seem on the surface to be orderly, with people in the neat box-like compartments called houses and with knowledge in its neat categories called disciplines. Yet the center does not hold. The boxes keep things apart, and whatever is inside a given box withers and dies. As we move toward a learning environment, there is an increasing awareness that mankind has only just been born, a growing realization of man's infinite possibilities, and an accelerating force for human development.

NOTES

1. The concept of "reflexive science" represents an extension of the concept of "reflexive sociology" developed in Alvin W. Gouldner, *The Coming Crisis of Western Sociology* (New York: Basic Books, 1970).

2. Some negative implications of the hierarchical relationship between scientist and subjects are portrayed in Charles Hampden-Turner, *Radical Man* (Cambridge, Mass.: Schenkman, 1970).

3. Max Weber, *The Protestant Ethic and the Spirit of Capitalism* (New York: Charles Scribner's Sons, 1958).

4. For an illustration of the literature on social indicators see Bertram M. Gross, *Social Intelligence for America's Future* (Boston: Allyn and Bacon, 1969).

5. See Edward Sapir, *Culture, Language and Personality* (Berkeley: University of California Press, 1962), pp. 78-119.

SUGGESTED READINGS

BONDURANT, JOAN V. *Conquest of Violence: The Gandhian Philosophy of Conflict.* Berkeley: University of California Press, 1965. The Gandhian "satyagraha" is at once a mode of action and a method of inquiry. Head, heart, and hand are involved in a way which is both creative and constructive. The author presents this developmental approach to political action within the context of Gandhi's life and thought.

KUHN, THOMAS S. *The Structure of Scientific Revolutions.* Chicago: University of Chicago Press, 1962. Scientific theories rest on paradigms or sets of assumptions frequently hidden from view, just as the ideas or behavior of the individual or group constitute only the visible portion of an iceberg. Kuhn demonstrates the power of scientific paradigms both for holding in check the development of science and for providing a basis from which investigation can proceed.

SCHAEFER, ROBERT J. *The School as a Center of Inquiry.* New York: Harper & Row, 1967. Schaefer argues that the public schools must be much more than places of instruction. They must also be centers of inquiry: producers as well as transmitters of knowledge. In addition to presenting this vision of a new kind of school, Schaefer describes some of the problems with existing schools which appear to point in this direction.

THEOBALD, ROBERT. *An Alternative Future for America II.* Chicago: Swallow Press, 1968. This collection of essays and speeches by Theobald is concerned with three questions, "What are the present realities, and what type of future do they imply?" "What would an alternative, humanized future look like?" and "How do we begin to invent this alternative future?"

Appendix

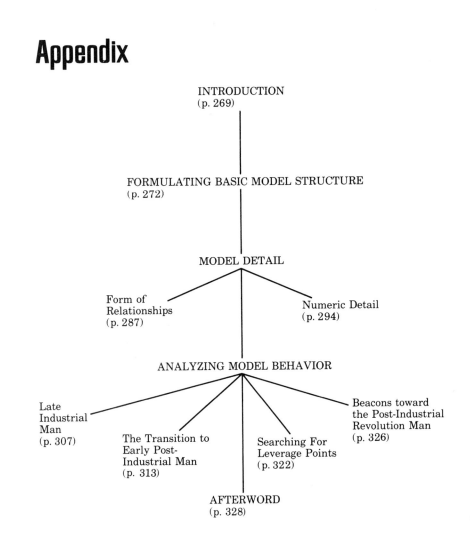

INTRODUCTION
(p. 269)

FORMULATING BASIC MODEL STRUCTURE
(p. 272)

MODEL DETAIL

Form of
Relationships
(p. 287)

Numeric Detail
(p. 294)

ANALYZING MODEL BEHAVIOR

Late
Industrial
Man
(p. 307)

The Transition to
Early Post-
Industrial Man
(p. 313)

Searching For
Leverage Points
(p. 322)

Beacons toward
the Post-Industrial
Revolution Man
(p. 326)

AFTERWORD
(p. 328)

From Beaker Metaphor to a
Dynamic Mathematical Model of
Human Development[1]

INTRODUCTION

The beaker metaphor, introduced in chapter 7, helped us to pull together a number of the fundamental ideas presented in this book. By employing this metaphor we could see how these ideas related to one another. Also, we could see things changing from moment to moment: the water level in the beaker might change only ever so slightly, yet the entire system of relationships was affected. This metaphor helped us to capture the idea of process, embodying it in a physical process which could be visualized. It helped us, because of its metaphorical character, to avoid endless quarreling over the definitions of concepts: instead of presenting an elaborate axiomatic schema, with its assumptions, propositions, and definitions, we simply conveyed a dynamic image. Of course, that image did imply assumptions, propositions, and definitions, but we were less motivated to explore these than to put the image to work. And we did just that in our ensuing discussion, exploring the transition from pre-industrial to late post-industrial society.

We have stretched the supply line from the beaker metaphor to the insights deriving from it quite far, and the time has come to construct a more substantial base of operations close to where we need it. This base will be a dynamic mathematical model. If the beaker metaphor led us to the frontier of understanding complex change emerging from a *system* of dynamic factors, all relating to one another, then mathematics can carry us beyond this frontier, into modes of discovery otherwise inaccessible. If the beaker metaphor helped us to get the feel of a process, then mathematics is admirably equipped to deal with processes in a much more precise way. And if that metaphor, via its visual qualities, gave us a shortcut to arriving at insights, then mathematics too can be presented visually.

Mathematics offers us a possibility for viewing ourselves as complex continuously changing beings. Ordinary language is shot through with a prejudice toward categorical structuring and static perceptions. The game language of continua and the beaker metaphor takes us a certain distance toward a comprehensive and dynamic view of human behavior. But if the rate of flow of water into or out of the beaker varies in a non-straightforward manner as the level of water changes, then we need a more precise model than the beaker metaphor provides. This is afforded by the mathematical concept of integration. Furthermore, to cope with a number of accumulation processes which are interrelated (that is, the level in one accumulation process may have an effect upon the actions taken in many other processes) we require a combinatorial capacity which the beaker metaphor does not possess. Once again we take recourse to a capacity of mathematics, this time one which can deal comfortably with complex combinations of accumulation structures.

In order to fully exercise these mathematical capacities free of the burden of excessively complicated mathematical technique, we require an approach toward the analysis of dynamic systems which is intuitively understandable and free of laborious calculations. For this we are indebted to the pioneering work of Jay W. Forrester in developing the methodology of System Dynamics.[2] This methodology skillfully exploits the digital computer to arrive at approximate solutions to the complicated models we shall develop. Mathematical techniques for arriving at final solutions for problems of the type we shall pose are nonexistent. These problems, involving complex situations which can be described by interrelated accumulation-feedback processes, are, however, amenable to computer-assisted analysis. With a computer we can attain "simulated" behavior of a dynamic model. This is not a solution, but an approximation to a solution, accomplished via elementary mathematics and the high speed computing capacity offered by the digital computer.

Such "approximations" are actually the most precise solutions of which we are presently capable. If we were to compare them to what we could come up with on the basis of ordinary language or of the beaker metaphor, then they are incredibly precise. Precision is a relative thing. Computer analysis does not imply the abandonment of mathematics but, rather, its extension to domains which otherwise would lie beyond its scope.

We do not mean by the foregoing to sing a hymn to the power of mathematics. It is all too easy to play Shell Game[3] with any tool of high repute, making its use an end in itself. The best remedy we know for guarding against this game is to keep in mind the purpose for which the tool is being employed: as a device for precise thinking about a system of dynamic factors. Some of us have already learned to use this device to deal with the physical universe, but it is safe to say that none of us has learned to use it for complex systems of accumulations which can describe human behavior. Mathematics is a stepping stone for attaining a new kind of consciousness, perhaps the kind which will characterize late post-industrial society.

If it is movement toward a consciousness of systems of accumulation processes and feedbacks which we are interested in, let us focus on just that and not on any particular solutions to particular problems. If presently we are steeped in a different kind of consciousness, one which conveys a narrow and static view of phenomena, then we must do what we can to alter that consciousness. One technique is to seek to balance the relatively narrow and static nature of ordinary language with diagrams emphasizing comprehensive and dynamic processes. We have included many such diagrams in this appendix. If they are to be effective, however, it is essential that the reader study each of them carefully and attempt to visualize the system of accumulations and feedbacks at work. The words which follow each diagram should be viewed merely as a supplement or guide to this activity, for they are unable to convey the dynamic relationship within a system of factors as well as the diagram can.

There are four major sections to this appendix: (1) Formulating Basic Model Structure, (2) Model Detail, (3) Analyzing Model Behavior, and (4) Afterword. We are presenting the fundamental structure, detail, and output of a mathematical model as a means for developing the theory contained in this volume and as a means for conveying this theory to the reader more precisely than our previous presentations. The afterword presents some basic assumptions for the technically minded reader. Modeling does not yield empirical verification, but rather is a tool for teaching the imagination to imagine in a precise fashion. What we are after—and this bears repeating—is a consciousness, a new way of thinking about human behavior, a path along which the reader can move toward his own discoveries. It is a path which the reader must construct for himself, largely unaided. Most things in his experience divert him from that path, and he should be forewarned of the difficulties involved.

FORMULATING BASIC MODEL STRUCTURE

The basic structure of our mathematical model will be presented under these headings: (1) The Rate-Level Diagram, (2) The Game Dimensions, (3) Calibration, (4) The System: Parallel Aspiring and Developing Processes, (5) The Environment: Its Effect on Aspiring Processes, (6) Interaction of Degree of Conformity and Environmental Effect, (7) Response to Environmental Pressure, (8) A More Thorough Definition of SHELL GAME–CONTINUING REVOLUTION, (9) An Internal Aspiring Mechanism to SHELL GAME–CONTINUING REVOLUTION, (10) Changes in Development Not Related to Aspiring Processes, and (11) The System: A Summary. We shall introduce each of these topics before proceeding to present them. Together, these topics cover the fundamental aspects of our model. When we present details of the model in the ensuing section, we will be going back over these fundamentals. And when we see the model at work in the final section, the output of the model will be a product of both the basic structure and the model details.

Our first three topics deal with basic mechanics of the modeling process and a general discussion of the game dimensions to be involved. The rate-level diagram looks deceptively simple, yet it will take considerable effort before the reader can expect to understand intuitively the idea of accumulation, a process we believe to be absolutely fundamental for understanding human behavior. The reader would do well to review the section on the beaker metaphor in chapter 7 in his efforts to gain this intuitive understanding, and he might attempt to apply that metaphor to processes which are already familiar to him. As for the dimensions of SHELL GAME–CONTINUING REVOLUTION and CONFORMITY–AUTONOMY, they are meant to illustrate the utilization of the game language within the modeling process. Let us not play Shell Game with these particular games but, rather, see them as illustrative of others. Also, let us not play Shell Game with the game language but, rather, see it as illustrative of a gradational view of phenomena. This gradational view, just like a gradational instrument such as a thermometer, must be calibrated if we are to make use of it. In a third topic we present the ways in which these two game dimensions are calibrated.

The fourth topic presents the system we choose to model. The basic dynamics of the system involve aspiring processes and developing processes. The manner in which states of aspiration affect activities of developing was established in chapter 7 using the beaker metaphor. The subsequent three topics probe factors affecting activities of aspiring. Topic 5 deals with the influence of the environment on the system's level of aspiration, an influence which is based on the ways in which the game dimensions are calibrated. In topic 6 we learn that a system modifies environmental effects, depending on its level of CONFORMITY–AUTONOMY. And in topic 7 we discuss a process by which the individual can respond to environmental pressures.

Topics 8 and 9 delve more deeply into SHELL GAME–CONTINUING REVOLUTION. In topic 8 we hypothesize that the individual's level of SHELL GAME–CONTINUING REVOLUTION determines how rapidly he can close a gap between a given aspiration and development relative to that aspiration. In Topic 9 we note the impact of a perceived change in the level of SHELL GAME–CONTINUING REVOLUTION on the aspiring process along this game dimension. In topic 10 we go out on a limb and hypothesize that an environment continually demands conformity, and that it continually pushes the system toward Continuing Revolution. The latter hypothesis is the singular element of model structure dealing directly with the premise that movement toward Continuing Revolution will characterize man's future evolution. Topic 11 is simply a visual summary of the preceding topics.

Let us now proceed with each of these topics in greater detail.

1. The Rate-Level Diagram

It will greatly expedite our tasks in this section to introduce a diagrammatic representation for the accumulation-feedback structure which is less cumbersome than that used in chapter 7. The diagram on the left of figure A-1 is the familiar beaker metaphor. On the right there is a representation of the same idea, known as the "rate-level" diagram. "Rate" refers to the concept of rate of flow, either rate of inflow or outflow. "Level" is the level of water in the beaker, the result of the accumulation of the rates of flow. The idea of a height of the beaker, symbolizing the goal of the accumulation process, is communicated in the rate-level diagram by the arrow from "goal" to the inflow rate.

Dashed arrows in both diagrams represent the feedback of information. However, the rate-level diagram shows information being "fed back" to both the inflow rate and the outflow rate, signifying

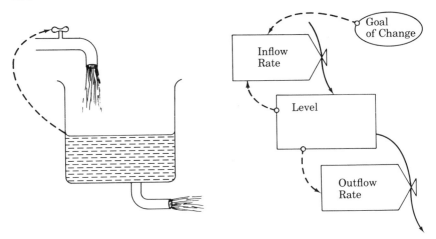

FIGURE A-1

that both are adjustable rates of flow capable of varying as a result of changes in the level. In chapter 7 we ignored the possibility of both inflow and outflow rates being adjustable in order to focus on the elements which determined the varying inflow. Now, we shall find it useful to have a diagram with more general representational capacities. We shall use dashed arrows in rate-level diagrams to indicate the impact of information about one system element upon another.

It may often happen that we shall wish to conceive of some action which can increase a level (act as an inflow rate) some times and decrease it (act as an outflow rate) at other times. In such a case we shall slightly modify figure A-1 to show a "bidirectional rate of flow," as illustrated by figure A-2. Furthermore, when many actions are converging to affect the way in which a level changes we will feel free to diagrammatically combine unidirectional and bidirectional flow to suit our purposes.

In a gross sense, what we are doing when we build a model is portrayed in figure A-3. There is both a model, which is changing, and an activity of modeling. We have tried in this appendix to convey the nature of building and analyzing a mathematical model as a total process, including both modeling and model. For example, the first draft of this book was somewhat abstract in its treatment of the various social systems of a null-A world. But it gave the author an accumulation of his consciousness of that world which was sufficient to push him to the activity of a more concrete presentation in the

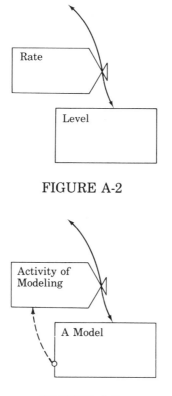

FIGURE A-2

FIGURE A-3

next draft. We encourage the reader to intermittently step back from discussion in this appendix and apply the structure of figure A-3 to better comprehend what is happening.

2. The Game Dimensions

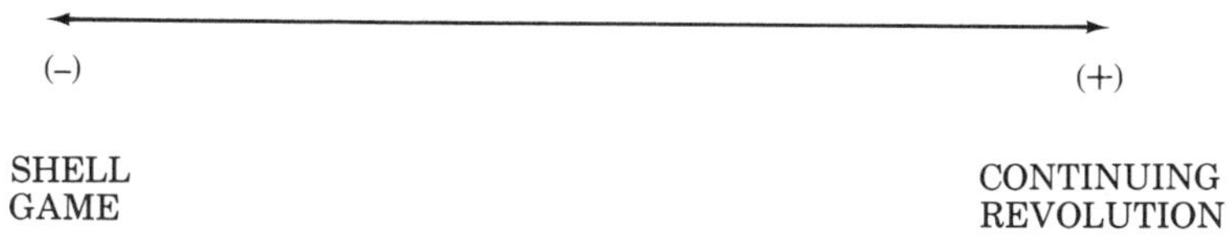

(−)   (+)

SHELL   CONTINUING
GAME   REVOLUTION

FIGURE A-4

In the process of accumulation the level varies over a continuum
of possible values, as illustrated in figure A-4. If we can clearly
distinguish movement along the continuum in one direction from
movement in the other, the continuum can be considered a dimension: a continuum with a positive and negative direction.[4] In this
appendix we shall deal with the game dimension of SHELL GAME–
CONTINUING REVOLUTION. One reason for choosing this dimension was that it was one along which man's developmental direction
seemed to us to be most clear. Because we are dealing with the game
dimension in connection with the process of accumulation, the discussion of any game implicates the dual concepts of an act of playing
the game and a resultant level or position on the game dimension.

It has been our intention from the onset of our modeling activity
to account for something of the environment's effect upon the individual. Thus, the game dimension of CONFORMITY–AUTONOMY
is of interest because it describes an aspect of human development
which is crucial at the interface of person and environment. By
"environment" we do not mean to specify any particular local environment. Rather, we refer to an abstraction; the general social context which includes both societal and local levels. However, we
might in the future wish to explore the implications of different
definitions of the environment, and we might even deal with other
systems than that of the individual.

By placing the two game dimensions perpendicular to each other,
as in figure A-5, we create a two-dimensional space in which a person's state can be located simultaneously along both dimensions.

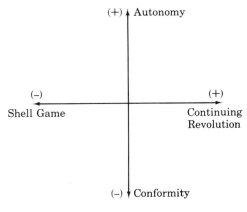

FIGURE A-5

The reader might pause to think about where he might locate
himself on these two dimensions at this very moment. To what

extent is he automatically adopting the views expressed here, or to what extent is he automatically rejecting them? Also, to what extent is he able to see his previous beliefs continuously from different perspectives and, on this basis, to what extent has he achieved a more comprehensive and better integrated view of phenomena?

3. Calibration

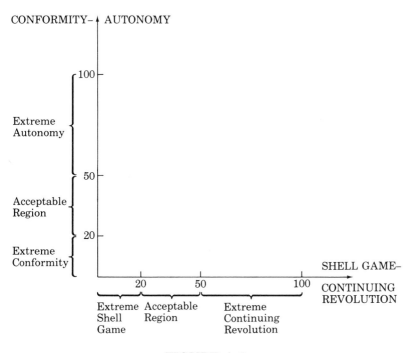

FIGURE A-6

We build a system using mathematics to express the process of accumulation and the relationships amidst elements of the system. The precision of mathematical expression demands a quantified vocabulary of concepts to be expressed. Thus, we must calibrate the game dimensions, as in figure A-6. We choose to identify regions which have meaning for us. These regions express the viewpoint of the environment faced by late industrial man. This calibration scheme is, of course, largely arbitrary. All calibration schemes are.

At this point we step back briefly from proceeding toward constructing a mathematical model to deal with an issue of singular import to applying mathematics to the study of human development. Our experiences in presenting the modeling process as a potential activity to students always seem to draw us into a position of fielding questions like, "How can you describe people by equations?" or, "How can you quantify human qualities?"

These questions are critical. We ask the reader to consider what it is that distinguishes a physical quality (such as one that has long been subject to quantification) from a "human" quality? To what extent is this the kind of dichotomy which obfuscates mathematical approaches to the study of human development and erects an impenetrable barrier isolating the human from the physical?

We believe that calibrating a "human" quality is, *in the sense of the form of the process,* indistinguishable from calibrating a "physical" quality. Once a continuum is identified calibration of that continuum is largely a matter of utility and convenience. What is, after all, the distinction between the quality of "hotness" (conceptualized along a continuum called temperature) as calibrated in degrees fahrenheit versus degrees centigrade? Once the application of a continuum to describe a quality is accepted, movement toward quantification has been largely accomplished. Just because there are, as yet, no numbers describing that quality, we should not be misled to believe that we have not already taken the step we were so afraid of.

4. The System: Parallel Aspiring and Developing Processes

The identification of the height of the beaker in chapter 7 as a driving force in development represented our basic premise of purposeful behavior. Thus, the system for this model involves the two game dimensions and the respective accumulation processes governing the formulation of aspirations relative to those dimensions, as illustrated by figure A-7. There is, in each case, an act of aspiring and an associated level of aspiration reflecting, to some degree, past acts of aspiring. Aspirations affect developing via the mechanism of an "aspiration development gap," as discussed in chapter 7. The dashed arrows from the levels of aspiration symbolize the effect of information about those levels which affects the game playing activities. What factors contribute to the acts of aspiring? This will be discussed later.

The reader should ask himself what his own aspirations are with respect to gaining a more comprehensive and better integrated perspective on human development from reading this appendix; that is, his current level of aspirations to SHELL GAME—CONTINUING REVOLUTION and his current activities changing that level. As will become increasingly clear, much of our work implicates aspiring processes as critical determinants of development: a low aspiration will tend to result in less development than a high aspiration.

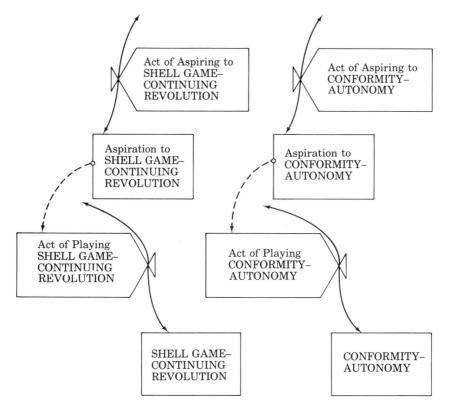

FIGURE A-7

5. The Environment: Its Effect on Aspiring Processes

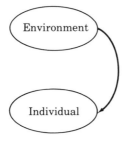

FIGURE A-8

Though the environment is, like the individual, changing, we shall
not attempt to explain why. We will focus on the effect of the envi-

ronment upon the individual, and not vice versa. Thus, we find in figure A-8 the arrow directing our attention to "one-way" causality from environment to the individual. In attempting to understand complex phenomenon via modeling we define a system which is inclusive enough to address questions of interest and exclusive enough to focus our attention on a reasonably small number of questions. Consider figure A-7. In order to address the individual's effect upon the environment, how many additional accumulation processes would have to be considered? As our facility with this model develops in the future, we intend to incorporate this kind of complexity.

Note that as we proceed to focus on specific relationships within the system we will not redraw all of figure A-7. It should be understood that this remains the system we are studying even if we diagram only a portion of it. One powerful mechanism of environmental impact upon the individual's processes of development comes about through an impact upon the individual's activities of forming aspirations, as illustrated in figure A-9. Combine the information in figures A-7 and A-9. The environment wishes to confine the individual's level of SHELL GAME–CONTINUING REVOLUTION and CONFORMITY–AUTONOMY within an acceptable region. Once the individual leaves that region the environment acts to return him to it. It acts by trying to appropriately

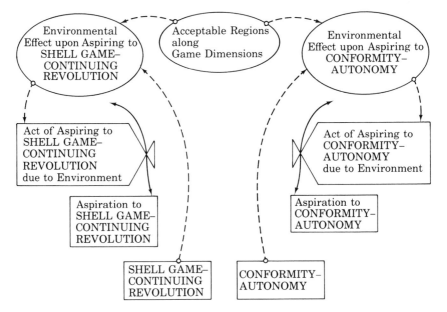

FIGURE A-9

influence a change in his aspirations, which will in turn influence
a change in his level of development in the direction desired by the
environment.

An "Acceptable Region" is neither a rate nor a level; thus, it is
placed in the ellipse in figure A-9. The dashed arrows, again, indicate
that information about one variable affects the value of another
variable.

6. Interaction of Degree of Conformity and Environmental Effect

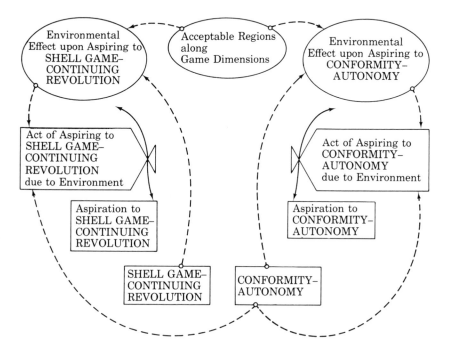

FIGURE A-10

Do the same environmental pressures affect all individuals equally?
We think not, and we think that whatever distinguishes the degree
to which different individuals are affected by the environment inheres in the game dimension of CONFORMITY–AUTONOMY. We
have come to define CONFORMITY–AUTONOMY in a purely functional manner: this level determines to what extent environmental
pressure to alter aspirations actually creates a rate of flow into or
out of a level of aspiration, as shown in figure A-10. Illustration: An
individual who encounters environmental pressure directed against

an extreme level of Continuing Revolution will be able to dampen that pressure to the degree that he has attained a state of extreme Autonomy.

In the process of building this model we are forced to be consistent in our definitions: CONFORMITY–AUTONOMY is just what we have described above and nothing more. We are not viewing movement in any particular direction along CONFORMITY–AUTONOMY, a priori, as developmental. If the individual views the environment as a threat to his development he shall attempt to become more autonomous from its effect. If he views it as a benefit to his development he shall attempt to become more conformist, to magnify its effect. It all hinges around whether the environment is encouraging movement toward Continuing Revolution or inhibiting such movement: this is the only measure of "developmental" in this model.

7. Response to Environmental Pressure

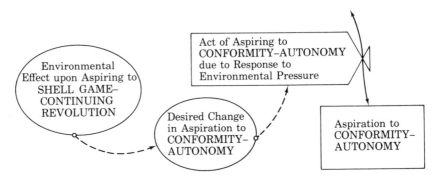

FIGURE A-11

We feel that the above paragraph implies a mechanism of response with which we have not as yet dealt, as shown in figure A-11. The individual desires to develop. He formulates a desired change in his Aspirations to CONFORMITY–AUTONOMY, a sort of meta-aspiration, to assist that development. Review the previous paragraph if the motivation for this mechanism is not clear. All we have added here is the notion that if an individual wishes to change his level of CONFORMITY–AUTONOMY, he may aspire in the direction of the desired change.

8. A More Thorough Definition of SHELL GAME–CONTINUING REVOLUTION

How does this game dimension affect development? Before we can answer that we have to understand somewhat better what it means. Movement in the direction of Continuing Revolution means an increasing ability to see the commonality of development in all areas of activity, which in turn frees the individual from excessive concern with any one area and allows him to value the very process of developing more than particular goals of development. This devotion to the process of developing lessens the likelihood of his playing Shell Game by getting mired down in any one narrow accomplishment, thereby encouraging him to develop with increasing rapidity. On the other hand, movement toward Shell Game represents a rigidifying of developmental activities: a general reduction in capacity to change, in either a developmental or nondevelopmental direction.

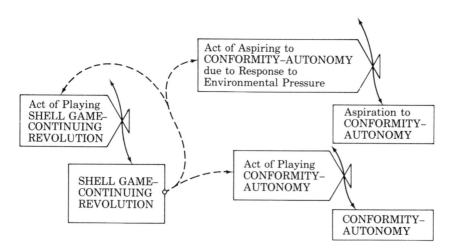

FIGURE A-12

The Acts of Playing SHELL GAME–CONTINUING REVOLUTION and CONFORMITY–AUTONOMY depend upon an aspiration-development gap of the sort we have dealt with since the first presentation of the beaker metaphor. We now hypothesize that it is the individual's level of SHELL GAME–CONTINUING REVOLUTION which determines how rapidly he is capable of closing any given aspiration-development gap: how quickly he can realize his aspirations in general. The structure of this relationship is presented in figure A-12. Movement toward Continuing Revolution allows a person to accelerate all of his activities of realizing aspirations. It should be noted that although there is no aspiration-development gap, as such, in the "Act of Aspiring to CONFORMITY–AUTONOMY due to Response to Environmental Pressure," the notion of a desired change in aspiration is directly analogous to such a gap, and the speed with which this change is accomplished can be affected similarly by change in the level of SHELL GAME–CONTINUING REVOLUTION.

9. An Internal Aspiring Mechanism to SHELL GAME–CONTINUING REVOLUTION

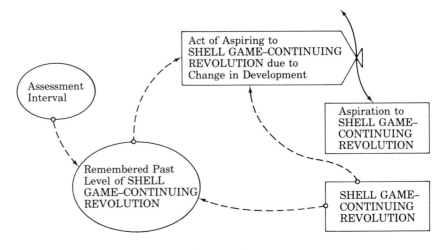

FIGURE A-13

In formulating activities which could change the level of aspiration to CONFORMITY–AUTONOMY, we identified both an act due directly to environmental pressure and an act of aspiring internal to the individual due to a response to environmental pressure. Aspirations to SHELL GAME–CONTINUING REVOLUTION are similarly changed as a result of an "internal" aspiring mechanism based upon the individual's assessment of his recent change in level of SHELL GAME–CONTINUING REVOLUTION, as indicated in figure A-13. He compares where he is with where he was and then aspires in the direction of that change. The period of time over which he makes this assessment is called the Assessment Interval. This activity is also subject to the level of SHELL GAME–CONTINUING

REVOLUTION, as were the activities indicated in figure A-13: aspiring goes on more rapidly as this level increases.

10. Changes in Development Not Related to Aspiring Processes

We have spent considerable time debating whether such mechanisms do in fact exist, and, we are currently of the opinion that two such mechanisms do operate to alter levels of development. The first is shown in figure A-14. An environment continually demands conformity. This force is structured into the basic nature of an environment and its presence is independent of the individual's level of CONFORMITY–AUTONOMY (though its magnitude is not). Even an environment oriented to the development of individuals within it demands conformity to its orientation. For example, we are pushing the reader to take seriously his own potentials for development.

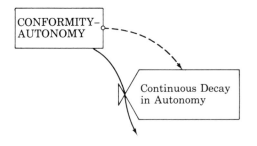

FIGURE A-14

The second mechanism is shown in figure A-15. In many ways this hypothesis may be the most controversial element of our model: we assume that there exists an ever-present force which is continuously pulling all individuals toward Continuing Revolution. The rate of change due to this activity is, for late industrial man, small in comparison to the rate due to the aspiration-development gap along SHELL GAME–CONTINUING REVOLUTION. One reason for this is that this rate depends upon the level of SHELL GAME–CONTINUING REVOLUTION which is, for late industrial man, generally low.

11. The System: A Summary

Before turning to the next section detailing the model structure we summarize all that has been said to this point in figure A-16.

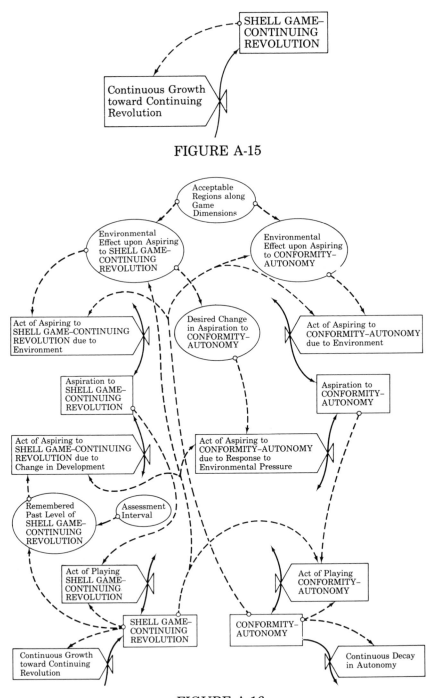

FIGURE A-15

FIGURE A-16

286

MODEL DETAIL

The structure developed in the preceding phase was painted in broad strokes. We now proceed to progressively more detailed expression. In doing so we will go through two phases, each representing a degree of specificity in expressing the ideas of the last section:

1. Determining the precise form of the relationships indicated in figure A-16, and
2. Numeric detail.

Form of Relationships

With respect to the form of relationships, we shall take up five topics: (1) Closing the Aspiration-Development Gap, (2) The Concept of a Time Constant and the Effect of the Level of SHELL GAME–CONTINUING REVOLUTION Upon the Speed of Gap Closing, (3) Time Constants which are not Affected by the Level of SHELL GAME–CONTINUING REVOLUTION, (4) The Environmental Effect and Its Interaction with CONFORMITY–AUTONOMY, and (5) The Individual's Response to Environmental Pressure. We shall introduce each of these at this point before presenting them.

Topic 1 has to do—in terms of the beaker metaphor—with the relationship between the rate of flow of the water and the size of the gap between the height of the beaker and the level of the water. There are many possible types of relationships. Three of these are discussed and one is selected for purposes of constructing the mathematical model. Hopefully the reader will be able to see how the development of a model forces one to become more precise than the beaker metaphor demands, leading one to ask questions which are not easily suggested by that metaphor. Topic 2 constitutes an elaboration of topic 1, going into detail on the one relationship that was selected. The focus is on the effect of the system's level of SHELL GAME–CONTINUING REVOLUTION on the speed with which the aspiration-development gap is closed.

Topic 3 deals with what we call continuous growth/decay processes: activities of game playing, independent of the individual's degree of awareness, which are ever-present. In our discussion of the basic structure of the model we put forward the ideas of a continuous decay in Autonomy on the part of individuals generally, and also that of a continuous growth toward Continuing Revolution. Here we simply add the idea that this hypothesized decay and growth can be described by a very simple mathematical relationship, that is, a linear one.

Topics 4 and 5 deal with the impact of the environment on the individual and the individual's reaction to this impact. We have already treated, in relation to the basic structure of the model, the idea that the environment attempts to return the individual to an "acceptable region" whenever the individual's levels of development fall outside that region. We have also discussed the idea that the impact of the environment depends on the system's level of CON-FORMITY–AUTONOMY. What remains to be taken up is the form of the relationships which describe these occurrences, since any number of possibilities exist. And having chosen from among these options, it remains for us to describe the precise ways in which a system will respond to environmental pressure to return to an acceptable region.

1. Closing the Aspiration-Development Gap. Our question, as presented in figure A-17, is this: How does the rate of playing vary as the gap between the height of the beaker (the individual's Aspirations to SHELL GAME–CONTINUING REVOLUTION) and the level of water (the individual's level of SHELL GAME–CONTINU-ING REVOLUTION) is closed? That is, what is the nature of the relationship between the rate of inflow and the size of this gap? To straightforwardly address this question, let us make the simplifying assumption that, for the moment, the height of the beaker is not changing. We will symbolize this fixed value of aspirations by the term "A_0"; likewise, we symbolize the initial value of the level of development of SHELL GAME–CONTINUING REVOLUTION "S_0."

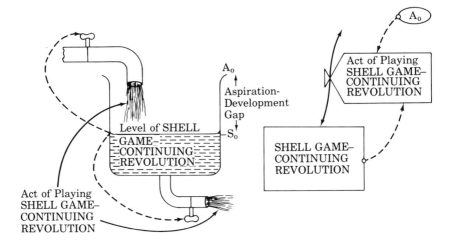

FIGURE A-17

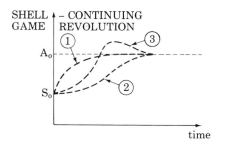

FIGURE A-18

Figure A-18 presents some possible changes in a system level (here, SHELL GAME–CONTINUING REVOLUTION) over a period of time. The quantity $(A_0 - S_0)$ is the initial aspiration-development gap. The dotted curves represent three possible alternative behavior patterns which could describe the process of "closing the aspiration-development gap." The reader should view each curve carefully to understand its implications. For example, curve 1 implies that the individual develops most rapidly initially (his rate of development is greatest), and his development gradually slows down as he approaches A_0.

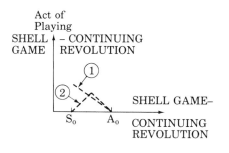

FIGURE A-19

Curves 1, 2, and 3 each imply a different form of relationship between the value of the level and the value of the inflow rate, as illustrated in figure A-19. The plots of curves 1 and 2 do not explicitly involve time; they describe alternative relationships between the two system variables of interest. There is no comparably simple relationship which can account for the third curve. Why?

If that question is a bit difficult to answer, the reader should first assure himself that he understands the unity between the structural relationships of figure A-19 and the resultant behavior of figure

A-18. Observe that curve 1 in figure A-19 portrays the Act of Playing SHELL GAME–CONTINUING REVOLUTION as greatest when the level equals S_0, and as continually decreasing in magnitude until it equals zero when the level equals A_0.

Now, we cannot draw a simple "one to one" relationship (between level of development and the act of playing) for curve 3 because it has the unique characteristic of rising past the level of aspiration and then falling back to it. Thus, it passes through a range of values for the level in excess of A_0, going up and then falling back down. If you do not see why a simple relationship is impossible for curve 3, try to draw one.[5]

We choose the first behavior pattern to describe this phenomenon of gap closing because it is the most elementary, and as such offers us a straightforward means of expressing the influence of the level of SHELL GAME–CONTINUING REVOLUTION upon the speed with which such gaps are closed. However, we also feel that both of the other behavior patterns bear attention in the future development of this model.

2. The Concept of a Time Constant and the Effect of the Level of SHELL GAME–CONTINUING REVOLUTION Upon the Speed of Gap Closing.

Relationship 1 in figure A-19 is a straight line and can be described by the following equation:

$$\text{Act of Playing S.G.–C.R.} = (-k)\,(\text{Level of S.G.–C.R.}) + b$$

where k and b are appropriate constants with values greater than zero; $-k$ is commonly called the slope of the line, and $+b$ the "y-intercept." Noting that $A_0 = b/k$ we can rewrite the above equation by substituting $k\,A_0$ for b and factoring out k:

$$\text{Act of Playing S.G.–C.R.} = (+k)\,(A_0\text{–Level of S.G.–C.R.})$$
$$= (1/\text{TC})\,(\text{aspiration-development gap})$$

where $k = 1/\text{TC}$
and TC is called the "time constant."

We could describe the last form of this equation verbally as follows: "the individual plays the game at a rate which at any particular point in time is a certain percentage, $1/\text{TC}$, of the aspiration-development gap." A relationship such as the one above, where the dependent variable (the rate) is proportionate to the independent variable (the level), is said to be linear. When such a relationship between a level and its inflow rate exists, a curve of the slope of curve 2 in figure A-18 describes the behavior. Such a curve is called an exponential curve.

What we are really interested in here is the idea of a "time constant." It is clear that if the value of TC were made smaller, the Act of playing SHELL GAME–CONTINUING REVOLUTION would proceed more swiftly to close the aspiration gap. This is illustrated in figure A-20. As one looks at each of the exponential curves starting with the one furthest to the right and moving to the left, it should be clear that each successive curve has a smaller time constant.

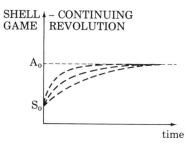

FIGURE A-20

Now, recall that we formulated the hypothesis that the level of SHELL GAME–CONTINUING REVOLUTION affected the rapidity with which each of four "gaps" were closed (see figure A-16). We can create a causal structure expressing this hypothesis with the aid of figure A-21. "TC" is taken to be the time constant characterizing the "gap closing" in each of the rates affected by this level. The figure on the right demonstrates the behavior involved in closing the (A_0-S_0) gap from time constants given by each of the points indicated in the relationship on the left. Looking at the left-hand relationship closely, we see that throughout the middle of the range of values for the level, the value of the time constant changes rather steadily, but it changes more drastically in the extreme values. This is to say that the relative effect of changes in the level of SHELL GAME–CONTINUING REVOLUTION is greater in these extreme regions.

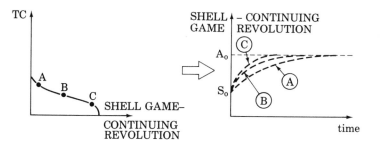

FIGURE A-21

3. Time Constants which are not Affected by the Level of S.G.–C.R. There are two such elements of structure (see figures A-14, 15), as shown in figure A-22: "DTC" and "TCCR," which stand for "decay time constant" and "time constant for Continuing Revolution" respectively. The relationship on the left is acting so as to pull the level of CONFORMITY–AUTONOMY to zero, while the one on the right does not involve any sort of "gap" and is continuously trying to increase the level of SHELL GAME–CONTINUING REVOLUTION. The notion of accelerating processes of change we expressed earlier, via the reduction of other time constants with increasing levels of Continuing Revolution, is intrinsic to the relationship of the right side of figure A-22: as the level rises, the rate of inflow rises, which causes the level to rise and so on. Thus, there is no motivation to make this time constant dependent upon the level of SHELL GAME–CONTINUING REVOLUTION.

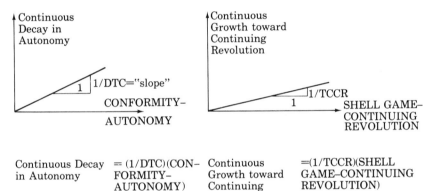

| Continuous Decay in Autonomy | = (1/DTC)(CON–FORMITY–AUTONOMY) | Continuous Growth toward Continuing Revolution | =(1/TCCR)(SHELL GAME–CONTINUING REVOLUTION) |

FIGURE A-22

4. The Environmental Effect and Its Interaction with CONFORMITY–AUTONOMY. There are two different "environmental effect" terms (see Figure A-9), one which responds to the level of SHELL GAME–CONTINUING REVOLUTION and one which responds to the level of CONFORMITY–AUTONOMY. We choose to conceive of these relationships as identical. They are presented in figure A-23.

Figure A-10 indicates that the environmental effect is one of two factors determining the "rates of aspiring due to environment." The other is the level of CONFORMITY–AUTONOMY. We feel that the following relationships between these factors express the essence of our notion of the "dampening or accentuating" effect of CONFORMITY–AUTONOMY:

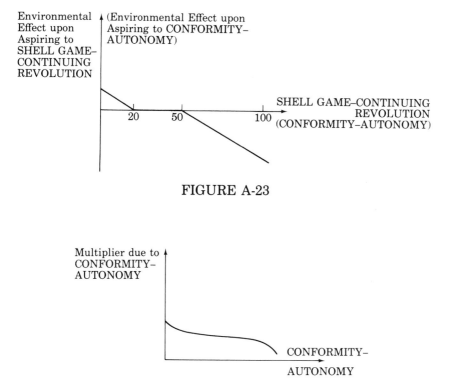

Act of Aspiring to SHELL GAME–
CONTINUING REVOLUTION $=$ $\begin{bmatrix} \text{Environmental} \\ \text{Effect upon} \\ \text{Aspiration to} \\ \text{S.G.–C.R.} \end{bmatrix}$ $\begin{bmatrix} \text{Multiplier} \\ \text{due to} \\ \text{CONFORMITY–} \\ \text{AUTONOMY} \end{bmatrix}$
due to Environment

Act of Aspiring to CONFORMITY–
AUTONOMY due to Environment $=$ $\begin{bmatrix} \text{Environmental} \\ \text{Effect upon} \\ \text{Aspiration to} \\ \text{CONFORMITY–} \\ \text{AUTONOMY} \end{bmatrix}$ $\begin{bmatrix} \text{Multiplier} \\ \text{due to} \\ \text{CONFORMITY–} \\ \text{AUTONOMY} \end{bmatrix}$

where the relationship between the Multiplier due to CONFORMI-
TY–AUTONOMY and the level of CONFORMITY–AUTONOMY
appears as in figure A-24.

FIGURE A-23

FIGURE A-24

When the multiplier is unity (which it would be, approximately,
throughout the middle region of the range of CONFORMITY–
AUTONOMY) it essentially has no effect (the Act of Aspiring to

SHELL GAME–CONTINUING REVOLUTION due to environment being equal to the Environmental Effect upon Aspiration to SHELL GAME–CONTINUING REVOLUTION). When it is less than one it is dampening the environmental pressure. Again we see that in the more extreme regions the multiplier changes more drastically.

5. The Individual's Response to Environmental Pressure. Figure A-11 tells the story here. The individual responds to environmental pressure to control his Aspiration to SHELL GAME–CONTINUING REVOLUTION by aspiring to become more or less autonomous from that environment, as portrayed in figure A-25. The environment tries to push his aspirations toward Shell Game (Environmental Effect less than zero) and the individual strives to become more Autonomous, and vice versa. Note the distinction between the relationship in the middle and extreme regions as compared to previous ones: here the Desired Change in Aspiration to CONFORMITY–AUTONOMY varies most drastically throughout the moderate values of the Environmental Effect. The individual's Desired Change in Aspiration becomes "saturated" at high values of environmental pressure. This does not necessarily mean that his ability to effectively respond becomes saturated at these high values of environmental pressure. Note figure A-12 indicates that this overall capability to respond also depends upon the degree of Continuing Revolution which has been achieved—this can greatly reduce the time constant governing the speed of response (figure A-21).

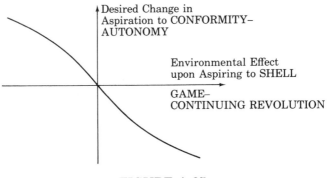

FIGURE A-25

Numeric Detail

Our major concern with numeric detail is that it not become a major concern. There are no such things as the "right numbers" or the "correct equations." Where no previous standards for quantification exist everything is truly relative. Our major task is to avoid making unwise choices in these matters.

We will encounter constraints of numeric detail at the following stages of specifying the model structure:

1. All of the relationships developed in the previous section must be expressed in terms of algebraic equations.
2. We must specify values for the time constants which do not depend upon the level of SHELL GAME–CONTINUING REVOLUTION and one other constant: the "assessment interval" for aspiring to SHELL GAME–CONTINUING REVOLUTION.
3. We must set "initial values" for the levels: the levels of SHELL GAME–CONTINUING REVOLUTION, CONFORMITY–AUTONOMY and the respective aspirations which we consider to be descriptive of the state of the individual at the beginning of the period of investigation.

In making the decisions involved in these numeric considerations we shall use the following guidelines:

1. the calibration of the game-dimensions set down in the section on Formulating Basic Model Structure;
2. a period of investigation of about one half year (25 weeks);
3. we are looking, initially, for numbers which can yield behavior representative of our most basic ideas about the behavior of late industrial man;
4. certain specific notions about what sort of behavior we are *not* looking for:
   a. the rise in level of SHELL GAME–CONTINUING REVOLUTION due to Force for Continual Growth toward Continuing Revolution should not be a major factor in determining the pattern of SHELL GAME–CONTINUING REVOLUTION behavior,
   b. the environment should have the capacity to prohibit dramatic rises in either of the game-dimension levels;
   c. the Continual Decay in Autonomy should not dominate change in the level of CONFORMITY–AUTONOMY.

In describing the process by which numeric detail is accomplished we shall greatly abbreviate its highly iterative nature. A great deal more has gone into choosing appropriately valued relationships and constants than we shall attempt to describe. However, our emphasis in the appendix upon the process of constructing a mathematical model dictates that a serious effort be made toward elucidating the form of the activity of achieving numeric detail, in addition to the results of that activity. For this reason we shall conclude this section with an illustration of one series of iterations we pursued in searching for appropriate behavior patterns for late industrial man, "Model Behavior and Numeric Detail."

The Effect of SHELL GAME–CONTINUING REVOLUTION upon Time Constants

Figure A-21 shows the general shape of this relationship, and figure A-26 provides specific calibrations. The points indicated on the curve are at intervals of 10 units on the horizontal axis. What is the value of the time constants at the low end of the "acceptable region" of SHELL GAME–CONTINUING REVOLUTION? The choice of two weeks as the time constant at this point is, of course, highly arbitrary. What is important is that the values of these time constants relative to the values of other model variables and constants be appropriate to the type of late industrial behavior we desire the model to generate.

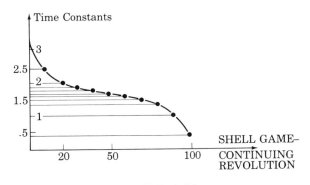

FIGURE A-26

The system flow chart, figure A-16, indicates the four rates where time constants are affected by the level of SHELL GAME–CONTINUING REVOLUTION. These time constants are:

1. time constant for closing aspiration-development gap in Act of Playing SHELL GAME–CONTINUING REVOLUTION;
2. time constant for closing aspiration-development gap in Act of Playing CONFORMITY–AUTONOMY;

3. time constant for achieving Desired Change in Aspiration to CONFORMITY–AUTONOMY in the rate Act of Aspiring to CONFORMITY–AUTONOMY due to Response to Environmental Pressure; and

4. time constant for aspiring on the basis of recent change in development in the rate Act of Aspiring to SHELL GAME–CONTINUING REVOLUTION due to Change in Development.

Environmental Effect on Aspiring to SHELL GAME–CONTINUING REVOLUTION

The shape of this effect, which depends upon the value of the level SHELL GAME–CONTINUING REVOLUTION, is shown in figure A-23. This environmental effect will contribute to the rate Act of Aspiring to SHELL GAME–CONTINUING REVOLUTION due to Environment; and this rate will compete with the rate Act of Aspiring to SHELL GAME–CONTINUING REVOLUTION due to Change in Development. For late industrial man the environment should play a strong role in determining behavior. Based upon estimates of likely magnitudes of the "internal" activity of aspiring we choose as values for this relationship those indicated in figure A-27.

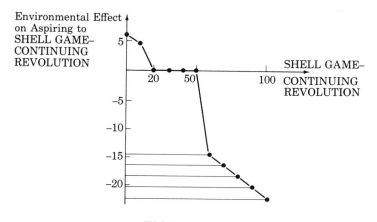

FIGURE A-27

The environment must respond abruptly to departure from the acceptable regions: the numbers shown above are chosen as a result of our expectations regarding the likely magnitudes of Act of Aspiring to SHELL GAME–CONTINUING REVOLUTION due to Change in Development as the individual enters the range of extreme Continuing Revolution.

Multiplier Due to CONFORMITY–AUTONOMY

The shape of this relationship is shown in figure A-24. We feel that
the individual attains the capacity to significantly dampen environmental effect only at extremely high values of Autonomy. The numeric relationship we have used is presented in figure A-28.

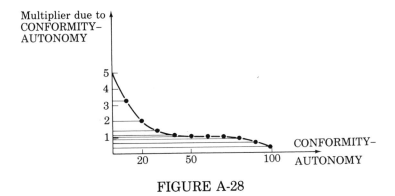

FIGURE A-28

It might be argued that we are somewhat biased toward the significance of the Conformity end of this dimension (note that the multiplier doesn't drop significantly below unity until the individual is
over 80 in CONFORMITY–AUTONOMY, while it is in excess of
unity for all values of the level less than 50). What are the hypotheses, implicit in these numbers, regarding the relative effects of different degrees of conformity and autonomy?

The Individual's Response to Environmental Pressure on His Aspiring to SHELL GAME–CONTINUING REVOLUTION

The shape of this relationship, between Environmental Effect of
Aspiration to SHELL GAME–CONTINUING REVOLUTION and
Desired Change in Aspirations to CONFORMITY–AUTONOMY, is
shown in figure A-25. Initially, we choose the following values for
this relationship indicated in figure A-29.

Environmental Effect upon Aspiration to CONFORMITY–AUTONOMY

The shape of this relationship, between the level of CONFORMITY–
AUTONOMY and the Environmental Effect upon Aspiration to
CONFORMITY–AUTONOMY, was also given in figure A-23. We do
not feel that late industrial man is characterized by extremely high

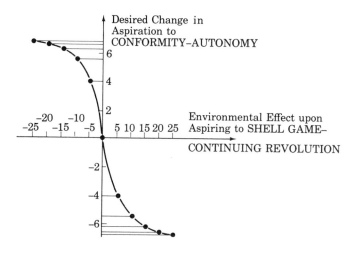

FIGURE A-29

values of Autonomy. Noting that the two rates which determine changes in the level of Aspiration to CONFORMITY–AUTONOMY depend upon this environmental effect and the Desired Change in Aspiration to CONFORMITY–AUTONOMY, respectively, we choose the same values for this environmental effect as were presented in figure A-23.

Time Constants not Affected by the Level of SHELL GAME–CONTINUING REVOLUTION

We choose the value of the Time Constant for Continuing Revolution as ten weeks. Compare this value to the range of values indicated in figure A-25. Should one expect the rate, Continual Growth toward Continuing Revolution, to play a major role in determining the pattern of behavior of the level of SHELL GAME–CONTINUING REVOLUTION?

The Continuous Decay in Autonomy should have an important, but not dominating, effect upon the level of CONFORMITY–AUTONOMY. We choose the Decay Time Constant to be three weeks.

The Assessment Interval

We feel that a reasonable "assessment interval" for evaluating one's development in SHELL GAME–CONTINUING REVOLUTION is one week. This is the period of time over which the individual assesses his change in development. This assessment, in turn, affects his aspirations for future development along this game dimension (see figure A-13).

Initial Values of Levels

Late industrial man should have values of the model levels which are initially within the acceptable regions of SHELL GAME–CONTINUING REVOLUTION and CONFORMITY–AUTONOMY. By "initial" we mean the values for these states at the beginning of the period of time we shall investigate. He also has a relatively narrow initial "aspiration-development gap" relative to SHELL GAME–CONTINUING REVOLUTION. Because the game dimension CONFORMITY–AUTONOMY is, in itself, a-developmental, we shall assume that the individual initially has no aspiration-development gap along this dimension.

The initial values for late industrial man we will use are:

1. SHELL GAME–CONTINUING REVOLUTION=25
2. Aspiration to SHELL GAME–CONTINUING REVOLUTION=30
3. CONFORMITY–AUTONOMY=25
4. Aspiration to CONFORMITY–AUTONOMY=25

Model Behavior and Numeric Detail

Figure A-30 is our first graph of model behavior. On the horizontal axis is time, in weeks. The vertical axis displays the four system levels with the same 0-100 scale as presented formerly when the game dimensions were calibrated. These four, along with the symbols representing them in figure A-30, are:

SHELL GAME–CONTINUING REVOLUTION=S
Aspiration to SHELL GAME–CONTINUING REVOLUTION=A
CONFORMITY–AUTONOMY=C
Aspiration to CONFORMITY–AUTONOMY=B

This figure is the first of a series of computer plots showing how the model as a whole performs over time. Our focus is on the four levels since it is these which define the general state of the individual—as we have modeled him—at a given time.

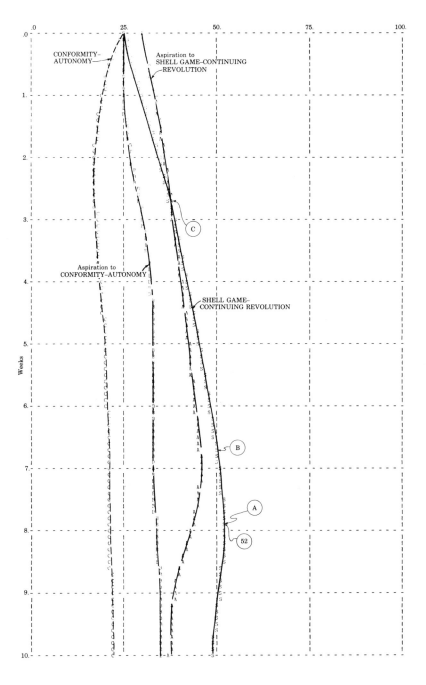

FIGURE A-30

301

In discussing graphs of model behavior we shall indicate particularly interesting points by encircled letters on the figure itself. Where useful we will also indicate the numeric values of peaks for the levels. For most of these figures we will focus on behavior over a ten-week period, occasionally looking at longer periods up to twenty-five weeks.

The thing which first disturbs us about figure A-30 is the behavior during the long gradual rise in the level of SHELL GAME–CONTINUING REVOLUTION. From time zero to about the end of the eighth week (point A) the level of development is continually rising, and only near the end of the rise does it exceed the acceptable region. Thus, there is no environmental force until about the end of week 7 (B) to pull aspirations down; yet at point C the level of development passes the level of aspiration and there is a "negative" gap from then on. Once this happens the environment never has to enter into the picture because this negative gap eventually curbs rising SHELL GAME–CONTINUING REVOLUTION with little help from the environmental effect (SHELL GAME–CONTINUING REVOLUTION peaks at a value of 52). Clearly, the presence of the Continuous Growth toward Continuing Revolution is causing the level of development to rise too rapidly in comparison with the level of aspirations.

Our first thought of corrective action is to increase the Time Constant for Continuing Revolution so that the level of SHELL GAME–CONTINUING REVOLUTION will not rise so rapidly and will be more dependent upon the aspiration-development gap. We alter this time constant to twenty weeks (twice its original value), with the result presented in figure A-31. The result is somewhat surprising. The pattern of behavior is practically unchanged, everything just occurs a bit slower. There is now an eleven-week interval between the time when aspirations fall below development (A) and when development ceases to rise during the sixteenth week (not shown in figure A-31, which is limited to a ten-week interval).

The result is quite similar when the time constant is increased to thirty weeks. What we have misunderstood is that when we increase the Time Constant for Continuing Revolution we not only slow the rise in SHELL GAME–CONTINUING REVOLUTION, but the rise in Aspirations to SHELL GAME–CONTINUING REVOLUTION as well. This is because the aspirations rise as a result of rises in the level of development over the one-week assessment time. This is clearly not the way to get out of this pattern of behavior.

We need a means of increasing the rate at which Aspiration to SHELL GAME–CONTINUING REVOLUTION changes relative to

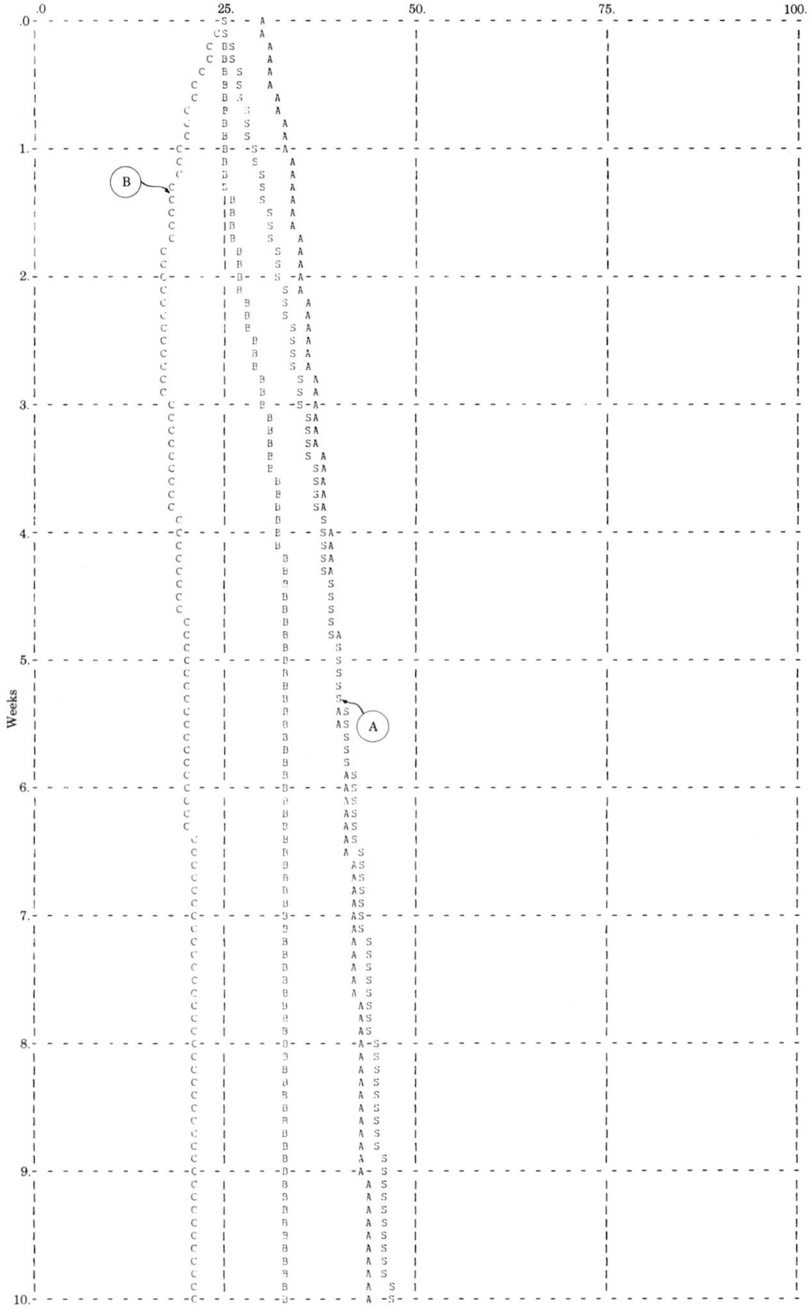

FIGURE A-31

303

the rate at which the corresponding level of development changes. We choose to alter the values of Time Constant for Realizing Change in Development, as determined by the level of SHELL GAME–CONTINUING REVOLUTION, to about one half their former values. This should speed up this aspiring process. This alteration is portrayed in figure A-32.

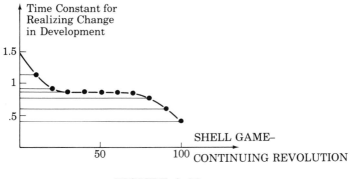

FIGURE A-32

Looking at Figure A-31 we are also dissatisfied with the behavior of the levels of CONFORMITY–AUTONOMY and Aspiration to CONFORMITY–AUTONOMY. With the exception of one brief period starting at B when the level of Conformity drops into the region of extreme conformity, and the environment acts to elevate Aspiration to CONFORMITY–AUTONOMY, neither of these levels varies to speak of. It is now apparent that there is no mechanism in our model to cause the level of Aspiration to CONFORMITY–AUTONOMY to vary if there is no environmental pressure either affecting those aspirations directly, or causing the individual to formulate a Desired Change in Aspiration to CONFORMITY–AUTONOMY. This seems to us a distinct shortcoming of the model.

As a consequence of figure A-31 we have reevaluated our ideas about the activities which alter level of Aspiration to CONFORMITY–AUTONOMY. Because CONFORMITY–AUTONOMY does not in itself carry developmental implications, there is an ever present tendency for Aspiration to CONFORMITY–AUTONOMY to decay toward the level of CONFORMITY–AUTONOMY, whether that level is above or below the level of aspiration. This structure is expressed in Figure A-33. We shall take the time constant for this decay to be four weeks, so that it is an important but not a dominant factor in influencing behavior. The results of these two alterations are presented in figure A-34.

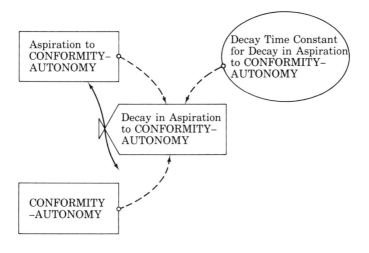

FIGURE A-33

Now, for the first time, the individual encounters the environmental pressure to a significant extent. When his level of SHELL GAME–CONTINUING REVOLUTION enters into the extreme region (point A) the environment responds by pressuring the associated aspirations until they are curbed at B. Whereupon, the level of development continues to rise for a short time and then tails off. This is more the pattern of behavior we were looking for in these two levels for late industrial man.

When the environment starts to exert pressure on the aspiring process to Continuing Revolution, the individual responds by trying to raise his level of Aspiration to CONFORMITY–AUTONOMY (C). We are still a bit dissatisfied with this aspect of the behavior our model is generating. In the interest of imparting the process of responding to environmental pressure with some degree of, at least, potential influence on behavior, we make two changes in numeric detail:

1. double the values of the Desired Change in Aspiration to CONFORMITY–AUTONOMY (figure A-28);

2. change the values for the Time Constant for Realizing Desired Change in Aspiration to CONFORMITY–AUTONOMY from the values of figure A-25 to those in figure A-32.

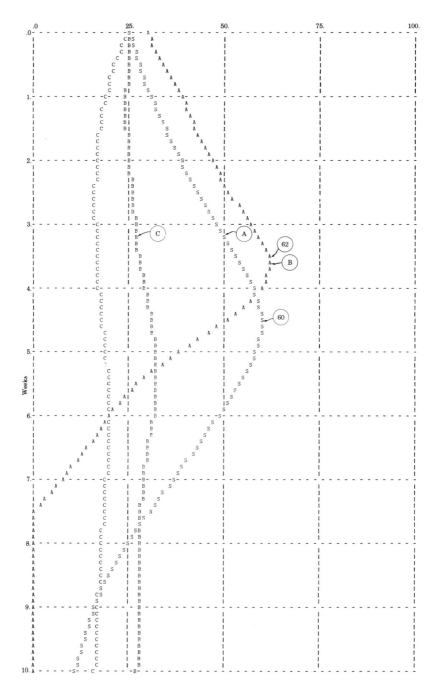

FIGURE A-34

306

The second change is also desirable because we now have the same relationship between the level of SHELL GAME–CONTINUING REVOLUTION and each of the Time Constants affecting aspiring processes.

The result of these changes is a pattern of behavior which we have chosen to identify as the basic behavior of late industrial man, a pattern presented in figure A-35.

ANALYZING MODEL BEHAVIOR

All of our modeling efforts to this point can be summarized in figure A-36.

Late Industrial Man

We begin our analysis by reexamining the basic late industrial behavior pattern portrayed in figure A-35, only this time we shall examine it over a twenty-five week period. The result is presented in figure A-37. This allows us to see a pattern of behavior characteristic of late industrial man: periodic oscillations of approximately equal amplitude (peak and nadir values) in all system levels.[6] The overall picture is one of rising development which encounters and is curbed by environmental pressure aimed at maintaining acceptable states along game dimensions. This pressure precipitates a period of declining development until extreme low values are entered, whereupon environmental pressure is exerted to raise development, and the pattern is begun anew.

The environment does not hold late industrial man in an obvious iron grip. Rather it tolerates "healthy" bursts of rising aspirations and development. The environmental cage within which late industrial man exercises his will to develop is a flexible one. It should be remembered as we proceed through analyzing model behavior over ten-week periods that periodic oscillations of the form shown in figure A-37 remain unless otherwise noted.

Now, we return to figure A-35 to take a closer look at behavior involved in the first period of rising and falling system levels. For the first three weeks the levels of Aspiration to SHELL GAME–CONTINUING REVOLUTION and SHELL GAME–CONTINUING REVOLUTION rise steadily. The level of development is being pulled up by the aspiration-development gap, and in turn the steadily rising level of development is resulting in further aspiring

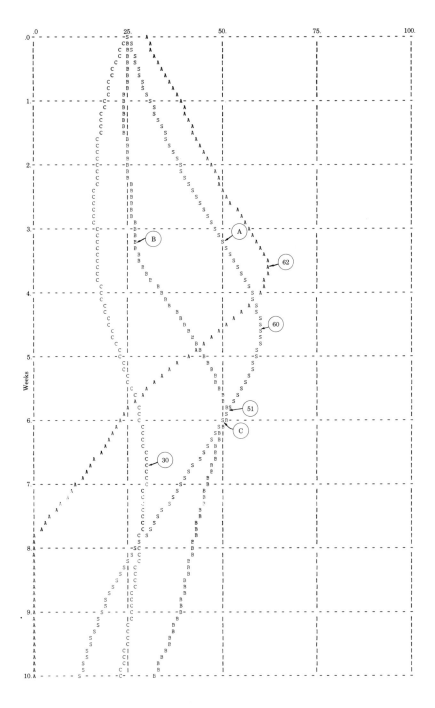

FIGURE A-35

308

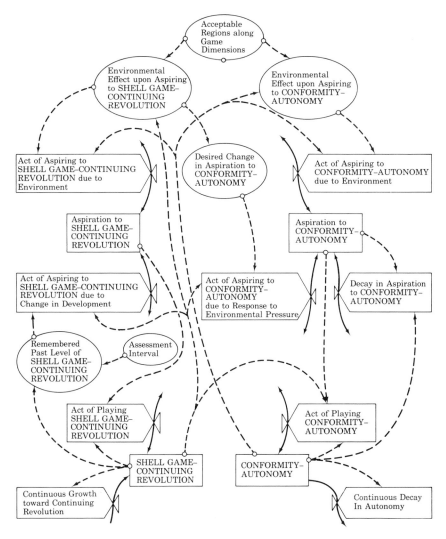

FIGURE A-36

to Continuing Revolution which steadily raises the level of aspiration. This is a reinforcing developmental cycle.

The environment for late industrial man is able to transform this pattern of self-reinforcing Continuing Revolution into a vicious circle of ever-increasing Shell Game. When the level SHELL GAME–

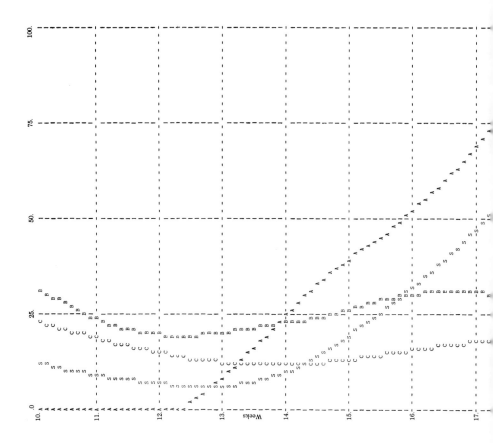

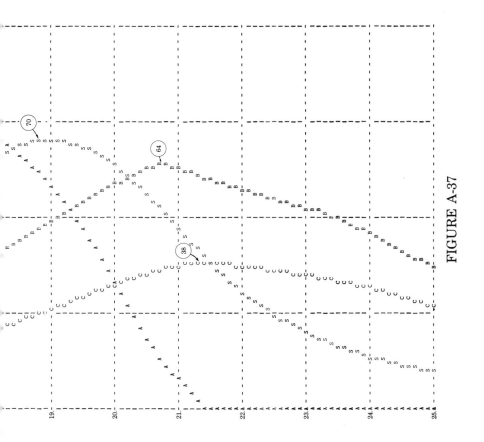

FIGURE A-37

311

CONTINUING REVOLUTION enters the extreme region of Continuing Revolution (point A) the environment begins to exert pressure on the aspiring process. Only slightly thereafter (point B) the individual begins to aspire to become more Autonomous, in the hope of dampening the environmental pressure. However, in this action late industrial man is "too late with too little": his response to environmental pressure results in only a slight rise in CONFORMITY–AUTONOMY, though his aspiration rises considerably higher, never approaching the extreme range of Autonomy.

The level of Aspiration to SHELL GAME–CONTINUING REVOLUTION peaks in the middle of the fourth week at a value of 62. The level of SHELL GAME–CONTINUING REVOLUTION achieves a delayed peak, due to the presence of the Continuous Growth toward Continuing Revolution, which allows development to continue until it is overwhelmed by the negative aspiration-development gap. As SHELL GAME–CONTINUING REVOLUTION starts to decline, the environmental pressure is reduced, and, in turn, so is the individual's Desired Change in Aspiration to CONFORMITY–AUTONOMY. Thus, the rising Aspiration to CONFORMITY–AUTONOMY peaks at point C, just as environmental pressure is diminishing to zero. Thereafter, this level of aspiration falls back gradually toward the level of CONFORMITY–AUTONOMY due to the Gradual Decay in Aspiration to CONFORMITY–AUTONOMY.

To more fully comprehend the vicious circle nature of the period of declining system levels, observe that the environmental pressure lasts for less than three weeks (from A to C). After the sixth week the environment is no longer pushing Aspiration to SHELL GAME–CONTINUING REVOLUTION downward. Now, the fact that the level of SHELL GAME–CONTINUING REVOLUTION has started to fall results in the individual aspiring to ever lower states of Shell Game (via the mechanism Act of Aspiring to SHELL GAME–CONTINUING REVOLUTION due to Change in Development). Furthermore, there is no possibility for the individual to break this cycle: falling aspirations pull down development which further lowers aspirations, and so on. Late industrial man's only mechanism for countering nondevelopmental pressures is his Desired Change in Aspiration to CONFORMITY–AUTONOMY. But this can only combat nondevelopmental spirals actively caused by external forces: if there is no active environmental pressure there is no motivation to become more Autonomous. After point C late industrial man's fate is in his own hands, a situation for which he is woefully ill-prepared.

The Transition to Early Post-Industrial Man

What are some of the characteristics of this transition? Paraphrasing what has been said earlier, early post-industrial man stands out in contrast to late industrial man on the basis of:

1. a rejection of the bureaucratic structure of late industrial society along with a concomitant
2. turning inward, seeking personal ground for cultivating less narrow life styles; and
3. groping toward self-togetherness: the schism for industrial man between intellect and emotion is identified, but there is more of a reaction against the former than a bridging of the two.

Overall, the early phases of the post-industrial era are characterized by many forms of "countering" dominant features of the preceding epoch, but the emphasis generally is on rebellion rather than a new direction capable of supplanting nondevelopmental aspects of industrial society. Our task is to translate these broad notions into plausible alterations in our model representative of late industrial behavior. In the course of these alterations in the structure and detail of the model we will study the accompanying changes in model behavior and, hopefully, come to better understand both the nature and potentialities of various means of effecting the transition to post-industrial society.

One alteration which we feel is basic to an individual's transition from late industrial to early post-industrial behavior is an elevation of his Aspiration to SHELL GAME–CONTINUING REVOLUTION and an accompanying lowering of his assessment of his state along this same game dimension. We shall first effect these alterations by appropriate adjustments in initial values of these two levels. We feel the former adjustment inheres in the general points 2 and 3 above: a deepening commitment, albeit relatively vague, to self-development. The latter alteration is accounted for as part and parcel of early post-industrial man's accentuated dissatisfaction with his world. In taking a more critical look at his world he cannot deny his place in and dependency upon that which he is criticizing, and thus he tends to assess his own development more critically than late industrial man.

We set the initial value of SHELL GAME–CONTINUING REVOLUTION at 20 and the initial value of Aspiration to SHELL GAME–CONTINUING REVOLUTION at 35, and observe the model behavior depicted in figure A-38. Have we effected any significant change toward more developmental behavior? Not really. SHELL GAME–CONTINUING REVOLUTION rises to a peak which is approximately 7 percent higher than that observed in figure A-37 despite the fact that its initial value was lowered 20 percent. Likewise, the aspiration along this dimension rises to a peak value 15 percent higher than previously. However, there are no significant changes in the pattern of behavior. The duration of time for which the level of SHELL GAME–CONTINUING REVOLUTION is in the extreme region is slightly greater: this accounts for the somewhat higher peak value of Aspiration to CONFORMITY–AUTONOMY. (This occurs because the longer the period of time in the extreme region, the longer the period of time in which the individual is trying to counter environmental pressure.)

Though this alteration, taken alone, does little to change significantly the individual's behavior, we nevertheless consider it basic to the transition to post-industrial behavior. It will be incorporated into all future alterations in the model investigated in this section, and figure A-38 will serve as a base of comparison for the remainder of this section.

Our model affords two alternative avenues for expressing early post-industrial man's characteristic opposition to his environment's nondevelopmental pressures. The first is to seek greater Autonomy at all times; the second is to respond more severely to environmental pressure curbing development. The first avenue, seeking higher levels of Autonomy regardless of environmental pressures, offers three possible model alterations:

1. alter the values of the Multiplier due to Conformity (figure A-27) to uniformly dampen environmental effect;
2. set the initial value of Aspiration to CONFORMITY–AUTONOMY higher and the initial value of the corresponding level of development lower; and
3. increase the Decay Time Constant (governing the rate of Continuous Decay in Autonomy) to slow down this decay.

We have defined the Multiplier due to CONFORMITY–AUTONOMY such that it has values of approximately unity (corresponding to no modification of environmental effect) throughout the middle ranges of CONFORMITY–AUTONOMY. To tamper substantially with these values is undesirable, since it would mask the environmental effect more than help us to understand the processes which might counter it.

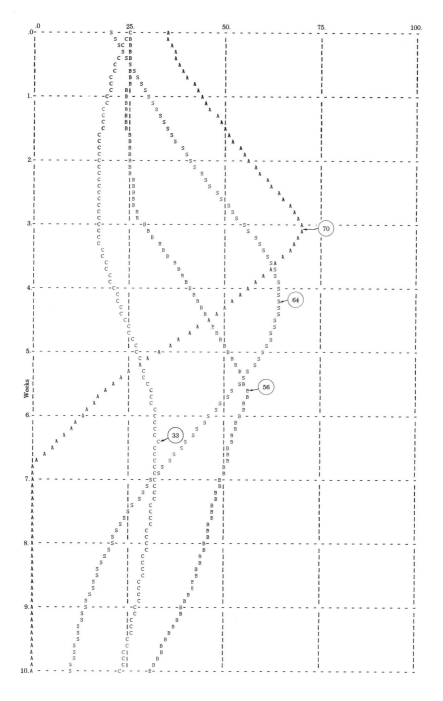

FIGURE A-38

315

The second possible alteration is reasonable. We have already made an analagous alteration in the initial values of Aspiration to SHELL GAME–CONTINUING REVOLUTION and SHELL GAME–CONTINUING REVOLUTION. Now, we set the initial value of Aspiration to CONFORMITY–AUTONOMY to 40 (feeling that a more dramatic alteration is called for here than in Aspiration to SHELL GAME–CONTINUING REVOLUTION) and the corresponding initial value of the level of development to 20 (following a line of reasoning analogous to that which led us to devalue the initial value of SHELL GAME–CONTINUING REVOLUTION above). These changes in initial values produce no noteworthy change in behavior. We now set the initial level of Aspiration to CONFORMITY–AUTONOMY to 50 and observe the resulting behavior in figure A-39.

Two points from this figure bear noting. The very large initial aspiration-development gap in CONFORMITY–AUTONOMY is relatively ineffectual because, until the level of SHELL GAME–CONTINUING REVOLUTION exceeds 50, there are no forces acting to change Aspiration to CONFORMITY–AUTONOMY except the Continuous Decay in Aspiration to CONFORMITY–AUTONOMY, which is acting to pull aspirations toward level of development along this game dimension. Thus, for almost the first three weeks the level of Aspiration to CONFORMITY–AUTONOMY can only decrease (until point A).

Second, what effect does the large initial aspiration-development gap CONFORMITY–AUTONOMY have upon development along SHELL GAME–CONTINUING REVOLUTION? In comparison to figure A-38, we see a 5 percent increase in the peak value of SHELL GAME–CONTINUING REVOLUTION, but no increase whatsoever in the peak value of aspirations along this dimension. However, the duration of time for which the individual is in the extreme region of Continuing Revolution is increased 17 percent (from three to three and one-half weeks). How can this change come about if the level of Aspiration to SHELL GAME–CONTINUING REVOLUTION rises to a peak no higher than previously? The answer lies in the fact that in figure A-39 the level of CONFORMITY–AUTONOMY is almost 50 percent increased (B) at the time when the environmental pressure to curb rising Aspiration to SHELL GAME–CONTINUING REVOLUTION begins. This pressure is sufficiently dampened to slow down the decline in aspiration and buy the individual a bit more time to continue developing. One offshoot of this model run is that we now pay closer attention to the duration of periods in extreme regions in addition to the peak values at-

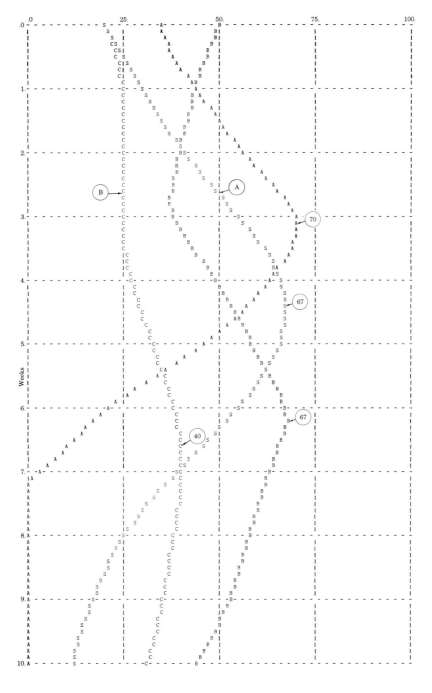

FIGURE A-39

317

tained–the two are often inseparably intertwined and we must guard against only noting the more obvious behavioral change.[7] However, increasing the duration in extreme regions is a two-sided coin; when the oscillations resultant from environmental pressure are slowed down the individual spends more time in the extreme region of Shell Game also.

For reasons similar to those surrounding the behavior in figure A-39, an alteration in the value of the Decay Time Constant, by itself, will not precipitate noteworthy behavioral change in the direction of more developmental behavior; and we will not take time here to discuss the ramifications of this alteration.

Clearly, unselective autonomy benefits the individual's quest to develop only perhaps in allowing him to broaden his peaks of extreme Continuing Revolution. It has not affected the values of those peaks to any significant extent, or, curiously enough, the peaks to which CONFORMITY–AUTONOMY rises. More importantly, it has done equally little to change the shape of behavior.

The second possible avenue for expressing early post-industrial man's characteristic opposition to his environment is through selective opposition: more rigorous opposition to nondevelopmental pressures, but no increased inclination to Autonomy in the absence of environmental pressure. The logical model element through which to approach this form of environmental opposition is the relationship between Environmental Effect on Aspiration to SHELL GAME–CONTINUING REVOLUTION and the Desired Change in Aspiration to CONFORMITY–AUTONOMY (figure A-28).

With the initial values of Aspiration to CONFORMITY–AUTONOMY and the level CONFORMITY–AUTONOMY back at their original values, we set the values of Desired Change in Aspiration to CONFORMITY–AUTONOMY to one and one-half their original values, and we observe an increase in the peaks of Aspiration to CONFORMITY–AUTONOMY and the associated level of development of about 30 percent. But we see no change whatsoever in the individual's behavior relative to SHELL GAME–CONTINUING REVOLUTION. Let us now double the values of the Desired Change in Aspiration to CONFORMITY–AUTONOMY and examine the results in figure A-40.

In comparison to figure A-38 we see that we have substantial increases in the peak values of CONFORMITY–AUTONOMY and Aspiration to CONFORMITY–AUTONOMY (on the order of 70 percent), but remarkably little change in either the peak values of SHELL GAME–CONTINUING REVOLUTION and associated Aspiration or the duration of time in extreme Continuing Revolution.

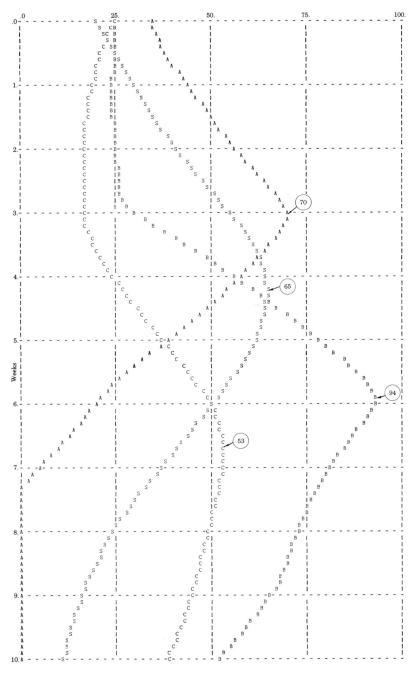

FIGURE A-40

This alteration has had even less impact upon developmental behavior than that which resulted in figure A-39.

Let us now explore the result of making all possible alterations expressive of early post-industrial man's sensitivity to his environment's capacity to curb his development. Here we:

> 1. increase the values of Desired Change in Aspiration to CONFORMITY–AUTONOMY to two and one-half their original values,
> 2. set the initial value of Aspiration to CONFORMITY–AUTONOMY at 50 and the initial value of CONFORMITY–AUTONOMY at 20, and
> 3. increase the Decay Time Constant for Continuous Decay in Autonomy to six weeks.

These alterations produce the simulated behavior in figure A-41.

In this figure we see the following changes, as compared to figure A-38:

> 1. the level of CONFORMITY–AUTONOMY rises to almost three times (300 percent) its previous peak value; this level remains in the region of extreme Autonomy for over seven weeks;
> 2. the level of Aspiration to CONFORMITY–AUTONOMY rises to a peak about two and one-half times (i.e., 250 percent) its previous value;
> 3. the peak value of SHELL GAME–CONTINUING REVOLUTION is 9 percent higher; this level remains in the extreme region of Continuing Revolution almost five weeks, an increase of about 60 percent from its previous duration in this region; and
> 4. the level Aspiration to SHELL GAME–CONTINUING REVOLUTION achieves a peak value 1.4 percent higher than previously.

The pattern of developmental behavior is affected amazingly little by all possible changes toward autonomous behavior. The only exception to this is, perhaps, the lengthening of the period of extreme Continuing Revolution, a minor improvement if any. The steep ascent (beginning of point A) of Aspiration to CONFORMITY–AUTONOMY allows the individual to continue aspiring in this direction for some time before the environment finally curbs his development (the level of Aspiration rises to a height of 130 before it is finally curbed by enormous environmental pressure). Yet this enormous leap in Autonomy is almost completely ineffectual.

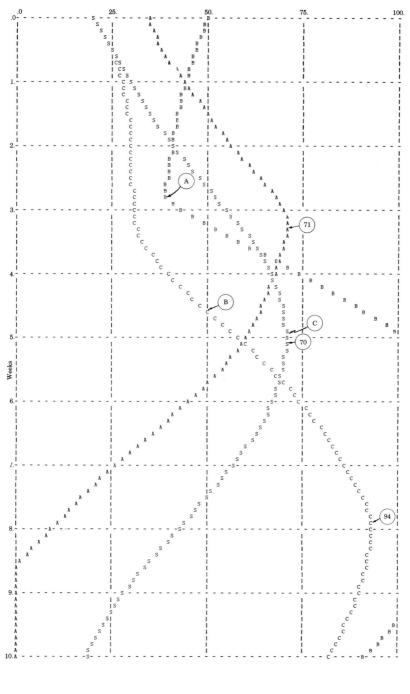

FIGURE A-41
321

Thus, we have the predicament of early post-industrial man: the ultimate bankruptcy of rebellion uncomplemented by a sense of developmental direction. Figure A-41 tells the story. The individual's Aspiration to CONFORMITY–AUTONOMY rises dramatically in response to the beginning of nondevelopmental environmental pressure. But, by the time the level of CONFORMITY–AUTONOMY enters the extreme region of Autonomy (B) and starts to dampen Environmental Effect upon Aspiration to SHELL GAME–CONTINUING REVOLUTION, the individual's battle to keep aspiring to Continuing Revolution has already been lost. The vicious circle of Shell Game has begun, and the only effect of the rising level of CONFORMITY–AUTONOMY is to delay the inevitable. All that early post-industrial man's autonomy rebellion can accomplish is just that—Autonomy—and even that is eventually doomed to succumb to environmental pressure. The structure underlying figure A-41 and the accompanying behavior throws light on, we feel, what we see today in the first waves of the post-industrial revolution.

Searching for Leverage Points

Can we put together some understanding from the preceding explorations which will point toward leverage points that are more effective than autonomous response to environmental pressure has shown itself to be? We think so.

In our discussion of the transition to early post-industrial man we noted that behavior during the first few weeks was critical in determining the pattern of long-run behavior. In particular, the time immediately following the individual's emergence into the region of Extreme Continuing Revolution is crucial, for it is then that he must successfully counter environmental pressure against his continuing development. Autonomous response is ineffectual because it is not sufficiently active during this period of initial environmental pressure.

Our first stop in searching for greater leverage on developmental behavior is the value of the Time Constant for Continuing Revolution. It will be recalled that this was originally set at ten weeks to prevent it from playing a major role in the behavior of late industrial man. A shorter time period, however, would give it a greater role. What effect upon behavior will a reduction of its value to five weeks have? Using figure A-38 once again as our basis for comparison, we find that this alteration produces a 9 percent increase in the peak value of SHELL GAME–CONTINUING REVOLUTION, and not much else. To more clearly assess the potential of this kind of alteration we now reduce this time to two and one-half weeks, one-fourth its original value.

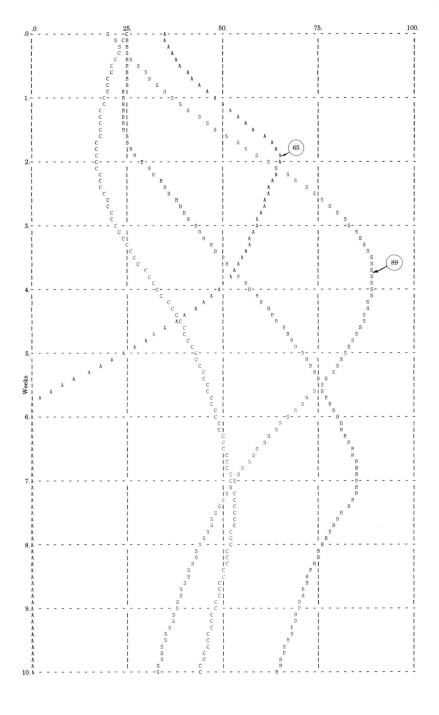

FIGURE A-42
323

In figure A-42 we see an increase in the peak value of SHELL GAME–CONTINUING REVOLUTION of almost 40 percent, and an increase in the duration of values within the extreme Continuing Revolution area of 80 percent. Yet, surprisingly, the peak value in Aspiration for SHELL GAME–CONTINUING REVOLUTION is 7 percent *lower* than previously. This unexpected change bears examination. Comparing figures A-42 and A-38 we see that, in the former, SHELL GAME–CONTINUING REVOLUTION enters the extreme region at about week 1.6 (as compared to 2.6 in the latter), and, more importantly, the net rate of growth toward Continuing Revolution (the slope of the SHELL GAME–CONTINUING REVOLUTION curve) at the time of encountering environmental pressure is much greater due to the increased Rate of Continuous Growth toward Continuing Revolution. This causes the environment to respond more severely to curb rising aspirations. (If this point is not clear, refer to figure A-26: as the behavior in figure A-42 more rapidly enters into the range of values of SHELL GAME–CONTINUING REVOLUTION above 50, the Environmental Effect on Aspiration to SHELL GAME–CONTINUING REVOLUTION likewise rises more rapidly to large values.) Thus, the ironic outcome: if taken alone, capacity to continually develop toward Continuing Revolution, when amplified to the extent discussed here, impairs capacity to aspire to Continuing Revolution.

Figure A-43 exhibits the most developmental behavior yet seen. The environment still maintains control to the extent that development is eventually curbed and the oscillating pattern is set in motion. Yet the peak value of SHELL GAME–CONTINUING REVOLUTION is 36 percent greater than that in figure A-38. This is due to an increase in peak value of Aspiration to SHELL GAME–CONTINUING REVOLUTION which resists environmental pressure for three weeks (point A to point B), allowing SHELL GAME–CONTINUING REVOLUTION to continue rising much longer than in any previous trial. The alteration which resulted in this pattern of behavior has addressed a critically important element of the model: how the individual aspires to SHELL GAME–CONTINUING REVOLUTION. It is here, as noted earlier, that behavior is determined. Figure A-43 resulted from altering the individual's Assessment Interval for evaluating his development in SHELL GAME–CONTINUING REVOLUTION, changing it from one week to one and three-fourths weeks.

In terms of the model, the lengthened Assessment Interval means that the individual evaluates his development over a longer period of time in the act of aspiring. When this period involves a rising level

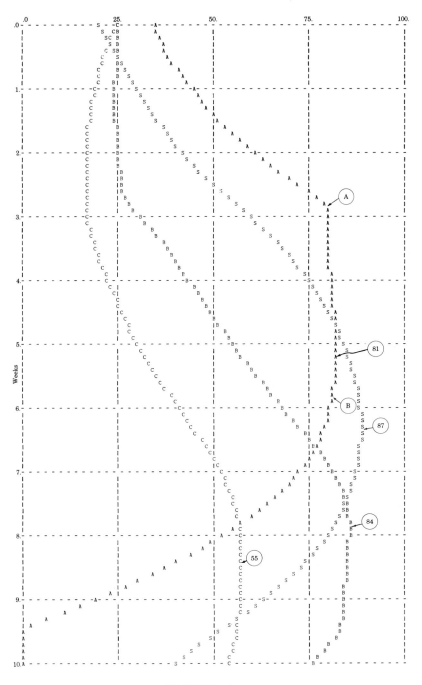

FIGURE A-43

of SHELL GAME–CONTINUING REVOLUTION it results in a greater force to aspire to Continuing Revolution. And, concomitantly, a reduced susceptibility to environmental pressure. The behavior of figure A-43 suggests that the individual does have capacities to resist (and, perhaps, overcome) environmental pressure, capacities which have yet to be tapped.

Beacons Toward the Post-Industrial Revolution

We are reticent to label one particular set of model alterations and accompanying behavioral changes as representative of late post-industrial man. Not only is labeling itself contrary to our purpose here, but it is also difficult to recognize something of which we have as yet seen only fleeting glimpses. Rather, we elect to briefly suggest some of the promising avenues for ushering in this transition, avenues which we are only gradually coming to understand.

The behavior of the model in figure A-44 is an outcome of a confluence of two now well-explored areas of model alterations. With the Assessment Interval maintained at one and three-fourths weeks, we set the values of the Desired Change in Aspiration to CONFORMITY–AUTONOMY at twice their original values, as done previously in figure A-40. In figure A-44 we encounter a new pattern of model behavior. We see, as in figure A-43, that at point A environmental pressure has effectively curbed the rising Aspiration to SHELL GAME–CONTINUING REVOLUTION. However, now, as a consequence of the individual's heightened capacity to respond to environmental pressure, his Aspiration to CONFORMITY–AUTONOMY rises much more rapidly upon encountering that pressure. For a period of about one week after point A, the level of Aspiration to SHELL GAME–CONTINUING REVOLUTION remains constant. Then, the rising level of CONFORMITY–AUTONOMY begins to tip the scales. Observe the following table of values of CONFORMITY–AUTONOMY after point A:

Time (in weeks) after A	Level of CONFORMITY–AUTONOMY in figure A-43	Level of CONFORMITY–AUTONOMY in figure A-44
1	21	25
2	28	40
2½	33	50
3	39	65

At point B (about two weeks after A) in figure A-44 the level of Aspiration to SHELL GAME–CONTINUING REVOLUTION begins

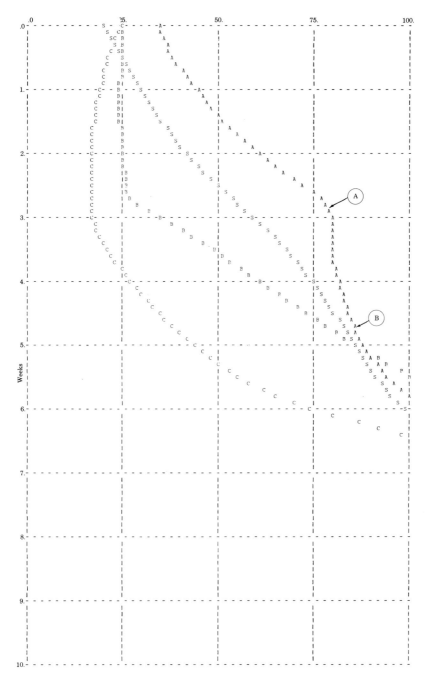

FIGURE A-44

a new cycle of self-reinforcing development. Environmental pressure has been sufficiently dampened by rising Autonomy to allow the effect of the one and three-fourths week Assessment Interval to push aspiration ever upward with the rising level of SHELL GAME–CONTINUING REVOLUTION. The level of SHELL GAME–CONTINUING REVOLUTION will not oscillate about the acceptable region when the model has undergone these alterations. This is the first time we have seen that behavior pattern broken.

Figure A-44 illustrates the complementary nature of two types of model variations. Of the two, we can fairly say that the alteration in Assessment Interval is more critical for getting into a new behavior mode. If Assessment Interval is increased to 1.9 weeks, a similar mode of behavior is observed even with the values of Desired Change in Aspiration to CONFORMITY–AUTONOMY at their original values. As shown earlier, no reasonable change in the latter will ever, by itself, have comparable effects.

We should also note that if Time Constant for Continuing Revolution is reduced sufficiently (to about one week), the oscillating pattern of behavior will again disappear. As observed in figure A-42, this will happen despite environmental control over rising Aspiration to SHELL GAME–CONTINUING REVOLUTION.

There are other potential means of effecting major behavioral change which we intend to explore in the future. For example, we have long been challenged by the apparent impenetrability of the vicious circle of declining Aspiration to SHELL GAME–CONTINUING REVOLUTION and SHELL GAME–CONTINUING REVOLUTION. Once the latter peaks and begins to decline there is no way, as currently expressed in our model structure, that the mutually reinforcing decline in system levels can be stopped until development has fallen so low that environmental pressure is exerted to raise it. What is needed is some form of personal ability to step back from this vicious circle, attain consciousness of a direction leading to development, and then aspire to it. In searching for a causal theory capable of accomplishing such aspiring, we hope to open up a new area for exploring the possibilities of this model and of the modeling process in general as it pertains to the dynamics of human behavior.

AFTERWORD: THE ASSUMPTIONS OF A STATE-DETERMINED SYSTEM

In constructing mathematical models based upon accumulation-feedback processes, we are making certain basic assumptions about the systems we study.

The state of a system is, in our terminology, the values of all of the levels at any point in time. Since the levels, in turn, determine the values of the rates, we can say that to know the state of the system at a point in time implies complete knowledge at that point in time of the values of all changing phenomena described by that system.

The essence of a state-determined system can be seen in the situation surrounding initial values of system levels. In Model Detail we said that it was necessary to choose initial values for system levels (SHELL GAME–CONTINUING REVOLUTION, Aspiration to SHELL GAME–CONTINUING REVOLUTION, CONFORMITY–AUTONOMY, and Aspiration to CONFORMITY–AUTONOMY), but we did not say why this was so. It is necessary to specify initial values of levels in order that the initial state of the system be known. In setting the initial values of the levels we implicitly set the initial values of the rates and other variables dependent upon the levels.

For a given system—that is, a given set of constants and numeric dependencies describing all interrelationships among the elements of a system—any specific set of initial values of system levels *uniquely* specifies all system behavior. If one does not alter the values of time constants, numeric relationships and such, the same initial state of a system will always produce exactly the same behavior. This is equally true if one looks at the state of a system at any point in time. At any point in time the state of the system uniquely determines a specific pattern (numeric values) of total system behavior extending forward and backward in time until such point as the system itself changes: thus, the name "state-determined system."

As a basic operating premise, the assumption of state-determinacy conflicts strongly with our less rigorous but more deeply ingrained assumptions about the indeterminacy of our behavior. We have long cherished the notion of will in the individual, and the heart of will is caprice. And caprice is the antithesis of determinacy. To accept that a given system is subject to moments of capricious behavior is to define a non-state-determined system: one which, in the time after reaching a certain state, will behave in one fashion sometimes and in another on different occasions.

In the juxtaposition of state-determinacy and caprice is illustrated a classic case of the disparities which inhere in our very process of thinking. The reconciliation of such disparate notions will help to accomplish the synthesis of human will and reason. Surely, man is both state-determined and capricious. Surely, these two abstract notions are intrinsically artificial, each distilling one prime trait from the universe of traits possessed by the human. Surely, we can understand ourselves better if we try to see state-determinacy and caprice as two widely separated points along a continuum describing the determinacy of human behavior. Surely, we do not *have* to view them as mutually exclusive alternatives.

It is our belief that the implementation of a new structure for constructing and analyzing mental models—the structure of the dynamic accumulation-feedback process—can be an important complement to our current techniques for achieving understanding of the complex worlds of human behavior.

NOTES

1. This appendix is based on a project funded by the Graduate School of Arts and Sciences, Boston University. It is an outgrowth of the collaboration of the author and Mr. Peter M. Senge. Mr. Senge is a graduate student in System Dynamics at Massachusetts Institute of Technology.

2. See for example *Industrial Dynamics* (Cambridge, Mass.: The M.I.T. Press, 1961); *Principles of Systems,* 2d preliminary edition (Cambridge, Mass.: Wright-Allen Press, 1968); and *Urban Dynamics* (Cambridge, Mass.: The M.I.T. Press, 1969).

3. Our convention in this appendix is to capitalize games only when both directions of the game dimension are mentioned. Otherwise, only the first letter will be capitalized. This differs from our convention, throughout the book, of capitalizing all games.

4. The reader should avoid inferring that certain values are associated with positive versus negative directions, unless specifically stated.

5. It can be demonstrated that to produce behavior such as that of curve 3, the Act of Playing SHELL GAME–CONTINUING REVOLUTION must be other than an algebraic function of the level of SHELL GAME–CONTINUING REVOLUTION.

6. The observed increase (of about 25 percent) in peak values from the first to the second set of peaks is not repeated in subsequent peaks.

7. This point was particularly impressed upon us in other model runs, which are not included here, where the level of SHELL GAME–CONTINUING REVOLUTION, though not rising to a significantly higher peak value, remains in the region of extreme Continuing Revolution for periods of eight weeks or more.

Name Index

Amosov, Nikolai, 7, 22n, 80, 82, 84, 88-90
Aristotle, 125, 136, 168, 187, 230

Bacon, Francis, 199
Becker, Ernest, 71n
Berger, Peter L., 72n, 113
Bergman, Ingmar, 49, 80, 82-83, 86-88, 90
Berne, Eric, 210
Bertalanffy, Ludwig von, 71n, 126
Bessemer, Henri, 30
Blumer, Herbert, 72n
Bondurant, Joan V., 267
Borge, Victor, 37
Bronowski, J., 71n
Buckley, Walter, 71n
Buddha, 117, 125, 234

Calley, William L., 216, 253
Camus, Albert, 125
Chardin, Pierre Teilhard de, 210n
Chase, Stuart, 123
Christ, Jesus, 124
Clarke, Arthur C., 72, 78-79, 82, 84-85, 90
Confucius, 117
Copernicus, Nicholas, 224
Curie, Marie, 30

Da Vinci, Leonardo, 125
Daguerre, Louis, 30
Dahrendorf, Ralf, 193, 210n
Darwin, Charles, 123-24
Dewey, John, 122-23
Dickson, William, 210n
Dionysus, 124, 131, 133, 135

Einstein, Albert, 125, 167, 217

Feiffer, Jules, 186
Fellini, Federico, 79, 81-82, 87, 90, 135
Fleming, Alexander, 30
Forrester, Jay W., 270
Freud, Sigmund, 117, 123, 130, 136, 204
Fromm, Erich, 115, 124, 149, 210
Fuller, Buckminster, 181-85

Galvani, Luigi, 30
Gandhi, Mohandas, K., 107
Gerth, H. H., 210n
Goffman, Erving, 72n, 113
Gonzales, Pancho, 175
Goodwin, Leonard, 71n
Gouldner, Alvin W., 71n, 72, 267n
Greenburg, Dan, 113, 113n
Gross, Bertram M., 71n, 267n
Guetzkow, Harold, 120

Subject Index